Brain Korea 21 Phase II

A New Evaluation Model

Somi Seong, Steven W. Popper,
Charles A. Goldman, David K. Evans

With Clifford A. Grammich

Prepared for the Korea Research Foundation

 EDUCATION

The research described in this report was prepared for the Korea Research Foundation and was conducted by RAND Education, a unit of the RAND Corporation.

Library of Congress Cataloging-in-Publication Data

Brain Korea 21 phase II : a new evaluation model / Somi Seong, ... [et al.].
    p. cm.
    Includes bibliographical references.
    ISBN 978-0-8330-4321-4 (pbk. : alk. paper)
    1. Brain Korea 21 (Project)—Evaluation. 2. Education, Higher—Korea (South)—Finance. 3. Government aid to higher education—Korea (South) I. Song, So-mi.

LB2342.4.K6B73 2008
379.1'214095195—dc22

2007052726

The RAND Corporation is a nonprofit research organization providing objective analysis and effective solutions that address the challenges facing the public and private sectors around the world. RAND's publications do not necessarily reflect the opinions of its research clients and sponsors.
RAND® is a registered trademark.

Published 2008 by the RAND Corporation
1776 Main Street, P.O. Box 2138, Santa Monica, CA 90407-2138
1200 South Hayes Street, Arlington, VA 22202-5050
4570 Fifth Avenue, Suite 600, Pittsburgh, PA 15213-2665
RAND URL: http://www.rand.org
To order RAND documents or to obtain additional information, contact
Distribution Services: Telephone: (310) 451-7002;
Fax: (310) 451-6915; Email: order@rand.org

Preface

The Brain Korea 21 program (BK21) of the Korea Ministry of Education and Human Resource Development seeks to nurture research manpower and strengthen graduate programs. The first phase of the program included US$1.4 billion in funding for Korean graduate departments and their students and research faculty. The current, second phase features US$2.1 billion in funding for a broader range of institutions, including regional schools.

The BK21 award selection process is highly competitive, and funding is a mark of prestige for its recipients. Since its introduction in 1999, the well-publicized program has elicited a passionate response from universities, researchers, policymakers, and the National Assembly, as well as interest in determining its effects on Korea and its universities. This monograph presents a model for assessing program effects, discusses program metrics and measures, and evaluates the measures. It should interest not only individuals and institutions involved in BK21 but also higher education policymakers in Korea and elsewhere who are concerned with nurturing globally competitive research manpower and research universities.

This research was sponsored by the Korea Research Foundation. It was conducted within RAND Education and reflects RAND Education's mission to bring objective analysis and effective solution to the national and international debate on education policy.

For further information on this research, contact Somi Seong, the principal author of this monograph, by mail at the RAND Corporation, 1776 Main Street, P. O. Box 2138, Santa Monica, California 90407, by email at Somi_Seong@rand.org, or by phone at 1-310-393-0411, extension 6379. For more information on RAND Education, contact Charles Goldman, the associate director, by email at charlesg@rand.org or by phone at 1-310-393-0411, extension 6748. More information about RAND is available at www.rand.org.

Contents

Figures

Tables

Summary

In the late 1990s, the Korea Ministry of Education and Human Resource Development (MoE), in response to concern over the relatively low standing of the nation's universities and researchers, launched the Brain Korea 21 Program (BK21).

BK21 seeks to nurture globally competitive research universities and graduate programs and to breed high-quality research manpower in Korea. It provides fellowship funding to graduate students, postdoctoral fellows, and contract-based research professors who belong to research groups (*sa-up-dan*) at top universities. Recipients are selected on the merit of the research groups and universities to which they belong, not on individual merit. Although the department-level research group is the unit of support, the program does not support the labor cost of faculty members participating in the research groups or capital costs of university research and development (R&D). These costs are supposed to be financed by sources other than BK21. BK21 funding for a selected research group is proportional to the number of graduate students and young researchers in the group.

The program has had two phases so far. In Phase I, which ran from 1999 to 2005, BK21 allocated about US$1.4 billion. In Phase II, which began in 2006 and is scheduled to run through 2012, BK21 will allocate an additional US$2.1 billion. The Phase I and Phase II programs are not much different from each other in their goals and missions, funding rules, and selection criteria. The few differences between the two phases are subtle and nuanced in emphasis. Whereas Phase I emphasized university-level excellence, Phase II emphasizes department-level excellence. Phase II emphasizes the university-industry link more than Phase I does, and institutional reforms are emphasized in Phase I more than in Phase II. A Phase II research group is based on a department of a single university, whereas Phase I research groups originally started with investigators from multiple universities in the same academic discipline—a leading university and one or more participating universities. However, during the course of Phase I, investigators in each university were regarded as a separate research group and each university accounted for its performance at the end of the Phase I program, which is basically the same as in Phase II.

BK21 has attracted a great deal of attention, in part because of its strategy of concentration that results in relatively large awards and because of the prestige it confers on recipients. Given the high profile of the program, there is great interest in the program and in determining its effects on universities and human resource development.

In this study, we develop an evaluation model to assess the net effect of the BK21 Phase II program. The evaluation model includes a logic model, a quantitative model, and evaluation metrics. We also suggest prototype database structures that would allow assessment of the BK21 Phase II program achievement in the future. Based on the findings of the evaluation model and database structures and also on our knowledge of research and educations systems in the United States, we derive policy implications for the future management of the program and for the university research sector more generally. The task of deriving broader policy implications beyond the findings of the evaluation model and database structures was specifically requested by the sponsors.

Lessons from Previous Evaluations

Although there were several evaluations of BK21 Phase I, they were not designed to answer the critical accountability question of the program's net contribution to R&D capability and manpower production compared with those of other programs. Data were generally limited to information gathered from institutions that received Phase I funding during the program period only and hence could not reveal net effects of the program. Previous evaluations largely lacked models that were sophisticated enough to show the program's net effects.

Previous analyses did suggest several options for improving evaluations. These included suggestions to improve the balance between quantity and quality indicators of the program performance, further development of the proper metrics to assess human resource development, focusing on a more narrow set of evaluation metrics for core performance indicators to measure quantity and quality of research outputs and manpower production, assessing net program effect instead of showing gross increase in performance indicators, and designing evaluation systems that will both measure the extent to which the program achieves its goals and monitor program progress.

A Logic Model to Identify Program Goals and Dynamics

We propose a logic model to identify the goals and missions, inputs, incentives, activities, outputs, and outcomes of the program and to explore the logical linkages among these elements (see Figure 3.1). Based on our review of relevant literature and interviews with BK21 stakeholders, we develop the logic model to understand underlying policy intentions and program dynamics. The logic model serves as a conceptual framework for identifying the goals of the study as well as for the evaluation metrics and quantitative assessment model we develop.

The goals of BK21 are (1) developing research manpower and (2) strengthening graduate programs to be globally competitive. Missions undertaken to accomplish these goals include improving the research capabilities of faculty and graduate students, enhancing the quality of research and training, and helping establish infrastructure of graduate schools. An additional mission, promoting regional universities, also seeks to build regional innovation clusters.

The goals and missions of BK21 direct the inputs, such as program resources and rules. The program allocates resources by using a concentration strategy, which results in awards much larger than those for other project-based funding programs. Even though the total BK21 budget is relatively small compared with other sources of R&D funding to universities, the concentration strategy makes the individual award size attractive enough for universities to put priority on obtaining BK21 funding—and hence on meeting the goals of the program.

BK21 also encourages specialization within the recipient universities so that they can concentrate their resources and support on selected areas of particular academic fields. Applicant universities are supposed to choose their academic areas of concentration, make a commitment to investing in the infrastructure needed to promote those areas of concentration, and plan for such reforms as improving the accountability over research funds and the faculty evaluation system.

Because award selection is based on academic and institutional merit rankings, the comparative rankings of universities and departments in Korea should become more obvious than before in Korea, which may induce stronger competition among them.

BK21 funding offers incentives for both recipients and those affiliated with them. For students, it lowers the expected cost of obtaining advanced degrees and thereby provides more incentive to pursue them. For postdoctoral researchers, BK21 funding provides stability in their transition to permanent academic jobs. For faculty, BK21 provides free manpower for research activities. For both faculty and universities, BK21 funding offers both prestige and incentives to align their decisions with the goals of the program. In addition, BK21 funding gives recipients flexibility to carry out broader research agendas and so develop university or department excellence.

Outputs and outcomes include impacts directly linked to the program as well as to its intended and unintended long-term effects. In addition to increased research, many program stakeholders claim that BK21 has led to structural reform of Korean universities, such as downsizing or closing weak departments and encouraging weak faculty members to leave the university, including those not gaining funding but seeking to do so in future rounds.

Some outcomes, such as greater international prestige for Korean universities, may take more time to emerge and may have broader causes than BK21 funding.

Quantitative Model for Assessing Net Program Effects

The quantitative model aims to assess the net effect of the program. It is specifically aimed at measuring the extent to which BK21 results in net improvements to the recipient groups' R&D outputs and human resource production compared with those of nonrecipients. We also discuss quantitative methods for isolating some of mechanisms by which BK21 affects various outcomes.

Several statistical methods could be used to examine treatment effects: ordinary least squares, matching, propensity scores, fixed effects, difference-in-differences, regression discontinuity, instrumental variables, and the Heckman selection correction.

We discuss the pros and cons of each method and conclude that the fixed-effects estimation procedure is the best strategy for examining the effects of BK21.

Despite being the best option, fixed-effects estimation does present some challenges. Compensatory funding changes, either for groups not receiving BK21 funding or in other sources of funding for BK21 recipients, can complicate estimation of the net effects of BK21, as can the effects of BK21 on both recipients and nonrecipients (such as those resulting from enhanced competition), other heterogeneous characteristics of both groups, and lags in program effects. For some of these problems, solutions are available; for others, awareness of model limitations is necessary to interpret the results appropriately.

The quantitative model used in the study is appropriate for a broad range of measures including, among others, total publications and high-impact publications, the faculty composition of research groups, number of PhD graduates, and number of patents. We demonstrate how the model will work in the future by using historical data on funding levels for both Phase I and Phase II, the number and quality of journal publications, and other quality indicators of Phase I. We explore some variations in the model specifications to evaluate Phase II impacts and to examine differential impacts by research area, lags in treatment impacts, and nonlinear treatment effects.

The analysis on quantitative model leads to several specific suggestions for database design. To understand fully the effects of BK21, data needs to be collected from universities and departments that received funding through the program, from those that applied but did not receive awards, and from those that never applied over the periods of pre-BK21, Phase I of BK21, and Phase II of BK21. The data requirements are broader than the scope of the data compiled in previous evaluations in Korea.

Evaluation Metrics and Measures

We next suggest relevant metrics and their measures that allow both quantitative and qualitative assessment of program effects. Metrics to evaluate BK21 Phase II program effects should be derived directly from the intended goals of the program. The evaluation must look at different levels of action and effect to make fully clear the degree to which BK21 has succeeded and through what means it has done so. Taking these two principles together, we suggest a set of metrics for both the outputs and outcomes sought within the context of the program's three major goals as shown in Table 5.1.

Having framed the evaluation metrics, we next construct appropriate measures. A metric is a criterion for evaluation; a measure is the practical means used to estimate the value of that metric. For a measure to be applicable to a particular metric, the necessary data must be available and the cost of collection should not be prohibitive. In addition, measures need to be valid, so that we are actually measuring the phenomenon we wish to measure. Finally, we may have to rely on proxy variables to represent what we can observe directly.

We propose at least one measure—often several—for each metric (Table 5.2). Multiple measures may provide a means of checking the accuracy of any one and allow evaluators to determine the level of detail at which to evaluate the metric. For example, to assess research quality, evaluators may wish to look at both the number of times a paper is cited by other researchers and peer assessments of the research (learned through surveys).

Prioritizing Measures

Not all candidate measures for evaluating BK21 are equally important. Evaluators should prioritize these measures taking into account the effort needed to assess them. We explore two ways for doing so. (Table 6.1). The first is assigning a relative raw importance to the measures, based on how closely related measures are to what evaluators consider to be most crucial. The second is determining the ease (or difficulty) of gathering the necessary data.

Measures that are the most important and for which it is easy to gather data could be given top priority. Those that are important but for which it is difficult to gather data could be given second priority; those that are less important but for which data gathering is easy could be given third priority; those that are less important and for which data gathering is difficult could be given the lowest priority. This system is notional and could be used as a starting point in assessing which measures to gather, but it is unlikely that the distinctions among measures will be so clear.

Obtaining comparative data from nonrecipients and nonapplicants may be a particularly vexing issue. Greater availability of data for applicants and recipients (through their program participation) could result in a structural bias in the evaluation. This suggests that evaluators will need to deliberate carefully before excluding a measure from the evaluation model because of difficulties in gathering the needed data or in using measures for which data are obtainable only from recipient institutions.

Database

The database of measures we suggest comprises four groups: (1) education, (2) noninstructional activities related to scientific and academic inquiry, (3) research and development activities with industry, and (4) other, or "general." In determining which data to gather, evaluators should assemble information that includes a unique identifier for each data series, an assessment of data-gathering difficulty, an ideal time period between observations or data collection, the evident qualitative differences (e.g., between BK21 recipients and nonrecipients), the level at which data are to be gathered, a listing of measures each data series would support, and possible data sources. We develop a suggested format for gathering this information, including a format for data series necessary to support the measurements presented in this report.

Future Development of BK21 and the University Research Sector

Although ultimate analysis of the BK21 Phase II program will have to await gathering of data to measure program effectiveness, BK21 program administrators also need to consider how to allocate program resources when making ongoing decisions. As the sponsor requested, we offer guidance on several topics related to BK21 and the research university system in Korea, including the research group (*sa-up-dan*) as the unit of support, award selection based on rankings of scientific merit, and the optimal number of research universities in Korea.

Addressing these topics required us to go beyond the findings of the evaluation model and database of this study. We base our analysis of these topics on our understanding of the BK21 program, the findings presented in this report, and other studies, particularly those in the United States, on research and education systems.

We recommend that Korea increase the role of merit-based competition in funding and award funds on an individual project basis. The *sa-up-dan* is not an optimal unit for support, even for graduate fellowships, because it does not promote full competition at the project and individual level. While there are valid reasons for the use of the *sa-up-dan* as a transitional strategy to improving academic and research capabilities, we recommend using smaller groups or individual projects to increase competition both among and within universities in the future. Project funding mechanisms, including size and length of funding, should be adapted to different fields of science. Although competition is important, it is also desirable to give researchers some stability in funding so that they can plan their programs. Awarding funds based on merit while allowing the best researchers to obtain grants of up to five years is a good way to balance competition and stability.

Similarly, granting portable fellowships for individuals to pursue graduate study will further increase competition and promote excellence. To finance infrastructure and facilities, Korea may also wish to promote the development of an efficient financial market where universities can borrow for construction. These loans would be repaid from overhead recovery on future projects performed in the new facilities. Until the required financial markets can operate effectively, however, Korean may prefer to use a competitive system of grants for facilities and infrastructure to spur university development in this area.

The U.S. system also offers some lessons to help more Korean universities attain research university status. The largest Korean universities currently have research expenditures on a scale similar to that of American research universities, but there is room for more Korean universities to reach this level. Given differences in the American and Korean economies, as well as in the composition of their populations, we estimate that Korea could support about 16 major research universities comparable with those in the United States. Korean university research could be stimulated further through a combination of competitive awards for project funding, fellowships for graduate students who select their universities, and university access to capital for construction of first-rate research facilities.

It may take a number of years to implement all these changes. Until that time, transition arrangements may be appropriate to encourage the university research system to become more responsive yet avoid abrupt shocks and dislocations.

Acknowledgments

This study benefited greatly from discussions with anonymous interviewees and policymakers at the Korea Ministry of Education and Human Resource Development (MoE), program evaluators and managers of BK21-NURI Committee (BNC) at the Korea Research Foundation, directors and managers of various university research laboratories, and researchers and consumers of BK21 program performance information. They generously provided insights and data for the study.

The authors would like to express special thanks to Mr. Gwangjo Kim, Deputy Minister for Human Resource Policy of MoE, Mr. Sanghyun Um, former Director General of the BK21 Planning Office of MoE, and Mr. Ik-hyun Shin, former Director of the BK21 Planning Office, for sharing their policy experiences and future visions of the BK21 program. Mr. Shin was a visiting fellow at RAND over the period of this study and provided invaluable comments and enthusiastic support for the study.

We also want to thank our reviewers, Brian Stecher, Francisco Martorell, Cathleen Stasz, and Susan Bodilly. Their thoughtful input did much to improve our manuscript. Miriam Polon skillfully edited the document, and Todd Duft guided it through the publication process. Myong-Hyun Go and Seo Yeon Hong provided efficient research assistance, and Regina Sandberg and Rochelle Hardison offered well-organized administrative support.

Finally, the authors are grateful to the Korea Research Foundation and the Korea Institute of Science and Technology and Evaluation Policy for their financial support.

Abbreviations

ARWU	Academic Ranking of World Universities
BK21	Brain Korea 21
BNC	BK21-NURI Committee
GNERD	gross national expenditure on research and development
GPS	Global Positioning System
GRF	graduate research fellowship
HR	human resource development
IPP	innovative products and processes
ISI	Institute of Scientific Information
ISIC	International Standard Industrial Classification
KAIST	Korea Advanced Institute of Science and Technology
KISTEP	Korea Institute of Science and Technology Evaluation and Planning
KRF	Korea Research Foundation
KRW	Korean won
MIC	Ministry of Information and Communication
MOCIE	Ministry of Commerce, Industry, and Energy
MoE	Ministry of Education and Human Resource Development
MOST	Ministry of Science and Technology
NURI	New University for Regional Innovation
OECD	Organization for Economic Co-operation and Development

OLS	ordinary least squares
POSTECH	Pohang University of Science and Technology
R&D	research and development
SCI	Science Citation Index
SD	standard deviation
SDR	Survey of Doctorate Recipients
SME	small or medium-sized enterprise
SNU	Seoul National University
S&T	science and technology
THES	*Times Higher Education Supplement*

CHAPTER ONE

Introduction

Background

In the late 1990s, the Korea Ministry of Education and Human Resource Development (MoE), in response to concern over the relatively low standing of the nation's universities and researchers, launched the Brain Korea 21 program (BK21). The program has had two phases so far. In Phase I, from 1999 to 2005, BK21 allocated about US$1.4 billion in funding.[1] In Phase II, which began in 2006 and is scheduled to run through 2012, BK21 will allocate an additional $2.1 billion.

BK21 Program Structure

BK21 seeks to nurture globally competitive research universities and graduate programs and to breed high-quality research manpower in Korea. BK21 funding is awarded to department-level research groups (*sa-up-dan*) in a stable lump sum over a seven-year period. BK21 recipient research groups are selected at the beginning of each seven-year phase. To qualify for BK21 funding, a research group must satisfy several conditions. It must have a doctorate program with enrolled PhD candidates. The number of faculty members participating in the research group must be at least seven for liberal arts and social sci-

---

[1] The Phase I program budget for the seven-year period was 1.34 trillion Korean won (KRW). The won has appreciated greatly since 1999. We used an approximate exchange rate of 950 KRW per one U.S. dollar in our calculations. As of August 16, 2007, the exchange rate was 950.50 Korean won to one U.S. dollar. The Phase II program plans to allocate 2.03 trillion KRW.

ence groups, ten for basic science groups, and 10–25 for applied science groups.[2] Participating professors must also produce or exceed a minimum average number of publications for the prior three years.[3] All research groups must secure matching funds from their universities equal to at least 5 percent of the level of BK21 funding that they seek. Applied science and interdisciplinary science research groups must secure matching funds from industry sources equal to at least 10 percent of BK21 funding. Regional university research groups must secure matching funds from local government equal to 3 to 5 percent of BK21 funding, depending on discipline.

BK21 funding covers scholarships and stipends for graduate students, postdoctoral scholars, and contract-based researchers but does not cover professors' labor cost or costs of equipment and facilities. BK21 funding is not project-based. Research groups are supposed to find other funding for research projects, equipment, and facilities.[4] The award size is basically proportional to the size of the department. BK21 recipients receive a fixed stipend every month.[5]

Although BK21 funds scholarships and stipends for individuals, individual recipients are not selected on their own merit but on the merit of their department and university. Award selection criteria are based on the qualifications of the research group to which the individuals belong, the excellence of their department, and their university's commitment to the department, institutional reform, and research infrastructure. Applicant universities are supposed to choose their academic areas of concentration, make a commitment to investing in the infrastructure needed to promote the selected areas of concentration, and plan for

---

[2] For applied science groups, the minimum number varies by discipline.

[3] For a basic science research group, for example, a participating faculty member should average at least three Science Citation Index (SCI) publication papers per person for the past three years.

[4] A one-time grant for a Seoul National University dormitory for graduate students in Phase I was the only exception.

[5] The minimum monthly payments are 500,000 KRW for a master's degree student, 900,000 KRW for a doctoral student, 2,000,000 KRW for a postdoctoral researcher, and 2,500,000 KRW for a contract-based research professor. As of August 16, 2007, the exchange rate was 950.50 KRW to US$1.

such reforms as improving accountability over research funds and the faculty evaluation system. Through these rules, the program seeks to induce changes across a university to increase global competitiveness.

Program funding allocations are made by academic discipline, geographical location, and scale of research group (MoE, 2006c). By academic discipline, science and engineering receive 85 percent of the Phase II funds for large-scale research projects; liberal arts, social science, and interdisciplinary fields account for the remainder. In science and engineering, applied science accounts for about three-fourths of resources and basic science for the remainder.[6]

By geographical location, about 25 percent of the total program budget is allocated for universities located outside the vicinity of Seoul. Regional universities compete in separate rounds in each academic field. Top universities, such as the Korea Advanced Institute of Science and Technology (KAIST) and the Pohang University of Science and Technology (POSTECH), although outside the vicinity of Seoul, are prohibited from applying for regional university support.

About 70 percent of the Phase II program budget is allocated to support department-level large research groups (*sa-up-dan*), in which 70 percent of the department's faculty members participate and the number of participating faculty exceeds the required minimum (which varies over different academic discipline).[7] Support for smaller-scale research teams accounts for about 20 percent of the BK21 Phase II budget, while support for professional schools and other expenses takes up about 10 percent.

Phase I and Phase II Comparison

The Phase I and Phase II programs are not much different from each other in their goals and missions, funding rules, and selection criteria. The few differences between the two are subtle and nuanced

---

[6] In BK21 Phase II, applied science is classified into seven areas: information technology, mechanical engineering, chemical engineering, material engineering, construction engineering, applied biological science, and interdisciplinary fusion science. Basic science includes five areas: physics, biological science, chemistry, mathematics, and earth science.

[7] The minimum number of faculty for each research group varies between seven (liberal arts and social science groups) and 25 (applied science groups).

in emphasis. Whereas Phase I emphasized university-level excellence, Phase II emphasizes department-level excellence.[8] Phase II emphasizes university-industry link more than Phase I. Institutional reforms are emphasized in Phase I more than in Phase II. A Phase II research group is based on a department of a single university, whereas the Phase I research groups originally started with investigators from multiple universities in the same academic discipline—one leading university and one or more participating universities. However, during the course of the Phase I, investigators of each university were regarded as a separate research group and each university accounted for its performance at the end of the Phase I program, which is basically the same as in Phase II. This study focuses on the Phase II program (2006–2012) and its program level performance evaluation model.

Significance of the Program

BK21 has attracted a great deal of attention—more, in fact, than its relative share of resources might at first seem to warrant. By our calculations, Phase I accounted for only 5 percent of government R&D expenditures, 10 percent of university R&D funding from all sources, and just 1 percent of gross R&D expenditures in Korea. Yet the program's strategy of concentration resulted in awards that were much larger than those of other, project-based funding programs. BK21 funding is also relatively stable for longer periods (seven consecutive years) than other funding is. As a result, the award selection process is highly competitive. BK21 funding is a mark of prestige for its recipients because the award is based on the comparative ranking of universities and departments.[9]

Given the high profile of the program, stakeholders—including universities, researchers, policymakers, and the National Assembly—

---

[8] The focus on department-level excellence in Phase II is based on one of the MoE's guiding principles in higher education policy—"specialization of universities." Instead of pursuing excellence in all fields, each university is encouraged to choose the areas where it wants to concentrate its resources and differentiate itself from other universities.

[9] For example, in Phase I of BK 21(1999–2005), about 90 percent of BK21 funding was allocated to 48 research groups in 14 universities in science and engineering. There are more than 216 four-year universities in Korea in 2006.

have all had great interest in it and in determining its effects on university R&D performance and human resource development. Unfortunately, key accountability questions have not been addressed well enough to satisfy all stakeholders; hence the extent to which BK21 is achieving its goals is still controversial.

Rapid growth in Science Citation Index (SCI) paper publication by Korean researchers is the most commonly used metric to demonstrate BK21 performance. However, whether the growth in SCI paper publication can be attributed to BK21, or to what extent, has not yet been proven. There are surveys and self-evaluation by recipient universities showing that BK21 has made a positive contribution. However, they are not well accepted as objective measures of program performance. In particular, the net impact of the program, i.e., the impact of the program above and beyond that of other concurrent trends and initiatives, has yet to be shown.

In its continuing search to find the best possible means for evaluating this important program, the MoE and the Korea Research Foundation (KRF) asked the RAND Corporation for advice on Phase II evaluation.

Objective of the Study

In this study, we develop an evaluation model to assess the net effect of the BK21 Phase II program.[10] Our evaluation model includes a logic model, a quantitative model, and evaluation metrics. The study will also suggest prototype database structures that would allow assessment of Phase II program achievement in the future. Based on the findings of the evaluation model and database structures, we make recommendations for future management of the program and of the university research sector more generally.[11]

---

[10] Phase I performance evaluation is beyond the scope of this study. Phase I evaluations were done by previous studies in Korea.

[11] The sponsors asked us to derive the broad policy implications beyond the findings of the evaluation model and database structures.

Approach

We begin with a logic model that shows major elements of the program and the links among them. The logic model is a diagram showing relationships among goals and missions, activities, incentives, inputs, outputs, and outcomes of the program. It serves as a conceptual framework for identifying the goals of the study as well as for the evaluation metrics and quantitative assessment model we later develop.

Our quantitative assessment model aims to evaluate the net effects of the BK21 Phase II program. In developing it, we consider critical issues that have been raised regarding the program evaluation during its implementation as well as those that will likely be raised in the future. We suggest options for metrics and measures that allow objective assessment of program effects.[12]

To execute the quantitative assessment model and the evaluation metrics, we suggest a prototype database structure. For the future assessment of the BK21 achievement, the prototype database will be structured to address some core questions of objective assessment. In designing the database, we explicitly consider practical issues concerning its use, such as accumulating data, evaluating performance, and monitoring the progress of the program.

As the sponsors requested, we also offer guidance on several topics related to BK21 and the research university system in Korea.[13] Some of these topics extend beyond the main objective of the study. We base our analysis of these topics on our understanding of the BK21 program, the findings presented in this monograph, and other studies on research and education systems, particularly those in the United States.

---

[12] In this monograph, a *metric* is defined as the ideal yardstick by which we would wish to evaluation Bk21 program performance, observed periodically to assess progress toward the program's goal. Metric is abstract higher level attributes mapped into BK21 logic model. A *measure* is defined as the practical means we may use to estimate the value of a metric. Measures are concrete and objectively measurable manifestation of the metric. Measurement is the activity of obtaining results for one or more measures.

[13] Chapter Seven contains the list of topics.

Outline of the Monograph

In the next chapter, we review existing evaluations of BK21's Phase I to incorporate their "lessons learned" into our new evaluation model. In Chapter Three, we present a logic model, based on our analysis of the relevant literature as well as comments of key BK21 stakeholders. In Chapter Four, we develop a quantitative method for identifying the impact of Phase II. In Chapter Five, we suggest metrics needed to evaluate the program and available measures for each metric. In Chapter Six, we present a database structure for assembling the measures necessary to evaluate program effects. Chapter Seven applies the findings of the earlier chapters and our knowledge of research and education systems to derive policy implications for the future management of the program and of the university research sector more generally. We present our conclusions and summarize recommendations in Chapter Eight.

CHAPTER TWO

Implications of Phase I Program Evaluations for Phase II Evaluations

In this chapter, we review the findings of Phase I evaluations[1] to derive implications for evaluating Phase II. The purpose of this chapter is not to provide a comprehensive survey of existing evaluations and the associated literature but to extract lessons for designing an evaluation model that can show the net effect of the Phase II program.

Previous Performance Evaluations of BK21 Phase I

Phase I had two types of evaluations: (1) annual and interim evaluations to assess how each recipient research group was progressing each year and (2) program evaluations to assess the program's overall effects. We review each of these below.

Annual and Interim Evaluations

Expert panels organized by KRF evaluated the progress of Phase I recipient research groups each year. These evaluations monitored the adherence to specific contractual terms and promises that had been made by the recipient groups before the award selection.[2] The interim

---

[1] See MoE (2005a) for a discussion Phase I program evaluation.

[2] Contractual terms in the Phase I award usually included qualifications of the recipient and implementation of institutional reforms such as reduction in undergraduate enrollments. Reduction in undergraduate enrollments was suggested by BK21 Phase I to divert resources to graduate education and research. Many observers criticized the forced reforms

evaluations in 2002 and 2004 assessed overall progress of the research groups in achieving their goals. Interestingly, the goals of the research groups are directed by the selection process. Therefore, evaluation metrics for the interim evaluations were constructed around the selection criteria.

At the end of Phase I, program-level achievements were presented as aggregated performance indicators for the individual research groups—e.g., number of papers published by BK21 recipients, summaries of survey results on how much influence the program had on its recipients, or national-level R&D and technology indicators, such as total number of papers published by Korean authors.

However, the sum of the recipients' performance indicators did not exactly show the extent to which Phase I had achieved its stated goals. Because the performance indicators were directed by the selection criteria, they did not necessarily measure the contribution of the program. The survey results reported as Phase I achievements did not show what difference the program made to the recipients as compared with nonrecipients. The national-level R&D and technology indicators did not distinguish the BK21 contribution from that of other programs or general trends.

The poor presentation of program achievements can be attributed to two facts, among many. First, there was no evaluation model sophisticated enough to show the net effect of Phase I. Second, there were no systematic efforts to compile data for objective analysis of program performance. The data compiled for annual and interim evaluations by the KRF were the main sources of available data, and these were limited to Phase I recipients. However, it is necessary to compile data for comparisons with a control group, as well as with statistics and trends on R&D, human resource development, and the higher education sector in general.[3]

---

for allegedly harming the autonomy of universities for goals that were seemingly disconnected from the program's goal of nurturing globally competitive research universities.

[3] These conditions are necessary but not sufficient for detecting BK21 effects. In Chapters Four through Six we discuss the data requirements in more detail.

Program-Level Evaluations

There were several efforts to assess Phase I, although they did not isolate its net effects. These studies sought to evaluate the achievements and challenges of the Phase I program and to provide suggestions for Phase II. We review each below.

Oh et al. (2005), one of three evaluations conducted under KRF auspices, surveyed research group leaders and collected statistics, exemplary cases, and opinions regarding Phase I program achievements. The survey asked the recipient research groups for both quantitative and qualitative information. Quantitative performance measures included human resource production (such as how many MAs and PhDs were granted), research capability, patents, collaborative research with industry, technology transfer to industry, research and education infrastructure, and international exchanges.[4] More-descriptive measures based on the survey included those concerning institutional reform, program goal achievement, opinions on whether the program should continue to Phase II, and the program's contribution to improvement in the research and education conditions of the recipient groups.[5] The survey was restricted to recipient groups from 2000 to 2004 and did not allow analysis of the marginal contribution of BK21.

B. J. Kim et al. (2005), another KRF evaluation, conducted a Delphi Survey of BK21 research group leaders on Phase I achievements and limitations.[6] The study also surveyed graduate students in recipient research groups on their satisfaction with research and education by faculty members, their own activities in research and education, educational infrastructure and facilities, faculty-student ratio, financial

---

[4] Quantitative measures are based on numbers and statistics.

[5] Descriptive measures are based on survey results, either in scales (such as "on a scale of 1 to 5 . . .") or in words.

[6] The Delphi method, originally developed by the RAND Corporation to forecast the impact of technology on warfare, is a structured group interaction process. Opinions are collected by conducting a series of surveys using questionnaires, with the results of each survey being used to construct the subsequent questionnaire. The key to Delphi is that anonymous summaries are presented between rounds to influence subsequent rounds without focusing on personalities.

and other support, international cooperation, university-industry collaboration, and other educational environment and services.

B. K. Kim et al. (2005), a third KRF evaluation, conducted focus group interviews with faculty members of nonrecipient universities and surveyed recipient research group leaders for their view of Phase I achievements and their suggestions regarding Phase II.[7] The study, however, did not explore performance differences between the recipient and nonrecipient groups or how recipients changed as a result of program participation. Rather, the study focused on improving operations for the Phase II program.

Lee et al. (2005) analyzed the BK21 program for the MoE. Their work summarizes opinions on the program's merits and failures as expressed in a series of expert meetings and discussions. The experts included seven Korean-American scholars active in science and engineering research in the United States as well as seven local scientists and engineers from academia and industry. Rather than a being systematic assessment, the study reflected the brainstorming of experts on identifying program successes and failures.

Lee, Lee, and Kim (2005) evaluated Phase I for the National Assembly Budget Office, analyzing consistency among different elements of the program using a logic model framework that included ultimate goals, intermediate goals, inputs, and program implementation and practices. They also analyzed some statistics compiled by the MoE and KRF. While they did not analyze the net contribution of the program to changes in these indicators, they did note the importance of such work for future evaluation research.

Chang and Chun (2005) examined labor market outcomes for BK21 program graduates. Unfortunately, their full report, sponsored by the KRF and the Korea Research Institute for Vocational Education and Training, is not publicly available. A MoE (2005a) summary of the study indicates that it surveyed 1,285 graduates about their first jobs and salary levels. Training indicators in the survey included length

---

[7]   B. K. Kim et al (2005) also sought to identify linkages between employment and human resources goals of the BK21 program, reviewing literature on the future demand for and supply of highly educated manpower.

of BK21 participation, number of publications during BK21 participation, and experience with international training. Labor market outcome indicators included choice between entering a PhD program and seeking a job,[8] length of job search, and level of wages.

KRF (2007) documents the history of the program from its inception to Phase I results. Performance indicators were based on data collected by KRF and MoE during the course of the program. This study describes Phase I program-level achievements by aggregating quantitative indicators at the research-group level.

KISTEP (2007) is a study sponsored by KRF and performed by Korea Institute of Science and Technology Evaluation and Planning (KISTEP) researchers in collaboration with experts at Media Research.[9] It takes a two-pronged approach, combining an analysis of performance indicators drawn from KRF (2007) and a qualitative assessment of the program through a Career Path Survey and Employer Survey. The Career Path Survey was conducted among research group leaders and faculty members participating in Phase I. It asked respondents to identify the kinds of jobs BK21 graduates took and the relevance of BK21 training to their career choices. For the survey's purposes, *BK21 graduates* were either those who obtained doctoral degrees or postdoctoral researchers who moved on to other work; master's degree students were not included. The Employer Survey collected employers' opinions on job performance of the BK21 graduates from science and engineering research groups. Of the 110 employers responding to the survey, 27 were from academic institutes, 66 were from industry, and 17 were from the public sector. The questionnaires, which covered such topics as the capabilities of program graduates and employer satisfaction with them, asked respondents to compare BK21 graduates with doctoral degree holders from nonrecipient universities.

Areas of evaluation commonly used in all these evaluations included R&D capability, human resource development, links to indus-

---

[8] The study does not appear to distinguish outcomes for master's and doctoral degree graduates.

[9] Because KISTEP (2007) is an ongoing study, we reviewed the interim report of the study as of April 2007, together with survey results compiled by Media Research.

try, infrastructure, institutional reform, and international exchanges. Performance indicators for these areas were generally similar. Appendix A summarizes the areas of evaluation and performance indicators used in the previous evaluations.

Findings from Previous Evaluations

We summarize two types of findings from previous evaluations: those regarding changes possibly resulting from the Phase I program, and suggestions for future evaluations.

Changes Resulting from BK21 Phase I

Among the changes resulting from BK21 Phase I program, the most frequently mentioned was a rapid increase in the number of SCI papers.

KISTEP (2007) reported that the annual growth rate in the number of SCI papers from 1999 to 2005 was 12.8 percent for the science and engineering research groups. This exceeded the 11.5 percent growth for all universities. Nevertheless, the annual growth rate in SCI papers for all BK21 participants was lower than that for all universities.

Oh et al. (2005) and KRF (2007) found that many science and engineering research groups in Phase I were comparable to benchmark universities in number of SCI papers per faculty member.[10] Many research groups published more than they had planned. The quality of papers by BK21 research groups, however, was below that of benchmark universities, as measured by impact factors.[11]

KISTEP (2007) found that SCI papers for postdoctoral researchers and research professors had increased by 33 percent during the Phase I

---

[10] For the Information Technology Research Group of KAIST, benchmark universities included MIT, Stanford, University of California, Berkeley, and the University of Illinois at Urbana-Champaign.

[11] The *impact factor* of a journal is defined as the number of references to articles appearing in that journal that are cited in papers published in other journals, divided by the total number of articles published in the first journal. It counts citations appearing two to three years after initial publication.

program period, and those for graduate students had increased by 32 percent—both greater rates of increase than the 9 percent increase for faculty members. Oh et al. (2005), Lee et al. (2005), B. J. Kim et al. (2005), and KRF (2007) also found that the quantity and quality of BK21 graduate student research had increased. B. J. Kim et al. attributed this to the greater opportunities for presentations and publications that BK21 graduate students enjoyed, as well as to the greater flexibility and motivation to produce research that BK21 grants provided.

Greater competition among universities and faculty members was also commonly seen as a positive result of the program. Lee et al. (2005) claimed that, prior to the BK21 program, lack of competition was a problem in university community. B. J. Kim et al. (2005), Lee et al. (2005), and KRF (2007) all found that the competition induced by BK21 led faculty members to become more committed to research. B. J. Kim et al. (2005) and B. K. Kim et al. (2005) also found that introducing performance-based faculty evaluation system further intensified competition for publication among faculty members.

The evaluations also cited improved research and education conditions. Lee et al. (2005) and B. J. Kim et al. (2005) found that departments receiving BK21 support had more teaching assistants and research assistants than before. Oh et al. (2005), B. J. Kim et al. (2005), and Lee et al. (2005) also found that as the number of post-doctoral and contact-based researchers increased, the student-faculty ratio improved.

Although the BK21 budget for international collaboration was relatively small, several evaluations noted that this part of the program was considered one of the most important. Lee et al. (2005) and B. J. Kim et al. (2005) found that graduate students greatly appreciated the benefit of international exchange. B. J. Kim et al. added that such collaboration gave graduate students more confidence to compete internationally and that international exchanges improved the quality of research and education in the recipient graduate departments.

Other areas of change mentioned included institutional reform and university-industry collaboration. Among institutional reform efforts induced by BK21, performance-based faculty evaluation systems and centralized management of R&D funds were among the most appreciated (Lee et al., 2005, KISTEP, 2007). Phase I changes to the university-industry link were not appreciated as well. Many of the existing studies even contended that weak emphasis of this link was one of the limitations of Phase I, while others said that Phase I helped establish a university-industry network.

Suggestions for Improving the Evaluation System

Several previous evaluations of BK21 suggested options for improving the evaluation system. Most frequently, these focused on performance indicators.

Many previous evaluations of Phase I suggested improving the balance between quantity and quality indicators. B. K. Kim et al. (2005), KRF (2007), and KISTEP (2007), found that quantity indicators, such as number of SCI papers, were the most commonly used yardstick in Phase I evaluations but that quality indicators, such as the quality of research papers, are equally important. They also suggested that more weight be placed on impact factors and that other appropriate quality indicators be devised.

Lee et al. (2005) suggested developing proper indicators to assess human resource development (HRD). They noted that it is problematic to use the number of BK21 grant recipients as a major HRD performance indicator.

Lee, Lee, and Kim (2005) and KRF (2007) contended that too many performance indicators were applied to Phase I recipient selection and performance evaluations. Too many performance indicators, they argued, may cloud the goals of the program. They therefore suggested a more narrow set of performance indicators that focused on the core outputs or outcomes of Phase II.

Oh et al. (2005), Lee, Lee, and Kim (2005), and KISTEP (2007) emphasized long-term evaluations of BK21. They suggested that it may be too early to assess the full effect of the program. Oh et al. (2005) and Lee, Lee, and Kim (2005) also noted the need for assessing net program effects in future evaluations.

KISTEP (2007) and KRF (2007) emphasized the linkage between the evaluation system and the behavior of recipients. Evaluations can help guide program changes; in fact, annual and midterm

Phase I evaluations influenced recipients' activities and decisionmaking. Evaluation systems should be designed both to help achieve goals and to monitor program progress.[12]

Limitations of Previous Evaluations

One of the most important purposes of program evaluation is to provide public accountability. In the case of BK21, this includes addressing such topics as the extent to which the program achieves its stated goals and the program's net contributions to R&D capability and R&D manpower production in comparison to those of other programs.

Unfortunately, previous evaluations did not address these accountability issues. With the exception of KISTEP's (2007) employer survey, they did not consider performance differences between recipients and nonrecipients.[13] None of the evaluations controlled for the influences of other programs or other general trends in performance indicators.

There were several reasons why Phase I evaluations were not able to show the Phase I program impact. First, they did not use proper data to show the net program effects of BK21. For example, data were generally limited to Phase I recipients for the period of the program. Data on increased numbers of SCI publications, for example, may have resulted from changing the importance of publication in faculty evalu-

---

[12] In the program evaluation literature, evaluations concerned with program improvement are called *formative evaluations*; evaluations that make an overall judgment about program effect are called *summative* evaluations. Patton (1980) suggests that "it is important at the outset of the evaluation process to clarify the extent to which the primary purpose of an evaluation is to make an overall judgment about the effectiveness of a program (summative evaluation) or to collect information that can be used primarily for ongoing program development and improvement (formative evaluation)." The primary purpose of our study is to suggest a model for summative evaluation of the BK21 program, although some of the metrics and measures suggested in Chapters Five and Six can be also used for formative evaluations.

[13] Some of questions in KISTEP's (2007) employer survey were constructed so that respondents could compare the job capabilities of BK21 graduates with those of graduates of nonrecipient universities.

ations or from possible increases in the number of publishers and journals in Korea.

Second, previous evaluations were not designed to consider net program effect. Quantitative analyses were usually characterized as preliminary analyses of the statistical characteristics of performance indicators. These analyses typically showed levels and changes in performance indicators for recipient groups during Phase I. The level of sophistication in these analyses, including those of the number of SCI publications, fell short of that needed for objective assessment of net program effect. Surveys and interviews are also lacking in the ability to distinguish BK21 program effect from the influence of other programs and trends. B. K. Kim et al. (2005) include focus group interviews with nonrecipients, but these interviews were not designed to compare the performance of recipients with that of nonrecipients. The KISTEP (2007) Employer Survey includes questions on both program participants and nonparticipants but does not account for variables beyond program participation that may have influenced worker performance; hence, it does not allow analysis of net program effects on job capabilities.

Third, previous evaluations lacked evaluation models that were logically consistent, theoretically sound, and practical enough to show net program effects. Existing evaluations generally did not question which metrics should be used to assess program performance, the strength of causality between the goals of the program and selected metrics, and how metrics are related to each other. Most of the studies seemed to assume that evaluation metrics were largely predetermined by the areas of program supports and the selection criteria. The Lee, Lee, and Kim (2005) study was the only one to examine the linkage among different elements of the program in a logic model framework. Still, it did not develop a full logic model for directing an objective assessment of the BK21 program impact. None of the Phase I program evaluations made the effort to establish a systematic model for objective assessment of the program's net contributions.

Fourth, previous evaluations did not develop program-level metrics and measures.[14] Most previous evaluations assumed that program-level performance is the sum of recipients' individual performance indicators. Typically, previous evaluations aggregated statistics collected at the research-group level to the academic discipline or subprogram level and then to the program level. Most previous evaluations used the same metrics for both the research-group level and the program level.[15] This is problematic because program goals are broader than the goals of individual research groups. As noted previously, research group goals are strongly influenced by the selection criteria. Selection criteria and contractual terms direct goals of recipient research groups, but these criteria and contractual terms are not necessarily identical to program goals. The selection criteria and goals of individual research groups may reflect some of the short-term outputs of the program but not necessarily its long-term outcomes. Therefore, program-level performance metrics should not be identical to those used to measure the performance of individual research groups.

Implications for Designing the Phase II Evaluation Model

The limitations of previous Phase I evaluations suggest directions for future improvement.

First, Phase II evaluations should be designed to show the net contributions of the program. The evaluation needs to consider explicitly the existence of other R&D programs and funds in Korea and their increasing investment in university so that it can assess BK21's net effect.

---

[14] In this monograph, metrics and measures are defined as follows. A *metric* is the ideal yardstick by which we evaluate BK21 program performance. observed periodically to assess progress toward the program's goals. A *measure* is the practical means we use to estimate the value of a metric. Refer to Chapter Five for the details of the definition.

[15] The study by Lee, Lee, and Kim (2005) is an exception. This study examines some macro statistics such as current account balance of studying abroad and also evaluates consistency between the program goals and the design of the program. These variables are not research-group-level metrics.

Second, a set of metrics and measures to assess national-level achievements beyond achievements of individual research groups, departments, or universities needs to be developed. The set of program performance metrics and measures may partially overlap the existing indicators but would not necessarily be the same. Program performance evaluation metrics and measures for Phase II should reflect the goals of the program and the paths that lead to achieving those goals.

Third, it is necessary to establish a database that will facilitate objective assessment of the program performance and the process of monitoring the program. The database should contain data for recipients and nonrecipients, as well as statistics and trends on R&D, HRD, and the higher education sector in general.

In the following three chapters, we propose an evaluation model that allows assessment of the net program effect of the BK21 Phase II program. The model includes a logic model, a quantitative model, and relevant metrics and their measures to allow both quantitative and qualitative assessment of program effect. Then, we suggest a database structure to facilitate assessment of program effect.

CHAPTER THREE

A Logic Model for Evaluating BK21

We begin by developing a logic model to specify the goals and missions, inputs, activities, incentives, outputs, and outcomes of BK21 and the logical linkages among them. This provides a conceptual framework for the quantitative assessment model we discuss in Chapter Four and the evaluation metrics and measures we discuss in Chapter Five.

In presenting the elements of our logic model, we seek to comprehend the underlying policy intentions, program structure, and dynamics of the program effects. In discussing program goals and missions, we want to identify implicit and explicit program goals by which performance will be evaluated and how those goals and missions are related to other elements of the program. In discussing program inputs, we seek to capture the structure of the program, including its resources and rules. In discussing program activities, incentives, outputs, and outcomes, we attempt to describe the program dynamics.

Literature Review and Focus Group Interviews

The logic model is based on two sources of information: our review of relevant literature and focus group interviews with key BK21 informants. Our review of relevant literature included both general material on identifying and evaluating the effects of research and educational programs, such as BK21, as well as documents and existing literature more specific to the program that concerned its policy intentions and the background of its structure.[1]

We conducted our focus groups with BK21 program managers and directors, key MoE officials, directors and managers of university laboratories, researchers, and consumers of performance information. During these interviews, we asked about

- the policy intentions behind the stated missions and goals of the BK21 Phase II program
- changes induced by Phase I program
- the suitability of Phase I effects as a benchmark for measuring Phase II effects
- interviewees' expectations of Phase II outcomes.

We sought to understand not only the implicit and explicit goals, objectives, and dynamics of BK21 but also to develop a keen sense of the debate about the program in Korea. Understanding the expectations of both program leadership and the public is critical for designing an evaluation framework.

We conducted our interviews with program participants, policymakers, and users of the university research education system in late 2006. For each interview, we followed a semi-structured interview protocol, presented in Appendix B, with questions derived from our initial logic model.

In total, we interviewed 20 individuals in seven group meetings. These included

- an administrator from a national university that was a "winner-winner" institution, gaining both Phase I and Phase II funding
- three university professors from "loser-winner" institutions, including two private universities and one national university, that gained only Phase II funding. All three, like the "winner-

---

[1] Literature reviewed includes Brewer, Gates, and Goldman (2002), Goldman and Massy (2001), Ruegg and Feller (2003), MoE (2005a, 2005b, 2006a, 2006b, 2006c), Chang (2005), Chang and Chun (2005), Kim et al. (2005), KBJ (2005), KISTEP (2006), Lee et al. (2005), Lee, Lee, and Kim (2005), and Oh (2005).

winner" university, are among the top five universities receiving the largest amount of BK21 funding[2]

- six BK21-New University for Regional Innovation (NURI) Committee (BNC) staff of the KRF, who are known as experts on all aspects of the BK21 program
- three members of the Program Management Committee of the BNC
- five officials at the MoE who lead the current Phase II program or were in charge of planning it
- a corporate executive of one of the largest employers in Korea who is knowledgeable about the BK21 program and is also a corporate member of the BNC
- a National Assembly member interested in education and research who was an education policy researcher before joining the Assembly.

Respondents participated under conditions of confidentiality. We sent them some specific questions from the protocol before the interviews. Their comments reflect both how the program operates in practice and changes that they believe the program should induce.

Developing the Logic Model

Developing the logic model required us to consider several questions. These included the following:

- *What is to be measured?* We intend to measure the extent to which BK21 is achieving its articulated goals. Ideally, evaluation metrics should reflect those goals.
- *At what level of aggregation should effects be examined?* Our charge is to evaluate program effects at the national level. How-

---

[2]   Combined, these four universities accounted for 40 percent of Phase II funding. Altogether, 74 universities (with 243 research groups and 325 small-scale research teams) won Phase II funding. We sought, but were unable to gain, interviews with representatives from universities winning neither Phase I nor Phase II funding.

ever, to understand the program's dynamics, we cannot overlook its influence on the activities and incentives of individuals and institutions.

- *How do we measure program effect?* Ideally, our evaluation should distinguish the contribution of Phase II from that of other programs funding university R&D and education.

Our logic model for evaluation, shown in Figure 3.1, reflects each of these questions in one way or another. Below we briefly review the major elements of the model, discussing each in further detail in subsequent sections.

Goals are what the program intends to achieve ultimately. *Missions* are operational tasks to achieve the goals. The stated BK21 Phase II

Figure 3.1
Logic Model for BK21 Phase II Evaluation

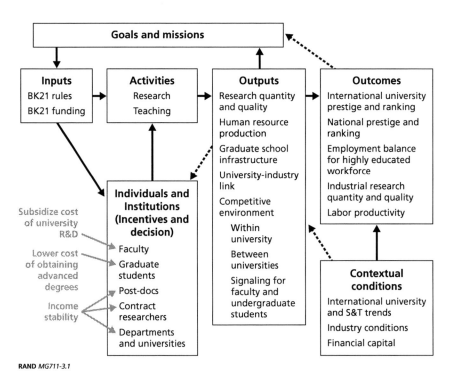

RAND *MG711-3.1*

program goals are nurturing next generation of research manpower and strengthening graduate school departments and programs in Korea so that they are globally competitive. Core missions of the program are to improve the research capability of faculty and graduate students, to enhance the quality of research and training, and to help improve the infrastructure of graduate schools.

Inputs are BK21 funding and the rules of the program to accomplish its missions and goals. BK21 funding is used to improve the research and teaching activities and decisionmaking of universities, academic departments, and individuals. It is intended to complement rather than substitute for other funding. Recipient departments may be able to leverage BK21 funding within the university to obtain other research funding, although the complementarity of the funding remains to be proven.

BK21 rules are principles and regulations that govern the conduct of participants and procedures for program implementation. The program rules include strategies of the program, policy instruments, funding rules, selection criteria, evaluation criteria, and other operational mechanisms.

Activities and *incentives* comprise the dynamics of the program. *Program inputs* influence incentives of individuals and institutions. Individuals include graduate students, postdoctoral researchers, contract-based researchers, and faculty. Institutions include departments and universities. Program inputs also influence research and teaching activities in universities directly or indirectly through changes in people's incentives. Some changes may be produced by program design; others may be unintentional.

Outputs are the products of research and teaching activities. They reflect the results of interaction among people and institutions involved. As activities and incentives change in response to BK21, program outputs may change in quantity, as reflected by the number of doctoral and master's degree holders, or in quality, as reflected by recipients' publications. Program outputs also may affect the infrastructure (e.g., operation, management systems) of graduate schools and the competitive environment within and between universities.

Outcomes include both the intended and unintended long-term effects of the program. They may have to do with international prestige of Korean universities in particular and of higher education more generally, as well as effects on labor productivity, workforce skills, and links between industry and universities. They may be affected not only by BK21 but also by efforts made by other universities and by the broader financial and science and technology (S&T) trends in the rest of the world that affect academic and professional opportunities. The causality between program inputs and outcomes may not therefore be as direct as that between inputs and outputs of the program.

In the next three sections of this chapter, we review in more depth the (1) goals and missions, (2) inputs, and (3) incentives, activities, outputs, and outcomes of the program.

Identifying the Goals and Missions

Ideally, the goals and missions of a publicly funded program should be articulated at the beginning of the program in a way that addresses public accountability questions. Many programs, however, fall short of the ideal. For BK21, various MoE documents state program goals and missions in different ways, but not in a way that facilitates evaluation. To identify the goals and missions of the program more clearly for the purpose of performance evaluation, we reviewed documents on BK21 and interviewed program leaders.

The MoE endorsed two documents on goals for Phase II. The *Plan for the Phase II BK21 Program* (MoE, 2006a), released shortly before the recipient selection process started, outlines program goals, implementation, procedures, and future agenda. The *Year 2006 Basic Managerial Plan for Phase II BK21 Program* (2006c), released after recipients were selected, elaborates the background and goals of the Phase II program, reports on its progress, and provides the year 2006 agenda of the program.

These publications do not state goals in a clear, consistent manner that can facilitate the evaluation process, much less link goals to other elements of the programs. Our interviews with BK21 stakeholders helped supplement our understanding of programs goals and missions as well as the debate over them.

Below, we describe the process of how we finally synthesized the goals and missions of the program and what they are to our best knowledge.

Goals

Although they have remained somewhat consistent over time, MoE goals for the program have also evolved, and linkages among goals and missions have not always been explained clearly. MoE (2006c) notes that the ultimate goals of the program are (1) nurturing creative research manpower for the future and (2) fostering research universities specialized in specific academic disciplines. "Creative" and "research manpower" are both key words for these goals, particularly in nurturing academic manpower specifically, and not just highly skilled workers generally, who can create new knowledge and new technology.[3]

Many respondents identified two similar, related goals for BK21: providing graduate education to the next generation of workers and increasing the quality and quantity of Korean university research. A number of respondents said that the two goals—the education goal and the research goal—sometimes conflicted. This is probably due to the trade-off in time allocation of faculty members between research and teaching.

Regarding the relationship between the two goals of nurturing creative research manpower and fostering research universities with specialties in selected disciplines, one of the respondents told us, "The BK21 Phase II program is a research training program. High-quality research training is the key element of BK21 Phase II. Research and human resource development cannot be separated for advanced degree programs. To supply top-notch research manpower, Korea needs high-

---

[3] MoE (2006a) offers a slightly different first goal. It notes the first goal as "producing globally competitive top-notch human resources," which appears to indicate a desire for a high-quality labor force in general rather than a specifically academic workforce. In interviews with the MoE BK21 leadership, we raised the issue of differences in stated goals between MoE (2006a) and MoE (2006c). In response, some leaders asked us to view the latter document as the most recent, and therefore the most authoritative.

quality graduate schools to train them. To foster high-quality graduate schools, there should be enough high-quality students and faculty and research activities." Other respondents told us that nurturing top research manpower (education) is the primary goal, a priority that MoE (2006a, 2006c) appear to confirm. Some respondents suggested a secondary goal, strengthening the Korean graduate school system in general, which differs from the official one of fostering globally competitive research universities with strong specialties.

We asked our respondents whether BK21 places a higher priority on increasing the number of advanced degree holders or on improving the quality of the workforce. They told us that both quantity and quality matter in developing knowledge workers. Highly qualified scientists and engineers are always in short supply in Korea, even with adequate numbers of science and engineering majors at the undergraduate level. BK21 seeks to have these undergraduates hold more-productive jobs. Low-end jobs are now filled by foreigners, while the number of middle-level jobs is static. Future employment for Koreans is therefore most feasible in high-end jobs. Our respondents saw the BK21 program as important for cultivating these high-end jobs. They did not identify a specific plan in the BK21 program for doing so but rather assumed that opportunities would be created as more qualified individuals become available to fill high-end positions.

When we asked whether the BK21 program was designed to alleviate possible mismatches between jobs and candidates for them, our respondents indicated that the BK21 program is intended to promote linkage to industry labor demand, hopefully through students and staff exchanges and codevelopment of curriculum, especially in applied science fields.

Does the program promote more locally conducted research by producing more doctoral and master's degree holders and keeping high-quality students in Korea rather than sending them abroad? Respondents indicated that while having more knowledge-intensive activities inside the country was always desirable, BK21 currently does not necessarily seek to keep every high-quality student in Korea. Rather, some first-tier students will continue to study abroad, but other students can be retained and developed in Korea, especially if graduate programs are competitive. Several respondents said that the program should ultimately try to keep talented Korean students in Korea for their graduate studies rather than having them go abroad, at least in the long run.

We also asked our respondents whether they intend, by creating global centers of excellence, to compete for, maintain, and recruit high-quality labor from all over the world and, if so, why foreigners are not encouraged to become BK21 recipients. They told us that BK21 seeks to provide research training for Korean students while other programs help support foreign students. They added that, in the short run, it is challenging for Korea to compete for high-quality labor in the world market, given language barriers, limited career opportunities, and the living environment in Korea. In the long run, however, our respondents said that recruiting talented students from all over the world should be a goal of the program.

We asked whether BK21 goals for arts, humanities, and social sciences, which receive about 10 percent of Phase II funding, are the same as those for S&T. Our respondents said they are, and one respondent argued that it is important for Korea to develop world-class talent in these fields as well. As another also said, the expected outcome of the program is "overall capacity building in highly skilled labor and high quality research."

In summary, we identify the goals of the program as (1) increasing the size and capability of the research manpower pool that can create new knowledge and technologies and (2) fostering globally competitive graduate departments and research universities.

Missions

To achieve program goals, Phase II sets forth three missions: (1) fostering world-class research groups to nurture next-generation scientists and engineers; (2) establishing infrastructure—both physical facilities and institutional arrangement, such as an improved faculty evaluation system and accountability over research funds—to help research universities meet their own needs for high-quality manpower as well as those of industry; (3) promoting regional universities that will lead to innovations in those regions.[4]

At first glance, the third mission may appear to be unrelated to the other two, particularly the first goal for fostering "world-class" research groups. Nevertheless, MoE (2006a) claims that promoting regional universities can serve the R&D and human resource needs of regional industry, particularly to the extent that certain academic specialties are developed to support regional industry. The third mission may also help address equity concerns, because most leading higher education institutions in Korea are in the Seoul area (KRF, 2007).

The regional university promotion mission (third mission) may be at odds with fostering a core of research groups and institutions that are globally competitive (first mission). This may create a central dilemma for policymakers and evaluators when they are thinking about the goals of the program and devising metrics with which to evaluate the program performance.

Interestingly, many respondents did not include regional university promotion as one of the core missions of the program. They identified three core missions for BK21: (1) improving the research capability of faculty and graduate students, (2) enhancing the quality of research and training at graduate schools, and (3) building graduate school infrastructure. These differ from the stated missions in MoE (2006a, 2006c). They match only the first two missions identified in MoE publications.

Some respondents recognized the conflict between the mission of promoting regional universities and that of nurturing world-class research groups. They noted, however, that the recipient regional universities are also selected for their academic excellence. Thus, regional universities that become among the best in the nation in their specialized fields could later become among the best in the world in these fields.

Although the second mission—infrastructure building—stated in MoE (2006a) includes strengthening the university-industry link to meet industry demand for highly skilled labor, it is not exactly part

---

[4]   MoE (2006a).

of the physical and institutional infrastructure for globally competitive graduate programs in general. While industry-university links may provide more research opportunities for certain academic disciplines, such as the applied sciences, they may not always be necessary for achieving the broader goal of the program.

Phase II emphasizes links between universities and industry much more than Phase I did. These links are stressed in the mission to meet industry demand for highly skilled labor, in the milestones for technology transfer, and in the selection criteria for recipient departments.[5] This emphasis stems from Phase I program evaluations (MoE, 2005a, MoE, 2006a, and MoE, 2006c) claiming that BK21 was biased toward research performance and hence undervalued links between universities and industry as well as the economic contribution of universities.

Emphasizing the economic contribution of universities may not be always compatible with the goal of nurturing globally competitive research universities in Korea. Perceived excellence, as reflected in rankings of prestige, and actual excellence, as demonstrated by publications, both matter to top international universities. Pursuing such excellence requires considerable long-term investment, with benefits that may not always be large enough to justify the cost of obtaining it (Brewer, Gates, and Goldman, 2002).

In summary, we identify the missions of the program as (1) supporting excellent research groups; (2) building the physical and institutional infrastructure for globally competitive graduate programs; and (3) enhancing university-industry links and strengthening local universities. We regard the mission of promoting regional universities as a subset of strengthening university-industry links because regional university promotion aims to establish regional industrial innovation clusters, according to MoE (2006a).

Performance Milestones

MoE (2006a) initially offered three milestones for assessing the effects of the Phase II program. First, the program should help yield ten "world-class" research universities in Korea by 2012 and improve the

---

5   Milestones and selection criteria will be discussed later in this monograph.

nation's SCI paper publication ranking from 13th in 2005 to 10th in 2012. However, the milestone of "world-class" research universities does not include a definition of such universities, nor does it offer standards for judging leading departments.[6] One of the respondents told us that having "ten globally competitive research universities by 2012" is political rhetoric rather than a serious objective, adding the real objective is to improve human resource production by improving the graduate school system in Korea. While Seoul National University could strive for university-wide excellence, other universities might best pursue excellence for selected departments.

Second, the program should double the rate of technology transfer from university to industry[7] from 10 percent in 2004 to 20 percent in 2012 and improve Korea's Institute for Management Development ranking in technology transfer from university to industry from 21st in 2004 to 10th in 2012. BK21 funds support technology transfer activities, but the level of support is highly limited. Therefore, the linkage between the milestone and program input is not strong enough, like that between goals and missions. The linkage between the technology transmission milestone and the program inputs occurs only through criteria for selecting recipients. Technology transfer records and plans of participating faculty members are included in the metrics for selecting applied science research groups.

---

[6] Some standards are available to evaluate the comparative ranking of universities and departments. In the United States, for example, the "Carnegie Classification," originally developed by the Carnegie Commission on Higher Education, is used to define university types, traditionally by the number of doctoral degrees granted annually and levels of research activity and funding. It is not clear whether this classification could be applied to Korean universities. The *Times Higher Education Supplement* World University Rankings also rates graduate programs and disciplines. The Academic Rankings of World Universities by Shanghai Jiao Tong University provides university-level global rankings based on research capability. Chang (2005) suggests there were 11 "research universities" in Korea in 2004.

[7] The rate of technology transfer from university to industry is defined by the number of technologies transferred divided by total number of technologies owned by universities. Technologies include technology patents, application patents, designs, technology information, and know-how. Refer MOCIE (2006) for definition details.

Third, the program should support more than 20,000 graduate students and young researchers annually. The program reached this milestone with the selection of 21,000 recipients in 2006.

Goals and Missions Identified for the Logic Model

Our reviews of stated goals and missions in BK21 publications and interviews revealed two goals, as shown in Figure 3.2.

The first goal of the program is to increase the size and capability of the research manpower pool that can create new knowledge and new technology. The second goal is to foster globally competitive graduate departments and research universities. While the first goal is national in focus, the second goal is focused on individual departments and universities. The first goal is affected by other educational environments not addressed in BK21, as well as by the second goal. The second goal is supported by the first, as well as by two program missions. The

Figure 3.2
Goals and Missions of Phase II BK21 Program

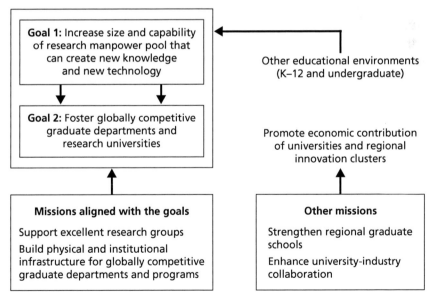

missions that are aligned with the goals are (1) supporting excellent research groups and (2) building physical and institutional infrastructure for globally competitive graduate departments and programs.

In other words, to supply creative research manpower (first goal), Korea needs high-quality graduate schools to train them (second goal). To have stronger graduate schools and programs (second goal), it is necessary to have better qualified graduate students and faculty that constitute excellent research groups (first mission of the program) and research and education infrastructure (second mission of the program).

Other program missions, such as strengthening university-industry links and promoting regional graduate schools, aim to promote the economic contribution of universities and to establish regional industrial innovation clusters.

In the next section, we examine how these actual goals and missions direct program inputs.

Program Inputs

Inputs are the BK21 funding and rules of the program to accomplish its missions and goals. Rules comprise the principles and regulations that govern participants and implementation procedures. They are reflected in the program's strategy, unit of support, selection criteria, evaluation criteria, and other operational mechanisms.

In this section, we explore inputs for BK21 Phase II by assessing official documents, press releases, and R&D statistics. We discuss each of the program inputs in turn.

BK21 Funding

The program provides stipends to graduate students, postdoctoral fellows, and contract-based research professors who belong to research groups selected from top universities.[8] BK21 funding is awarded to

---

[8]   Research group qualification details are discussed in the subsection entitled "Recipient Selection Criteria."

department-level research groups (*sa-up-dan*) in a stable lump sum over a seven-year period.[9] BK21 funding is not project-based. Research groups are supposed to find other funding for research projects, equipments, and facilities. Through this process, BK21 funding may serve as financial leverage for recipients to obtain other funding, especially by signaling academic excellence.

As noted previously, the total BK21 budget for the seven-year period of Phase II is about US$2.1 billion, resulting in an annual appropriation of about US$300 million. BK21 funding accounts for only a small portion of R&D expenditures of Korean universities and of Korea in general. In 2004, the MoE BK21 program provided 180 billion KRW in funding, as shown in Table 3.1. This was less than

Table 3.1
Korea's R&D Expenditure, 2004

		Amount (billion KRW)	Share (%)
GNERD composition	University	2,201	9.9
	Industry	17,020	76.7
	Public research institutions	2,965	13.4
	Total GNERD	22,185	100.0
University R&D funding sources	Government	1,437	65.3
	Other public	406	18.4
	Private	350	15.9
	Foreign	8	0.4
	Total university R&D	2,201	100.0
Composition of government R&D funding to universities	MOST[a]	365	25.4
	MOCIE[a]	291	20.3
	MIC[a]	33	2.3
	MoE academic research promotion program[a]	226	15.8
	MoE BK21 program[a]	180	12.5
	Other	342	23.8
	Total government funding to university R&D	1,437	100.0

SOURCE: MOST and KISTEP (2005), pp. 18–19.
[a] MoE internal data.

---

[9] The funding scheme described in this subsection is common to both Phase I and Phase II.

1 percent of the Gross National Expenditure on Research and Development (GNERD) total of 22.2 trillion KRW that year, and only 8 percent of the 2.2 trillion KRW contribution made by universities to the GNERD. Even among government funding sources for university R&D, which totaled 1.4 trillion KRW in 2004, BK21 is relatively modest. Funding from programs of the Ministry of Science and Technology (MOST) and the Ministry of Commerce, Industry, and Energy (MOCIE) both exceeded BK21 funding. Even the MoE's own Academic Research Promotion Program funding exceeds that of BK21. The Ministry of Information and Communication (MIC) also contributed to university R&D, albeit at about one-sixth the level of BK21. Although Phase II BK21 funding is 50 percent greater than that of Phase I, it still likely accounts for less than 2 percent of GNERD.

Program funding allocations are made by academic discipline, geographical location, and scale of research group (MoE, 2006c). The details of the program funding structure were explained in Chapter One.

The grant structure of each BK21 award is as follows. About 70–80 percent of BK21 funds goes for scholarships and stipends to graduate students, postdoctoral researchers, and contract-based research professors.[10] The remainder is spent on international collaboration and other expenses, much of which also benefit recipient students and researchers. BK21 funding can support professors for their participation in international workshops and seminars only when they accompany graduate students. Therefore, professors who participate in the BK21 program need to find other project-based funding to cover their other research costs, including those for their own labor, travel expenses, equipment, and other overhead costs.

While BK21 funds are not tied to specific projects, other government R&D programs provide project-based funding. In other government programs, professors are the award recipients who are contrac-

---

[10] Grant allocations among recipients vary by academic fields. For example, applied science research groups are supposed to allocate about 60 percent of their BK21 funding to graduate student stipends, about 20 percent to post-doctoral researchers and contract-based research professors, and about 20 percent on international collaboration and other expenses. See MoE (2006a, 2006b) for details.

tually responsible for the award and who allocate the research funds over such different expenses as labor costs and equipment.

University presidents are contractually responsible for BK21 funding; leaders of the research group have practical responsibility for deliverables—that is, for the results of the research supported by the BK21 grants. The university receives the grant and pays the monthly stipends to graduate students, postdoctoral researchers, and contract-based researchers of the selected department.[11] Although faculty members of the selected departments can use the free labor of students and researchers supported by BK21 grants in their research, they do not have direct control over the allocation of funds. The lump-sum grant, however, is not earmarked for specific identified students. Research group leaders and their departments can at least decide on who will get the scholarships and stipends that BK21 provides.

Strategy

BK21's official strategy is to pick "winners" and concentrate support on them. Our interviews with representatives of universities, however, revealed substantial disagreement over whether BK21 ought to concentrate its funding on a relatively small number of institutions and graduate students or whether it should seek to fund a larger number of both. The evolution of BK21 reflects this concern: Phase I funding was mostly concentrated in Seoul National University (SNU), providing an opportunity for SNU to upgrade its research and graduate training. Phase II funding, however, is spread over a much larger number of institutions.

The top five recipients of Phase II funding were SNU, Yonsei University, Korea University, Sungkyunkwan University, and Pusan National University.[12] These schools account for 44 percent of the Phase II program budget. During Phase I, the top five recipient

---

[11] Minimum monthly payments are 500,000 KRW for a master's degree student, 900,000 KRW for a doctoral student, 2,000,000 KRW for a post-doctoral researcher, and 2,500,000 KRW for a contract-based research professor. See MoE (2006a, 2006b). As of December 28, 2006, the exchange rate was 930 KRW to US$1.

[12] There are 171 four-year universities in Korea; 142 of them had graduate schools in 2004.

universities—SNU, KAIST, Korea University, POSTECH, and Yonsei—accounted for 53 percent of the BK21 program budget, with SNU alone accounting for 34 percent (Table 3.2).

The strategy of concentration appears to be a natural option, given BK21's limited resources and the large-scale investment needed for a graduate school to become globally competitive. Brewer, Gates, and Goldman (2002) show that universities successfully seeking to gain prestige pursue a concentration strategy, whereas universities that have already obtained prestige tend to distribute resources more evenly. Indeed, as noted earlier, one of our interviewees suggested that BK21 funds be considered as seed money for top graduate schools that might help their universities become more competitive.

Barring poor performance, BK21 provides sizable and stable funding to recipients over the seven-year program period. The scale of each award is much larger for an individual group than that of other project-based research funding programs. For example, a science and engineering research group is eligible for annual funding between 1.5 billion and 7 billion KRW in the Phase II BK21 program. During Phase I (1999-2005), annual average funding for a science and engi-neering research group was 1.77 billion KRW, with a maximum award of 6.82 billion KRW and a minimum of 0.38 billion. In contrast, other project-based research funding to universities is quite small. The KSF's Basic Science Research Program, for example, provided average fund-ing per project of less than 0.1 billion KRW (about US$100,000) in 2005. By concentrating its support on a few selected groups, BK21 can account for a significant portion of the total research funding of a recipient university. For the top five recipients of Phase I funds, BK21 funding accounted for 5–14 percent of total research funding, as shown in Table 3.2.

BK21 encourages specialization" within the recipient universities so that they can concentrate resources and support on selected areas. Applicant universities are supposed to choose their academic areas of concentration, make a commitment to investing in infrastructure needed to promote the selected areas of concentration, and plan for

Table 3.2
Share of BK21 Funding in Total Research Funds of the Top
Five BK21 Phase I Recipients, 2005 (billions of KRW)

University	Total Research Funds (A)	BK21 Funds (B)	BK21 Share (%) (B/A)
SNU	246.5	33.6	13.6
KAIST	108.3	15.3	14.1
Korea University	86.7	7.8	9.0
POSTECH	77.2	8.6	11.1
Yonsei	123.0	6.3	5.1

SOURCE: Total research fund data are from MoE (2006d). BK21
funding data are from KRF (2007).

NOTE: BK21 funding for SNU does not include the BK21 support for
building the graduate student dormitory. Annual appropriation for
the SNU graduate student dormitory was 35 billion KRW in 2005.
If this is included, the BK21 funding reaches 27.8 percent of SNU's
total research funds in 2005.

reforms, such as improving accountability for research funds and the
faculty evaluation system.[13]

BK21 seeks to induce changes across a university. While the unit
of support is a department-level research group, recipients are selected
not only for the excellence of their department but also for their university's commitment to the department, institutional reform, and
research infrastructure.

To secure the university-level changes intended by the program,
BK21 suggests that the leader of the research group serve as department chairman in order to lead decisionmaking within the department
and participate in university decisions.

BK21 mechanisms are relatively unique in their combination of
stipend and research funding selection on the basis of department and
university merit. BK21 funds are designed to subsidize a university's
R&D costs, lower the cost of getting PhDs and master's degrees, and
stabilize the income of post-doctoral students and young researchers in
early career transition. While BK21 funds scholarships and stipends for

---

[13] Specialization is one of the MoE's guiding principles for higher education policy.

individuals, individual recipients are not selected for their own merit but on the merit of their department and university.

Unit of Support

BK21's unit of support is the department-level research group. Students and young researchers are matched with faculty members to form a research group. To qualify for BK21 funding, a research group must satisfy several conditions.[14] It must have a doctorate program with enrolled PhD candidates. Liberal arts and social science research groups must have at least seven participating faculty members; basic science groups, at least ten; applied science groups, ten to 25.[15] Most faculty members of the department should participate in the research group.[16] The leader of the research group should be a faculty member who can lead the group until the end of the BK21 program period; that person should not lead other large-scale government-funded research projects. Participating professors should also have had a minimum average number of publications in the prior three years.[17] Participating graduate students should spend at least 40 hours weekly on research and education. All research groups need to secure matching funds from their universities equal to at least 5 percent of the level of BK21 funding that they seek. Applied science and interdisciplinary science research groups must secure matching funds from industry sources equal to at least 10 percent of the BK21 funding. Regional university research groups must secure matching funds from local government equal to 3–5 percent of BK21 funding, depending on the discipline.

Not all individuals participate in a department's BK21 program. The bottom third of faculty and graduate students in the department (as determined by such measures as number of publications) do not

---

[14] Multiple academic departments can constitute one research group in the application stage but their funding must later be administered by one department or program.

[15] For applied science groups, the minimum number varies by discipline.

[16] About 70 percent of the faculty members in a department participate in the research group in Phase II.

[17] For a basic science research group, for example, a participating faculty member must have an average of at least three SCI publications during the past three years.

participate, but individual participants can be replaced over time, so as to ensure performance from each team member. The leader is the only permanent member of the research group.

Recipient Selection Criteria

Selection criteria are announced before the selection process starts so that applicants may estimate their expected rankings[18] by research merit, training, links to industry, university reform and specialization, and, for regional university groups, regional development.[19]

Award selection is based on the ranking of merit—BK21's "competition rule." Research groups are ranked within each academic discipline. Ranking criteria are weighted differently for different groups. For applied science groups, criteria are weighted equally. For basic science groups, educational and R&D excellence are weighted equally and given slightly more weight than university reform and specialization, while industry links are not considered. Appendix C summarizes the selection criteria for applied science research groups.

Many of our interviewees emphasized that the competition rule made comparative ranking of universities and departments in Korea more obvious than before, which induced stronger competition among departments and universities.[20]

The level of requested funding is not subject to review in the selection process. Research groups choose their own funding level. Each group winning funding receives the amount it requested as long as (1) it meets general guidelines on distribution and (2) the total amount requested by all groups in each academic panel[21] is within the range of

---

[18] According to the MoE, this is one reason why the ratio of applicants to selected groups is not high. Universities that would not be highly ranked do not apply.

[19] Contribution to regional development is considered in particular in selecting regional university research groups.

[20] We examine how BK21 induced a more competitive environment for universities below when we discuss outputs and outcomes.

[21] There are three academic panels for large-scale research groups: Basic Science, Applied Science, and Arts and Humanities.

pre-announced funding. BK21 award size is basically proportional to department size.

Performance Evaluation Criteria

Performance evaluation criteria for the research groups have not yet been established for Phase II. MoE (2006a) has stated that diversity of academic disciplines will be considered in evaluating Phase II research group performance; its Phase I evaluations were criticized for applying uniform measures, such as number of publications, across all academic disciplines. To accommodate the diversity in goals and areas of specialization of the research groups, Phase II evaluation will adopt more-qualitative measures than those used in Phase I. Phase II research groups are to set their own goals in their application and to manage their performance by their own milestones in a "management by objectives" approach. Recipient universities and research groups are also required to consult domestic or foreign institutions and experts on evaluation.

Research groups will be evaluated annually for their adherence to contractual terms and their progress in proposed work plans (MoE, 2006a). In the 2008 evaluation, research groups that are performing at the bottom of their field will have to compete with new entrants to stay in the program. The 2011 evaluation may be used to adjust or halt support for research groups that are performing extremely poorly. In 2012, when Phase II ends, there will be a final evaluation of both research groups and the entire program.

Other Operational Mechanisms

Evaluation and management governance structure of Phase II is as follows: BK21 is under the jurisdiction of the MoE, which determines the program's core elements and operational mechanisms. The BK21 Planning Office had responsibility for Phase II before its launch; since then, the MoE Academic Research Promotion Division has had responsibility for it. The MoE entrusts administrative work of the program to the KRF; within the KRF, the BK21-NURI Committee, created to manage the Phase II program, has day-to-day responsibility for it. Members of its Program Management Committee, who include experts from universities, industry, think tanks, and government, supervise Phase II management and evaluation, assisted by full-time experts who analyze program performance and develop new evaluation tools.[22]

Summary

The goals and missions of the BK21 program influence the inputs, such as program resources and rules. The goals and missions affect resources by effectively requiring a concentration strategy that results in awards much larger than those for other project-based funding programs. Even though the total BK21 budget is relatively small compared with other sources of R&D funding for universities, its concentration strategy makes the individual award size attractive enough for universities to put priority on obtaining BK21 funding—and hence on meeting the goals of the program. BK21 funding also provides flexibility to recipients in carrying out broader research agendas and in developing university or department excellence. The goals and missions may have the most effect through the competition rule.

Because BK21 award selection is based on merit rankings, comparative rankings of universities and departments are more obvious than before in Korea, which may induce stronger competition among departments and universities. Phase II funding has broadened the pool of recipients, which may promote competition among a broader range of graduate schools in Korea. The competition rule is further extended to performance evaluation of Phase II awardees. Interim evaluations of Phase II in 2008 and 2011 will allow for adjustments through replacement of poorly performing participants with others. In the next section, we consider more closely how these inputs have affected program activities, incentives, outputs, and outcomes.

---

[22] See MoE (2006a, 2006b, and 2006c) for further details.

Incentives, Activities, Outputs, and Outcomes of the Program

BK21 program dynamics are best observed through changes in incentives for individuals and institutions and their activities, and the outputs and outcomes of those activities. Such changes illuminate linkages from the program inputs to its outputs and outcomes.

As of this writing, it is too early to observe the effects of changes made by BK21 Phase II, launched in early 2006. We therefore used Phase I as a benchmark to understand the changes that Phase II may induce. This requires understanding the changes Phase I produced, how they differed between recipients and nonrecipients, and how Phase II program dynamics might be expected to differ.

Phase II is similar to Phase I in its goals and missions, funding rules, and selection criteria. But whereas Phase I emphasized university-level excellence, including institutional reforms, Phase II emphasizes department-level excellence, including links to industry.

Incentives

Incentives are designed to motivate actions. Incentive design is embedded in the program structure. Stipends for graduate students, postdoctoral researchers, and research professors comprise the chief incentives of BK21. These may have differing effects for differing individuals and institutions.

For students, the availability of BK21 funding lowers the expected cost of obtaining doctoral and master's degrees, thereby providing an incentive to pursue an advanced degree. The financial stability provided by BK21 may induce recipient graduate students to devote more time to producing research. The BK21 program also provides guidance to students selecting a graduate school by signaling which departments and universities are national leaders. BK21 funding may also make the option of staying in Korea for graduate studies more attractive than before.

For postdoctoral scholars and contract-based researchers, BK21 funding provides income stability in their transition to permanent academic jobs. It may also expand job opportunities for postdoctoral researchers and young researchers as departments and universities try to hire more of these researchers in an effort to increase research production and thereby continue to receive BK21 funding.[23] BK21 funding, by paying for much of the costs of postdoctoral scholars and contract-based researchers, may increase flexibility in the Korean academic job market.

For faculty, BK21 funding provides free manpower to use in their research activities. Because BK21 recipient graduate students, postdoctoral researchers, and contract-based researchers are paid in advance, it becomes cheaper for a professor at a BK21 institution to lead research. In other words, BK21 subsidizes or lowers university R&D cost. Research outputs per unit of professor time may increase given this availability of additional labor. At the same time, by providing such incentives for research, BK21 may force a trade-off between faculty teaching and research. BK21 also confers prestige on faculty members. A faculty member's participation on a BK21 project may signal his or her productivity in research and other activities. Such signaling may spur faculty to produce more research or to attract more students.

For academic departments and universities, BK21 funding is a very attractive financial opportunity because the awards are sizable and stable over time. BK21 funding gives departments and universities an incentive to align their behaviors and decisions, including those related to research infrastructure and operation and management of departments, to support the standards that the BK21 program seeks to foster. Departments may try to recruit more faculty members with better research capability and to establish incentive systems that reward faculty members with higher research productivity. Departments may also seek to hire more post-doctoral scholars and researchers in order to publish more in the short term to take advantage of BK21 funding availability. Nonrecipient graduate departments may face more challenges when recruiting high-quality students.

Our respondents indicated that the BK21 graduate stipends were small compared with tuition and fees at private institutions but considerably larger compared with tuition and fees at public institutions. As

---

[23] Continued funding is contingent on production during the award period.

shown in Table 3.3, the average annual tuition at private universities was more than twice as large as that at national and public universities in 2007. BK21 support for a graduate student in a PhD program is about three times of the tuition at a public university, so that the student may be able to cover both tuition and living expenses from the BK21 stipend. However, if the recipient is in a PhD program in a private university, the person is left with a very small amount after paying the tuition.

Respondents generally agreed that without some sort of fellowship graduate students would find it difficult to enroll in programs and make good progress because the tuition cost would either discourage them from enrolling or compel them to work at distracting part-time jobs. Private university respondents added that BK21 helped them compete with national universities in attracting students, and that increases in the per-student stipend would level competition even more.

Several respondents suggested that Korean students are less motivated to work hard because of the country's significant economic advancement and that they are therefore less inclined to pursue graduate science and engineering degrees, which may be more difficult than other paths they could choose. BK21 could influence these decisions

Table 3.3
BK21 Support Compared with Average Annual Tuition at Four-Year Universities in Korea, 2007

Type	Thousands of KRW
Average annual tuition	
National and public universities	3,370
Private universities	6,890
BK21 minimum stipend per recipient per year	
Graduate student in MA program	6,000
Graduate student in PhD program	10,800
Postdoctoral fellow	24,000
Contract-based research fellow	30,000

SOURCE: Tuition statistics are from *Herald Economic Daily,* July 19th, 2007. Data for BK21 support are from MoE (2006a).

NOTE: Tuition in the same university varies over academic discipline. Average tuition for private universities by academic discipline is available from the Web site of the Korea Foundation for the Promotion of Private Schools (http://infor.sahak.or.kr).

by providing funding for graduate science and engineering training and also by increasing the prestige of these pursuits.

Activities

BK21 is designed to change behavior by young students, faculty and research workers, and administrators of an institution. Some changes may be produced by the program design's; others may be unintentional. Research and teaching are the main activities of the universities. Program inputs and incentives influence research and teaching activities in universities either directly or indirectly through changes in people's incentives.

Several BK21-NURI committee members stated that BK21 has increased the emphasis on research and decreased the emphasis on teaching, with top professors becoming less engaged in teaching.[24] In national universities, each professor is obliged to teach 18 credits per year. When research infrastructure had yet to be established, a trade-off between research and teaching was inevitable because that professors wanted to produce as many papers as possible. Respondents said that the sacrifice of undergraduate education may have been more serious because graduate education complements research somewhat.

BK21 has had only a limited effect on international collaboration because funding is restricted to sending Korean graduate students to international events. The program does not emphasize co-authoring papers with international scholars or recruiting international faculty and students for Korean institutions. Such support is needed for true international collaboration.

BK21 has changed the activities not only in recipient universities but also in nonrecipient universities, according to our respondents. Nonrecipients of Phase I made desperate efforts to enhance their research productivity so that they could be eligible for Phase II. This was due to the following reasons. Most Korean universities depend heavily on tuition as their revenue source and usually lack the financial resources for scholarships and stipends for graduate students. BK21 often accounts for a significant portion of a recipient university's

---

[24] This is one of the unintended consequences of the program.

research funding. Respondents from loser-winner universities admitted that, without the BK21 "brand name," they were at a significant disadvantage in attracting high-quality graduate students or could not recruit as many as they needed.

One respondent from a national university told us of hiring more research professors for finite terms outside the civil service system. These professors provide added flexibility in the academic job market and have contributed to research productivity growth, but they are considered "second-class" faculty.

A number of respondents felt that professors had had an unhealthy relationship with graduate students before BK21, with students like "slaves" to the professors. BK21 funding gives students more power in the relationship, although they still depend on their professors (as in most graduate education systems). One respondent said that while relations between professors and graduate students are businesslike, it would be good if they were more collegial.

Outputs

Outputs are the products of research and teaching activities. They reflect the results of interaction among the people and institutions involved. As activities and incentives change in response to BK21, program outputs may change in quantity, as reflected by the number of doctoral and master's degree holders, or in quality, as reflected by recipients' publications. Program outputs also may affect the infrastructure (e.g., operation, management systems) of graduate schools and the competitive environment within and between universities.

Research Quantity and Quality. Many respondents said that the research capabilities of faculty and graduate students have improved significantly because of BK21's contribution to funding and the subsequent competition among universities and faculty members.

In particular, because the number of papers as recorded in the SCI was a main evaluation metric in the BK21 screening process, that number increased in universities participating in the program as well as in those trying to improve their position to compete for funding. A representative of a university that failed to win funding in Phase I but subsequently won it in Phase II said that the university's annual number of SCI papers in the past decade had increased from 90 to 1,600. Another said that the BK21 program was a "publication drive" program comparable to the "export drive" economic growth during Korea's development era. It is notable that BK21 increased the research productivity not only of recipient universities but of nonrecipient universities as well.

A representative of a university that won both Phase I and Phase II funding mentioned increased concern about the trade-off between quantity and quality. After the explosive increase in number of papers published, the university is now trying to focus on quality rather than quantity.[25] Other university respondents agreed that Phase I put too much emphasis on number of SCI papers, and that mass production of papers often sacrificed quality.

Human Resource Production. Although BK21 is intended to increase the number of graduate students in several fields, university representatives that we interviewed said that other government regulations may have limited this effect.

The Ministry of Construction and Transportation, for example, limits the number of students in Seoul and its vicinity, as part of its broader effort to promote growth elsewhere in the nation.[26] Private universities in the Seoul area can, within MoE requirements on student-faculty ratios, reduce their undergraduate enrollments so as to admit more graduate students, but they are usually reluctant to do so because of the importance of undergraduate tuition to university revenue. Regional private universities can be more flexible in adjusting their enrollments, but these universities are not always attractive to students.[27]

---

[25] According to ARWU (2006), the SCI score of this university (64.2) is close to that of MIT (67.1), but its number of papers in *Nature* and *Science* (14.3) is far behind that of MIT (66.4).

[26] About one-quarter of Korea's population lives in Seoul and vicinity. Economic and social activities are highly concentrated in metropolitan Seoul.

[27] One university respondent noted that BK21 may be inadvertently lowering the quality of entering graduate students at regional universities. Some regional universities receiving BK21 funding that once had difficulty attracting students for their programs are now able to recruit students more easily, but it is not clear such students should be in graduate school.

To admit more students, national universities must also increase the number of faculty to maintain their student-faculty ratios. However, national university faculty members are civil servants, and their numbers are under tight control by the Ministry of Government Administration and Home Affairs. The maximum enrollment can be changed with MoE approval, but such approval is not easy to obtain given that the number of faculty is tightly controlled by the regulation.[28]

Competitive Effects and Structural Change. Many respondents indicated that BK21's design strongly supports structural reform in academic departments. By making explicit judgments about quality and linking those judgments to funding, universities will be more able to downsize or close weak departments and encourage weak faculty members to leave. Several respondents mentioned that increased competition in the BK21 Phase I program led many faculty members to retire or leave their positions, with some even suffering medical problems because of the stress of competition. The overall impression is that the BK21 system is promoting the departure of weak faculty members, although some strong faculty may also be leaving.

According to MoE respondents, structural reform is seen by MoE as necessary to improve the quality of Korean universities and to align university programs with the needs of local and national society. The traditional structure of Korean higher education insulates weak faculty and departments from market forces (such as those that operate in the United States). Several respondents said that there is a common presumption that all Korean universities should pursue the same research-focused model, rather than having some universities concentrate on research leadership while others focus more on undergraduate teaching and service to the local economy, especially to small- and medium-

---

Our respondents said that lower-quality PhDs from some regional universities would likely face difficulty finding the academic jobs they prefer and that industry may not be able to absorb a new supply of doctoral and master's degree holders. One of the respondents said that some BK21 students are working for research group leaders who are not well qualified, especially in regional universities.

[28] MoE is currently planning to turn national universities into nonprofit organizations so that they would be free from the regulations applied to government organizations.

sized suppliers to the large companies (the latter usually have their own research facilities and do not need help from universities as much).

Two representatives of universities that won Phase II but not Phase I funding said that their initial failure led to structural reform, thus matching an aim that MoE officials intended for the program. Representatives of these universities said their institutions changed significantly as a result of the BK21 program, with increased recognition of the importance of top talent and lower tolerance for mediocre performers. These changes were a result of both the competitive system established by the program and the actual funding. For instance, one respondent reported that his university offers bonuses to professors who publish in top journals and had also established a special scouting fund to recruit top professors by paying salaries exceeding US$100,000 (rather than Korea's usual top salary of $60,000). Another said that, when his university failed to get Phase I money, it raised a $5 million scholarship fund for 1999–2005 and a $21 million specialization fund for 17 academic areas during 2001–2005. These universities also hired more postdoctoral researchers to increase the number of publications produced by their institutions.

Representatives of these universities perceived Phase I as targeted toward SNU, noting that many other universities boycotted the competition because of this perception. Despite these concerns, these universities still chose to compete for Phase II funding, in part because the lack of Phase I funding led students to enter other programs and in part because they perceived that the second phase would be targeted more broadly and would give them a better chance.[29]

A representative from a university winning both Phase I and Phase II funding noted that BK21 provided an opportunity for his institution to leap forward because research funds increased significantly. At its peak, BK21 accounted for about 30 percent of total research funding at his university.

---

[29] Unfortunately, as noted previously, we were not able to interview representatives from universities that failed to receive funding in either phase. Their views on program dynamics, particularly the changes they may have undertaken after they failed to win funding, would be useful in assessing whether competitive dynamics affect differing programs in the same way.

In addition to strengthening some programs, some of our respondents suggested BK21 should ultimately try to reduce the number of graduate programs in Korea. One respondent noted that 90 percent of Korean universities have graduate schools and suggested that this number ought to be reduced. Another respondent said, "Graduate school is an ornament to make the university look picture perfect." He argued that the quality of graduate schools varies widely and that BK21 should help graduate schools evaluate and improve their programs.

The BK21 selection process has made the comparative ranking of universities and departments much more obvious. University respondents all agreed that BK21 created a competitive environment both among and within universities. The competitive environment was introduced in part through the "signaling effect" of the program—i.e., within the Korean higher education system, receiving BK21 funding was a signal of excellence. Respondents from Phase I nonrecipient institutions said that, without the BK21 "brand name," they were at a significant disadvantage in attracting high-quality graduate students and could not get as many as they needed. According to our respondents, universities that already have enough funding still pursue BK21 funding because of the prestige attached to the award. They agreed that the signaling effect may have been stronger for the second-tier graduate schools than for the top schools that are already well known as prestige schools.

Changes in University and Department Infrastructure. BK21 intends to address the adequacy of physical infrastructure. Although the program does not provide funding for establishing physical research infrastructure (except for a one-time grant for a SNU dormitory for graduate students), recipient universities are supposed to make such investments on their own.[30] Such investments are needed for a department or university to become globally competitive, but they are a challenge for Korean universities, which depend heavily on tuition revenue and have limited financial options. Our respondents agreed that a sig-

---

[30] As mentioned previously, BK21 applicant universities are supposed to choose their areas of specialization and show a commitment to invest in the facilities and equipment needed to promote those areas.

nificant improvement in the physical infrastructure of Korea universities can only be attained in the long term.

University-Industry Links. A corporate executive who is knowledgeable about the BK21 program and whose firm is one of the largest employers in Korea confirmed that industry sees universities as a source of human resources and, to some extent, basic and generic research. The main areas where industry expects to benefit from links to universities are recruitment, staff retraining, and corporate image enhancement. He noted that large companies have little incentive to cooperate with universities to perform product-related research but prefer to fund basic and generic research. In his view, basic research is generally useful to industry and, perhaps more important, helps train the next generation of researchers who can be employed in industry labs.

The industry respondent expressed frustration with the matching funds process of BK21 and with any programs that is intended to foster specific interaction between universities and industry. He noted that large companies run their own labs and have no immediate need for university research. He also suggested that BK21 focus on sectors in demand in the Korean marketplace and not fund oversupplied sectors, such as humanities and the arts.

University respondents also expressed difficulty in meeting the industry matching fund requirement of BK21 Phase II. Universities often had to transfer previous university-industry collaboration projects and funds to BK21 to meet the BK21 requirement. Funds from industry are usually quite flexible because industry sponsors university research mainly for recruitment of higher-quality graduates who are better suited for its work. In contrast, BK21 Phase II funds are highly restrictive, particularly in its encouragement of university-industry collaborative research rather than general research and education.

One of the university respondents even suggested that BK21 is not expected to promote industry-university collaborative research. Because BK21 funding is not based on projects, it cannot be expected to fill the gap between what is useful to industry and what universities want to do. Project-based funds from MOCIE, MOST, and MIC are more suitable for promoting industry-university collaborative research.

In contrast, our government-side respondents indicated that the main reason for having a link with industry is cooperation in human resource development, not collaborative research. According to respondents from MoE and KRF, the Phase II program intends to promote collaboration in the areas of curriculum development and student and staff exchanges, so that universities can meet industry's demand for high-quality labor and alleviate the mismatch in labor supply and demand over the long run. Misunderstanding by both industry and universities may be partly due to the fact that the level of industry matching funds is one of the award selection criteria that is relatively easy to measure. However, the intention of Phase II is not to increase the level of industry matching funds. It is only one of the indicators showing industry's commitment to collaboration with universities, stated our respondents. In fact, MoE (2006a) indicates that the emphasis on the university-industry link in Phase II is a response to criticism from universities and industries that Phase I did not put enough effort into strengthening the university-industry linkage.

Outcomes

Outcomes include both the intended and unintended long-term impacts of the program. They may include international prestige of Korean universities in particular and of higher education more generally, as well as effects on labor productivity and workforce skills. These may be affected not only by BK21 but also by efforts made by other universities and broader financial and S&T trends in the rest of the world that affect academic and professional opportunities. Causality between program inputs and outcomes may not therefore be as direct as that between inputs and outputs of the program.

The true effect of BK21 in improving the size and quality of the pool of knowledge workers in Korea and increase in Korean universities with international prestige will only occur over time.

Perceived excellence (prestige) as well as de facto excellence matters to top international universities. The number of published papers in top journals is an indicator of de facto academic excellence, but it does not necessarily bring prestige in the short run. Pursuit of prestige involves a large scale investment for a long time.[31]

Our respondents said BK21 has had some success in improving the stature of Korean universities, but lacks the resources to achieve some of its workforce goals.

The representative of the university winning both Phase I and Phase II funding said students now perceive its science and engineering schools to be competitive with the top 25 to 30 universities in the United States. He also contended that the engineering school, especially, is competitive with that of Tokyo University, although Tokyo produces more publications because of its larger faculty (about twice that for his university) and the greater emphasis SCI places on Japanese-language journals.

Regarding the Phase II goal of nurturing manpower that can create new technology, one respondent said that BK21 does not have a mechanism to improve the mismatch between the supply and demand for scientists and engineers. BK21 selection and evaluation criteria do not address employment balance for the S&T workforce. However, MoE officials said the Phase II program intends to improve the mismatch by introducing a new academic panel for "interdisciplinary fields in science" and by generally promoting university-industry collaboration.

Other Observations

Regarding possible changes in program dynamics, many respondents said Phase II, like Phase I, will continue to signal academic excellence and to make academic rankings of universities and graduate programs obvious. As Phase II covers more institutions, these respondents expect more universities to become competitive.

A few respondents suggested that the outputs of the Phase II programs will be influenced greatly by the evaluation system and metrics used. Quantitative metrics, such as numbers of papers and patents, are easy to measure. Nevertheless, they contend, improving the quality of doctoral degree holders and their career paths—a much more important goal—is more difficult to measure and will require a systematic,

---

[31] Refer to Brewer, Gates, and Goldman (2002).

qualitative approach, such as eliciting researchers' opinions about institutional quality.[32]

Respondents made a number of suggestions for improving BK21. Several said that the program should concentrate its support on fewer groups. One respondent suggested funding research infrastructure and faculty recruitment. Another said that BK21 should support foreign students because globally competitive Korean companies recruit all over the world.

Summary

In our interviews we found broadly similar views on actual and desired activities, incentives, outputs, and outcomes, but a few differences as well. Some of these differences may stem from the differing perspectives of our respondents.

The chief incentive of BK21 has been the stipends offered to participants. Respondents agree that students would find it harder to pursue graduate education without them. Some respondents also noted that, because BK21 provides an independent source of funding, it has helped improve relations between students and professors. The effect of BK21's incentives differs between private and public institutions, given their varying levels of tuition and fees. Difficulties that schools have in adjusting their enrollments mitigate the effects of these incentives on the numbers of graduate students.

Many respondents also agree that the BK21 competition has led to structural reform of Korean universities. Schools that were not able to win Phase I funding reformed themselves successfully to win Phase II funding. While some respondents indicated that broader coverage of Phase II funding spurred these reforms, others suggested that BK21

---

[32] In this monograph, *qualitative evaluation* means evaluation based on qualitative data in the form of words rather than numbers. Qualitative data often generated from survey of opinions or peer reviews. In contrast, *quantitative evaluation* means evaluation based on measures constructed from numbers and statistics.

should be targeted more narrowly to help reduce the number of graduate schools in Korea.

BK21 aims to improve links between universities and industry, especially in the areas of curriculum development and student and staff exchanges, so that universities can meet industry's demand for high-quality labor and alleviate the mismatch in labor supply and demand over the long run. The industry representative we interviewed preferred basic research as a means to develop future workforce talent. University respondents also expressed difficulty in meeting the industry matching fund requirement of the BK21 Phase II.

BK21 has succeeded in boosting scientific output of Korean universities as measured by publications. In the views of some, it has also helped boost the stature of the universities. This, many believe, has helped keep Korean students at home. At the same time, some respondents said that while quantitative measures of output and outcomes—such as number of publications—have shown an improvement, more qualitative measures of the program's effects, such as changes in quality of research and education, are needed.

CHAPTER FOUR

Quantitative Model to Assess BK21 Program Outcomes

Introduction

Our previously presented logic model for BK21 expresses the relationships between inputs, incentives, activities of individuals and institutions, outputs, contextual conditions, and program outcomes. Some of these relationships are easier to measure and test than others. For example, assessing research quantity and even research quality (as measured by means of the reputation of journals in which research is published) is more straightforward than measuring the subjective competitive environment or a university's prestige (which can take decades to change). Those outputs or outcomes that are difficult to quantify may still be evaluated using other methods, as we explore in Chapter Five.

In this chapter, we develop a quantitative model to examine the relationships most conducive to quantitative measurement. Figure 4.1 highlights elements of the logic model that we judge most conducive to quantitative evaluation. Less-conducive elements of the logic model are those that are more challenging to measure (such as the competitive environment) or for which the link from BK21 to the outcome is relatively distant (such as labor productivity for the overall Korean economy). We use "number of publications" as the principal output because these data are most readily accessible for both BK21 winners and other research groups. Nevertheless, the methods we demonstrate may also be applied to other quantitative measures of interest to the program, such as number of graduated PhDs, number of patents, or number of industry-academic collaborations.

Figure 4.1
Logic Model Elements Most Conducive to Quantitative Measurement

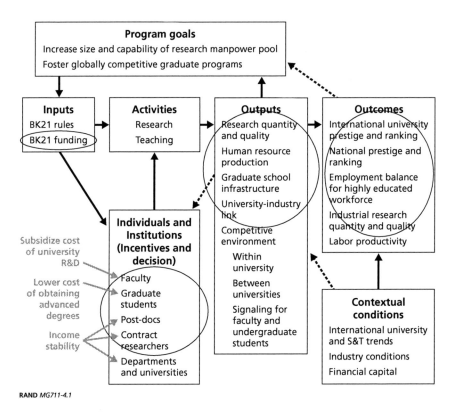

RAND *MG711-4.1*

Because Phase I of BK21 has been completed, we can use data from that time period to examine what quantitative model would be most appropriate for evaluation. We do not have data on many of the possible quantitative indicators appropriate to the areas marked in Figure 4.1, particularly for losers and nonapplicants. The one source that does cover these groups is data on publications, so we use that source to illustrate how the quantitative model functions for them and to make recommendations on the best modeling strategies. The examples related to publication data are not intended to diminish the importance of evaluating effects based on the other quantitative indicators.

First, we summarize some basic quantitative information about Phase I to inform the best choices of quantitative models for Phase II.

Second, we lay out various potential quantitative models for examining the impact of BK21 funding on publications or any other quantitatively measurable output or outcome. Third, we lay out the best options for evaluation given the data and explore some of the challenges in using these methods. Fourth, we describe the data from BK21 Phase I that we use to validate the quantitative model. Fifth, we use these historical data to demonstrate how the model will work in the future with Phase II data. We recognize that validating models this way has limited value because of the differences between Phase I and Phase II, particularly the concentration of Phase I funding on relatively few institutions and the wider distribution of funds in Phase II. Nevertheless, Phase I data are still the best option available for validation of our model and will, given appropriate caveats, yield significant insight into the appropriateness of the quantitative model. Sixth, we discuss the implications for what metrics we should use for evaluation and the implications for database design.

Summary of Phase I Statistics

Figures 4.2 through 4.6 show recent trends in the number of science publications for SNU, KAIST, other universities that received BK21 Phase I funding, universities that did not receive funding, and all Korean universities.[1] Ideally, we would like to compare trends in publications for research groups, rather than universities, before and after program initiation, but we do not have data on group publications before the program began. Later, in the section on validating our model, we discuss how to approximate data on group publications.

---

[1] Included in BK21 schools are Seoul National University, Korea Advanced Institute of Science & Technology, Yonsei University, Korea University, Sungkyunkwan University, Hanyang University, Pohang University of Science & Technology, KyungPook National University, Kyung Hee University, Ajou University, Ehwa Woman's University, Gyeongsang National University, and Myongji University. Gwangju Institute of S&T is excluded because it is new and had no publications previous to BK21. Included in non-BK21 schools are *those that applied for BK21 funds in S&T* but did not receive them: Pusan National University, Chonnam National University, Chungnam National University, Sogang University, Konkuk University, Pukyong National University, Sunchon National University.

Figure 4.2
All Korea Science Publications, 1996–2005

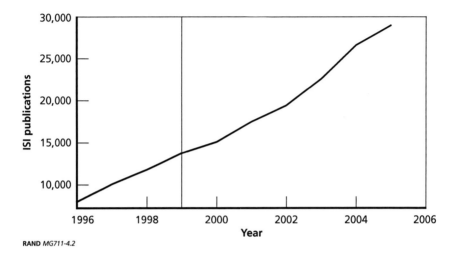

RAND *MG711-4.2*

Figure 4.3
SNU Science Publications, 1996–2005

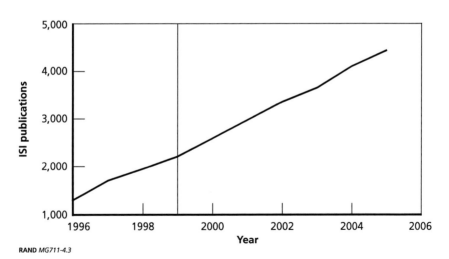

RAND *MG711-4.3*

Figure 4.4
KAIST Science Publications, 1996–2005

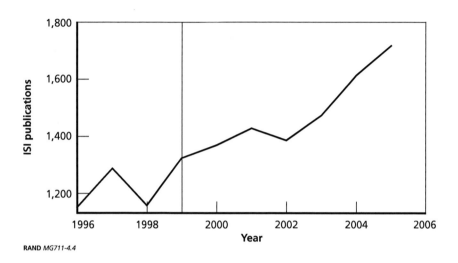

Figure 4.5
Total Science Publications for BK21 Schools, 1996–2005

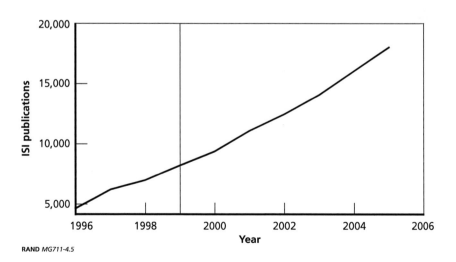

Figure 4.6
Total Science Publications for Non-BK21 Schools, 1996–2005

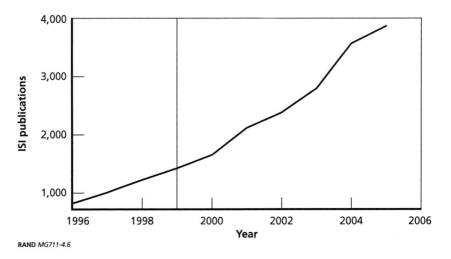

RAND *MG711-4.6*

BK21 has sometimes been criticized for increasing the quantity of publications but not their quality. One way to assess the quality of science publications is to examine the number appearing in the two top science journals, *Science* and *Nature*. Unfortunately, Figure 4.7 shows that very few Korean researchers have published in these journals, although their number is increasing. Figure 4.8 shows more publications but a similar trend for the number of Korean articles appearing in the top 15 science publications, as rated by Institute of Scientific Information (ISI) impact factor.

By themselves, these figures are a poor way to examine the impact of BK21, in large part because so much of the Phase I funding went to SNU. Later, after validating our quantitative model for analysis, we discuss how to use them to estimate the effect of BK21 funding on publication quality.

Potential Approaches

The first step in evaluating the impact of BK21 is identifying the treatment effect to be measured, which in turn suggests the appropriate comparison group. Comparing the BK21 group to this ideal

Figure 4.7
Korean Articles in *Science* and *Nature*, 1996–2005

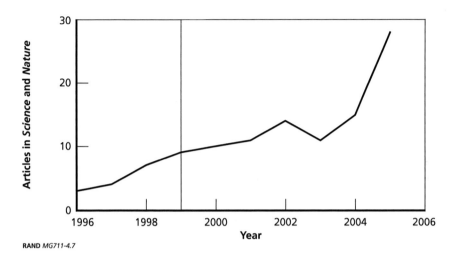

Figure 4.8
Korean Articles in Top 15 Science Publications, 1996–2005

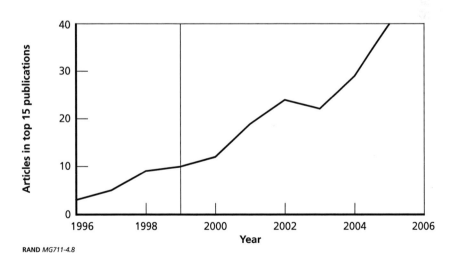

comparison group would yield the effect of the program, although in most cases the ideal comparison group is not available and must be approximated.

The BK21 program suggests two potential treatment effects: (1) the effect of BK21 funding relative to no such funding, and (2) the effect of the BK21 program structure (i.e., this particular set of competitive rules) relative to BK21 funding if it had been distributed through the pre-BK21 funding structure. Table 4.1 presents ideal comparison groups for testing each effect.

For testing the effect of BK21 funding, the ideal comparison would be to observe the research groups that received BK21 funding as they would have been without such funding and to compare the performance of these groups across all relevant variables. For testing the effect of BK21 program structure, the ideal comparison would be to observe the research groups that received BK21 funding as they would have been, had BK21 funding not been conditional on a competition. Of course, we cannot observe these alternative realities. The next-best solution would be to randomly select a group of schools to receive the program and another group of schools not to receive the program. Randomization is optimal for evaluation because the schools in each group would be similar; thus, any difference between the groups after the delivery of BK21 funding could be attributed to the funding rather than to differences between schools. However, in many public policy contexts, randomization may be impossible or undesirable.

Lacking the ability to employ the best or next-best comparisons noted above, we seek statistical methods that might be used to approxi-

Table 4.1
Treatment Effects and Their Implied Comparison Groups

Group	Treatment Effect 1: BK21 Funding	Treatment Effect 2: BK21 Program Structure
Treatment group	Research groups that receive BK21 funding	Research groups that receive BK21 funding
Ideal comparison group	Same research groups in the absence of BK21 funding	Same research groups with BK21 funding levels but allocated according to pre-BK21 programs

mate ideal comparisons. Research groups that applied for BK21 funding but did not receive it may, with some assumptions, serve as a comparison group in measuring the first treatment effect. Because they also applied for funding, they may be quite similar to groups that received funding. No completely satisfactory comparison group is available for examining the second treatment effect because all institutions were exposed to BK21 incentives. Thus, for the second treatment effect, qualitative measures may be best suited for evaluating the perceived impact of the BK21 program structure. As a result, this chapter will focus on quantifying the impact of BK21 funding rather than the structure of the BK21 program. Later in this chapter, we briefly explore non-BK21 applicants as a potential comparison group for examining the size of the second treatment effect.

A number of methods—from unadjusted comparisons to comparisons using sophisticated statistical methods—might be considered for evaluating the effect of BK21 funding. We review these below.

Unadjusted Comparisons of BK21 Winners and Losers

One starting point for comparing the effects of BK21 on research output would be to analyze it before and after the program began in 1999 (see, for example, Moon and Kim, 2001). We might, for example, compare the number of science publications by Seoul National University researchers from 1996 to 1998 with that from 2000 to 2002. The ISI science citation index (SCI), a prominent index of academic publications (ISI Web of Knowledge, 2007), shows that SNU had 4,951 publications between 1996 and 1998 and 8,912 between 2000 and 2002, representing an 80 percent increase (Figure 4.9). Yet as noted previously, this increase could be due to variables other than BK21 funding, such as growing faculty research experience or other sources of support to produce publications.

A second approach would be to compare research groups that received BK21 funding with those that did not. For example, we could compare numbers of S&T publications (i.e., all publications in the SCI) by each group. The comparison reveals that, on average, each group winning BK21 funding produced 206 S&T publications annually from 1999 to 2005, while the groups not winning such funding had only 121 publications annually (Figure 4.10).

Figure 4.9
SNU Science Publications

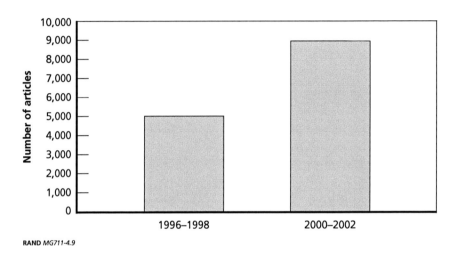

RAND *MG711-4.9*

Figure 4.10
Annual S&T Publications for BK21 Winners and Losers, 1999–2005

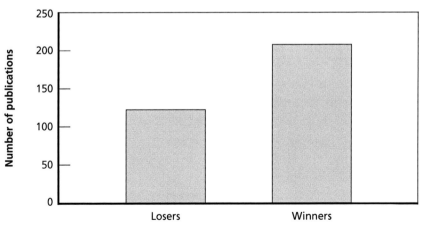

RAND *MG711-4.10*

The principal problem with this comparison is that BK21 research groups were chosen because they are the best research groups in the country, so even in the absence of BK21, they might be expected to produce more (and better) research than those that did not receive such funding. Indeed, the data support this hypothesis; In 1997, before BK21 began, the future BK21 schools had far more publications on per school than non-BK21 schools.

These examples demonstrate two challenges to evaluating BK21: (1) separating the impact of BK21 from preexisting trends, and (2) eliminating confounding differences between BK21 research groups and those to which they will be compared.

Ordinary Least Squares, Matching, and Propensity Score[2]

Three methods that can be used to adjust comparisons of BK21 winners and losers for observable differences between the two groups are ordinary least squares estimation, matching, and propensity scores. None, however, is completely satisfactory.

With ordinary least squares (OLS), an evaluator would compare groups that did and did not receive BK21 funding and seek to control for differences between the groups not attributable to such funding by using measures of these differences. An OLS regression would be used to identify the relationships between BK21 funding (and other characteristics) and the number of publications a group publishes in a given year through

$$
\begin{aligned}
(publications)_{it} &= (research\ group\ characteristics)_{it}\, \beta_\Gamma \\
&+ (BK21\ funding)_{it}\, \gamma + \varepsilon_{it},
\end{aligned}
\tag{4.1}
$$

in which i refers to the research group and t refers to the year, *publications* is the number of publications for a given group in a given year, and *research group characteristics* is a vector of observable characteristics of the group (such as size or whether it is public or private). *BK21 fund-*

---

[2]   Angrist and Krueger (1999) provide an intermediate survey of most of the methods examined in this chapter. Wooldridge (2002) provides more technical detail.

ing may be measured as the level of funding in that year, the average level of funding over the past several years, or in some other way. If, for example, BK21 funding is measured as the total cumulative funding received, then γ captures the difference in annual publications by research groups receiving BK21 funding and those that did not, controlling for research group characteristics (e.g., size, preexisting budget, specific field), which are also included in the equation. Controlling for research group characteristics in the equation makes OLS a significant improvement over simple comparisons between BK21 recipients and nonrecipients.

Nevertheless, there are problems with OLS analyses. The principal objection to OLS in this context is the difficulty in controlling for all essential characteristics of BK21 recipients and nonrecipients. In other words, we are still unable to eliminate confounding differences between the two groups. For example, suppose that in addition to the characteristics for which the model is able to control, entrepreneurship among the faculty is a major contributor to publications: Some faculty members may simply be better at getting projects done. Because entrepreneurialism is difficult to measure, it is likely to be omitted from the regression. Yet omitting such an important variable that is correlated with both other measures of research characteristics and the ultimate number of publications may affect, or bias, the calculated impact of the program (γ in Equation 4.1). In this case, the omission will bias the impact upward, inflating the perceived impact of BK21.

Because it is difficult to measure everything important about a research environment, OLS is likely to lead to other significant biases. Analysts using OLS are not likely even to be able to predict the direction of the net bias of all omitted variables, leading to uncertainty about true program impact. OLS also requires strong assumptions about "functional form." For example, the evaluator must decide whether research group size affects publications linearly, through a quadratic relationship, or in some other way, even when there is no way of knowing the true relationship between the two.[3]

---

[3] A *linear* effect would mean that one additional research group member has the same effect on publications whether the total group size is five or 50. A *nonlinear* effect would occur if

Matching and propensity score models can overcome that last weakness of OLS estimation. Matching models, rather than controlling for various characteristics, compare research groups that are exactly the same across the various characteristics *except for* BK21 funding. They do not require the evaluator to make assumptions about functional form. Research group size may affect publications linearly or in some other way and the results will be unaffected. Nevertheless, matching models have the same problems as OLS models—unobserved or unmeasured characteristics could still bias the estimates. Propensity score models have the same advantage as matching models, but, rather than requiring exact matching across characteristics, they use those characteristics to predict the likelihood of program participation and then match groups on that likelihood. Like matching models, they share the disadvantages of OLS in not accounting for unobserved or immeasurable variables.

Fixed-Effects and Difference-in-Differences Models
The principal problem with the methods we have examined so far is their inability to sufficiently control for differences between the two groups, thereby inadvertently attributing some preexisting differences to the impact of BK21. One solution to this problem is to use a diference-in-differences or—similar in principle but implemented differently—a fixed-effects strategy. This compares differences in outputs before and after the program for those who receive BK21 funding and those who do not. Given certain assumptions (discussed below), changes in the difference between treatment and comparison outputs can be attributed to the treatment, i.e., to BK21 funding.

The advantage of this method is that it allows the evaluator to ignore preexisting differences in the outcome variable of interest, no matter what the cause of those differences. For example, Figure 4.11 (left side) shows that the BK21 groups were publishing more than non-BK21 groups before the onset of BK21. The common trends assumption implies that the change in publications for non-BK21 groups (c–a)

---

an additional group member has less effect on publications as the number of persons in the group increases.

would equal the change for BK21 groups (d–b) in the absence of BK21. With BK21 (right side of Figure 4.11), we see that the BK21 groups experience a positive shift in publications: The trend for BK21 groups is now (e–b), which is greater than (d–b). The estimated impact of BK21 is then (e–b) minus (c–a).

This strategy makes two essential assumptions. First, it assumes that the BK21 research groups and the non-BK21 research groups would have followed the same trend in the absence of receiving BK21 funding. This assumption might not be true. Rather, these groups may have differing trends before and after the introduction of funding, as the left-hand diagram in Figure 4.12 shows. Second, this method assumes that treatment impacts are evident in a shift in the trend rather than a change in the slope of the trend, whereas a shift in slope may more accurately capture the impact (demonstrated in the right-hand diagram in Figure 4.12).

In some situations, the assumption about similar trends in the absence of treatment is unrealistic. One way to determine whether it is reasonable is to examine trends for several years before the policy inter-

Figure 4.11
Difference-in-Differences Estimation

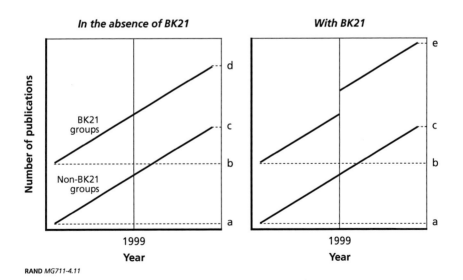

Figure 4.12
Two Violations of Difference-in-Differences Assumptions

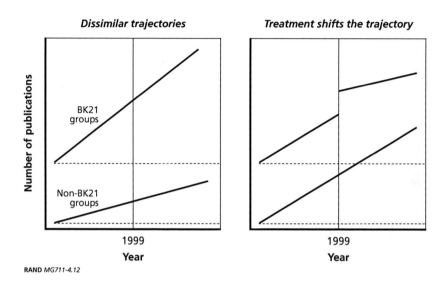

vention. If the trends in publications for BK21 and non-BK21 research groups from 1996 to 1998 are similar, for example, then it is more likely that those trends would have continued to be similar in the absence of BK21.

A regression equation using difference-in-differences estimation to assess the impact of BK21 funding would take the form of

$$\left(publications\right)_{it} = \beta_0 + \beta_1\left(after\,1999\right)_{it}$$
$$+ \beta_2\left(BK\,21\,participation\right)_{it}$$
$$+ \beta_3\left(after\,1999 \times BK\,21\,participation\right)_{it} + e_i . \qquad (4.2)$$

where β_3 gives the annual increase in publications due to participation in the program.

A fixed-effects regression, in this case, is similar to difference-in-differences except that, rather than merely comparing before and after for BK21 and non-BK21 research groups, the evaluator includes a separate dummy variable for each research group. This captures the fixed differences between each group.

One key difference between fixed-effects estimation and difference-in-differences is that the latter usually deals with a binary treatment (in which groups either participate or do not), whereas fixed-effects estimation can also deal with more nuanced treatments, such as varying levels of BK21 funding. Hence, we expect fixed effects to be more appropriate for assessing the effects of funding. We will discuss these methods more fully in the section on model validation. Because these methods eliminate many concerns about preexisting differences, and because one can test whether the common trends assumption is likely to hold, these estimators are good candidates for use in an evaluation.

Regression Discontinuity

This approach is often used when research groups are assigned to participate or not participate based on some kind of score with a clear cutoff point (for example, research groups above the cutoff point participate in a treatment). The central assumption is that if a program were to create a discontinuous jump in performance, then the groups immediately above and below the cutoff point would likely be very similar except for the treatment. For example, in Figure 4.13, the left-hand panel shows the relationship between the score and some outcome, such as number of publications. In the right-hand panel, the introduction of a policy intervention for those above the cutoff score creates a jump (or discontinuity), which can be attributed to the policy (BK21, in this case).

There are several ways to estimate a regression discontinuity design. One way (suggested by Bloom et al., 2005) is

$$
\begin{aligned}
(publications)_i &= \beta_0 + \beta_1 (score)_i \\
&+ \beta_2 (BK21\,participation)_i + e_i .
\end{aligned}
\tag{4.3}
$$

In this case, the *score* variable captures the consistent increase in quantity stemming from higher-ranked research groups; the *BK21 par-*

Figure 4.13
Regression Discontinuity Design

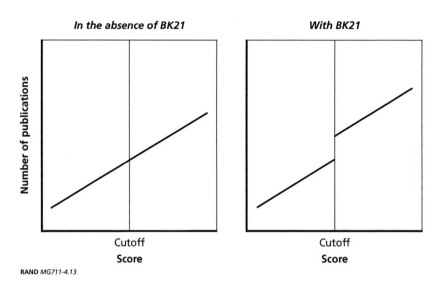

RAND MG711-4.13

ticipation variable captures the discontinuous treatment effect of the program.

In the BK21 selection process, a score was assigned to each research group based on various criteria and was used to determine whether the group received BK21 funding. This makes regression discontinuity a potential strategy for evaluating the effects of funding. Although these scores differ by, and therefore are not comparable across, academic fields, we could compare scores of research groups within individual disciplines through the use of normalized scores that note how many standard deviations an individual research group is from the mean of the average score within that discipline.

A disadvantage of regression discontinuity design is that it only identifies impacts for groups just above and below the discontinuity. It cannot be used to estimate the impact of BK21 for research groups that easily win (such as many at SNU or KAIST). Furthermore, close examination of the BK21 program reveals that while groups with better scores were more likely to receive funding, there is no consistent cutoff point at which to take advantage of a discontinuity. Table 4.2, for example, shows that, in Phase I, the normalized cutoff score for chemistry was below that for chemical engineering (i.e., groupsreceiving Phase I funds in chemical engineering were relatively stronger compared with their competitors than were groups receiving funds in chemistry). In Phase II, the normalized cutoff score for biology was lower than that for agriculture and veterinary biotechnology.

Other Strategies

Other strategies are available for program evaluation. An instrumental variables strategy can be used when there is some characteristic that affects the likelihood of program participation but does not affect the outcome except through increasing or decreasing that likelihood (Johnston and DiNardo, 1997).

Another is the Heckman Selection Correction, designed to correct for differences between those who participate in a program and those

Table 4.2
Variation in Cutoff Points in Scores for Funding

Field	Actual Scores		Normalized Scores (within field)	
	Highest Unfunded	Lowest Funded	Highest Unfunded	Lowest Funded
Phase I				
Agriculture & veterinary biotechnology	354.8	392.7	−.74	.47
Biology	411.1	418.6	.30	.45
Chemistry	407.1	419.7	−1.03	−.16
Chemical engineering	347.9	407.3	0.09	1.04
Information technology	343.6	391.8	−1.44	.32
Phase II				
Agriculture & veterinary biotechnology	180.5	192.2	−1.62	-0.82
Biology	185.9	187.2	−1.32	−1.28
Chemistry	210.1	210.6	−1.19	−1.15
Chemical engineering	179.8	208.0	−1.73	−0.69
Information technology	207.3	222.8	−0.98	−0.57

NOTE: Normalized scores are computed by subtracting the mean score for all applicant groups in a field from an individual group's actual score and dividing the difference by the standard deviation of actual scores.

who do not (Heckman, 1976). In this method, the researcher first uses a set of variables to estimate the probability of participation in BK21, and then includes a mathematical transformation of that probability (the Mill's ratio) in a second regression to estimate the impact of the program. If there is a variable that predicts the probability of participation but does not affect the outcome of interest (e.g., an instrumental variable), the researcher can use it in the Heckman Selection Correction. There is no obvious candidate BK21 characteristic for either strategy, so neither of these approaches seems appropriate.

Quantitative Model

Given the available analytic options, the most appropriate methods seem to be fixed-effects and difference-in-differences estimation. Both of these, given certain conditions, have significant advantages over OLS, matching, and propensity-score estimators. Neither relies on controlling for differences. Rather, they eliminate fixed differences between groups when estimating the treatment effect. If, contrary to the assumptions of fixed-effects estimation, BK21 and other groups would not have maintained similar trends in the absence of the program, then fixed-effects estimation can magnify biases in estimates of its effects. For example, if BK21 winning research groups were growing at much faster rates than BK21 losing research groups *before* BK21, then a fixed-effects estimate would mistakenly attribute the preexisting differential trend to the impact of BK21. It can also exacerbate problems of measurement error in the covariates (Green, 2005)—for example, if the level of funding is not well reported. We provide evidence below suggesting that we can be confident in the assumption of common trends and that the principal covariate of interest, funding, can be measured with limited error. Nevertheless, while these approaches are the best available options, there are significant challenges to using them. Some can be overcome, but others can only be recognized and accepted.

One important issue to consider in these (or other) strategies is contamination. This occurs when the comparison group receives some other treatment—for example, if other government agencies distributed additional funding to institutions that did not receive BK21 funding as BK21 was being rolled out. In this case, the comparison institutions would have received some level of "treatment" (not BK21 funding, but funding nonetheless).

Whether this creates bias depends on the exact interpretation of the treatment coefficient. If the coefficient on BK21 funding were interpreted to mean the impact of an additional dollar of funding on publications, then contamination would lead the evaluator to *underestimate* the impact of BK21. We demonstrate this in Figure 4.14.

In this case, the true impact of BK21 is demonstrated (in the left-hand panel) by (e–b) minus (c–a). With contamination (the right-hand panel), the treatment effect appears to be (e–b) minus (f–a). This is smaller than the true treatment effect because the non-BK21 groups also had a "treatment" resulting from the compensating funds.

If the coefficient on BK21 funding were interpreted as the impact of an additional dollar of BK21 funding (specific to the environment of the program), then the contamination would not lead to bias because

Figure 4.14
Difference-in-Differences Estimation

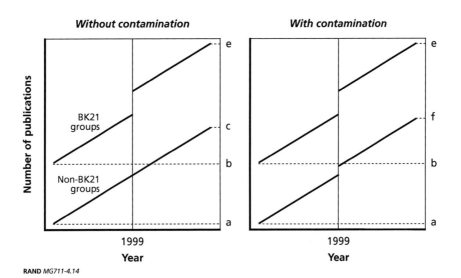

the compensation that comparison schools receive could be seen as part of the treatment effect. In other words, BK21 would have less of a differential impact on treatment versus comparison schools than one would expect in the absence of such compensatory funding, but the compensatory funding is one of the results of the program.

Conversely, if BK21 funding were to attract other funding, with, for example, non-BK21 institutions receiving fewer funds than they would otherwise because funding is focused on BK21 research groups, then resulting biases would lead to an overestimation of the specific impact of the BK21 program. Crowding-out and its effects on analyses of the program may also occur if BK21 recipients were to seek less private funding than they would have otherwise, so that funding for treatment groups rises by less than the total amount of BK21 funding.

Other effects that difference-in-differences estimation cannot capture include those that BK21 has on the research environment more generally. These are sometimes called general equilibrium effects. The competitive nature of BK21 may, for example, inspire competition that leads universities to perform at a higher level than previously in hopes of being involved in future phases of the program. Standard program evaluation strategies, including difference-in-differences estimation, cannot account for this and any other effect that impact all research groups. Qualitative evaluation, including analysis of perceptions of change in the competitive research environment (as discussed in Chapter Three), may be more appropriate to understanding such effects.

Another analytical concern is accounting for possibly heterogeneous effects of BK21 in different research areas. Fixed-effects models allow the evaluator to explore the distinct policy impacts of BK21 in various fields, either by running separate regressions for each field or by including indicator variables and interaction terms to create a difference-in-differences model, as in

$$
\begin{aligned}
\left(publications\right)_{it} &= \beta_0 + \beta_1 \left(after\,1999\right)_{it} + \beta_2 \left(BK\,21\,participation\right)_{it} \\
&+ \beta_3 \left(after\,1999 \times BK\,21\,participation\right)_{it} + \beta_4 \left(chemistry\,group\right)_{it} \\
&+ \beta_5 \left(chemistry\,group \times after\,1999 \times BK\,21\,participation\right)_{it} \\
&+ \cdots + e_i \, .
\end{aligned}
\tag{4.4}
$$

Here, the estimate of β_5 gives the differential effect of BK21 funding to a chemistry research group relative to research groups in other fields. The number of indicators that may be included in an equation is limited by the number of data observations. In this case, the number of data observations is not likely to be particularly large, somewhat limiting the specificity of the model.

Timing of the BK21 effect poses another challenge, particularly estimating when it could be expected to occur. If there were a clear indication of how long it would take for the program to have an effect, then the evaluator could simply designate that year as the "treatment" year and test for outcomes then. For example, if BK21 were expected to take two years from the 1999 implementation, or until 2001, to have an effect on publications, it could be estimated through

$$(publications)_i = \beta_0 + \beta_1 (after\ 2001)_i + \beta_2 (BK21\ participation)_i$$
$$+ \beta_3 (after\ 2001 \times BK21\ participation)_i + e_i \ . \qquad (4.5)$$

This estimation replaces the treatment year (1999) with the expected year of the onset of the impact (2001). If the time for effects to show is uncertain, then more than one specification (or year) should be tested. Estimating such delayed effects will work only if no other significant policy interventions have been introduced in the meantime. The longer the lag, the more likely that other interventions and events will make it difficult to pick up effects that can be attributed to the program.

Heterogeneous Funding

In describing potential strategies, we have emphasized the fact that BK21 offered heterogeneous, i.e., varying levels of, funding. One reason for this is the variation of department size for program recipients, with larger departments that have more graduate students and junior research faculty receiving more funding. Yet even when we control for department size, there appears to be a large variation in per-capita funding.

The fixed-effects estimation model captures fixed differences in performance resulting from research group size. An alternative approach is to include an interaction between initial group size and funding in the estimation model to estimate distinct treatment effects by group size. Without data on group size for nonparticipating groups, however, we cannot use this approach.

The Power to Identify Impacts

Even with strategies that seem theoretically appropriate for evaluating this program, it is impossible to know with certainty whether one will be to identify the impact of BK21 with statistical significance.[4] While BK21 is a major investment at the project level, at a broader level—e.g., across a university—its funding, as discussed earlier, does not constitute a large percentage of the whole. Nevertheless, given the higher levels of median funding in Phase II, we expect that a fixed-effects strategy will be able to identify effects, although this depends on the relationship between funding and outcomes.

Data for Use in Validating the Model

To test the appropriateness of the fixed-effects model, we draw on data on research groups in both the time preceding and the time during Phase I of BK21.

ISI Data

To measure numbers of publications, we use ISI SCI data on publications from 1990 through 2005. As noted above, these data provide information on publications by university, but not by BK21 research group. While it is possible to use these data to tabulate publications by research group, the number of professors sharing the same surname make such calculations extremely labor intensive. The Ministry of

---

[4] Statistical significance refers to the likelihood that the observed differences between groups are not due to random variation. In this document, we identify varying levels of statistical significance, including 90%, 95%, and 99% (the latter implying a 99% probability that the difference between groups is not due to random variation).

Education has provided data on publications by research group, but only for participating research groups during the period of the program and the prior year. Ideally, our analysis should include data on both participants and nonparticipants both during the program and for several prior years.

SCI does allow identification of publications by both university and subject area, so for most of our analysis we match the SCI general subject areas to the BK21 research group as closely as possible.[5] Table 4.3 shows how we grouped some SCI fields. In evaluating Phase II, the government could obtain data directly from research groups.

Because the data from this exercise only approximate the publications for winning and losing research groups, readers should consider

Table 4.3
Relationship Between BK21 Field and SCI Fields

BK21 Field	SCI Fields Included
Agriculture & veterinary biotechnology	Agriculture, dairy and animal science Food science and technology Plant sciences Veterinary sciences
Biology	Biochemistry and molecular biology Cell biology Biotechnology and applied microbiology Microbiology Biology
Chemical engineering	Engineering, chemical Biochemical research methods
Physics	Physics, applied Physics, multidisciplinary Physics, condensed matter Physics, particles and fields Biophysics Astronomy and astrophysics Physics, atomic, molecular, and chemical Physics, mathematical Physics, fluids and plasmas Physics, nuclear

[5]   In the process of data compilation and classification, we consulted Korean experts including members of BNC at KRF.

our results to be demonstrative rather than definitive. To truly evaluate the impact of BK21 Phase I funding, we would need actual data on the exact research output of groups winning and not winning BK21 funding.

Ministry of Education Data

All other data we employ come from the MoE. This includes funding data for Phase I and Phase II, the list of groups that applied for and received funding, and other statistics about BK21 participants.

Validation of the Model

We use some Phase I data to explore the validity of the best-choice estimation models. Previously, we proposed either a difference-in-differences model or a fixed-effects model. We expect the fixed-effects model to be most effective, because it can capture the nuanced treatment of varying funding levels (rather than a simple funding versus no-funding treatment).

One potential challenge to validating the quantitative model using Phase I data is that several research groups teamed up with research groups in other universities to improve their competitive chances. This challenge, however, is more apparent than real; most of these partnerships were unsustainable and dissolved early in Phase I. This practice was not permitted in Phase II. We therefore treat each research group as a separate entity.

Evaluating Phase II is likely to be easier than evaluating Phase I. Phase II, with wider disbursement of funds, had similarly greater variation in inputs, thus generating a larger treatment group and increasing the statistical power of subsequent analyses. In Phase I, research groups at the top five recipient universities accounted for 91 percent of BK21 funds; in Phase II, the top five universities only account for 48 percent of funding.

Pre-Treatment Trends

Although fixed-effects estimation overcomes differing *levels* in the outcome variable between the treatment and comparison group from the treatment effect, it does not overcome different *trends*. One strategy to examine the likelihood of bias resulting from these disparities is to examine the trends in outcomes in the years previous to the program and determine whether the treatment and comparison groups are on similar or different trajectories.

Using data from 1990 to 2005, we compare publications of S&T research groups that received BK21 funding in 1999 with those that did not. Although we are examining the appropriateness of this strategy for evaluating Phase II (which did not begin until 2006), we use the original treatment and comparison groups from Phase I because changes in treatment in Phase II were affected by Phase I funding and competition and so were still post-treatment. We examined the common trends assumption using data from both pre-BK21 and Phase I because an unbiased fixed-effects estimator relies on common trends in both periods, although a discrete break in trend is permitted. We did not include a distinct term for a break in trend at Phase I because our specification (below) allows for differential treatment effects *each year*.

Note that although this is the best available test for common trends, it is not without weaknesses. The lack of statistically significant differences between the treatment and comparison groups indicates either that these groups are similar *or* that our data do not contain the statistical power to precisely identify differences.

In addition to examining trends in the total number of articles, we examined a semi-log specification, which uses the logarithm of the output variable and the absolute level of the treatment variable. Using the logarithm of a continuous output, such as publications, in a regression allows us to interpret the coefficient estimate as the *percentage change* in the output for a *unit change* in the treatment.

Figure 4.15 suggests that, prior to BK21 implementation, groups that won funding had greater growth than nonrecipients in absolute number of publications. Figure 4.16, however, suggests that both recip-

Figure 4.15
Phase I Trend in Total Publications in S&T: Winners Versus Losers

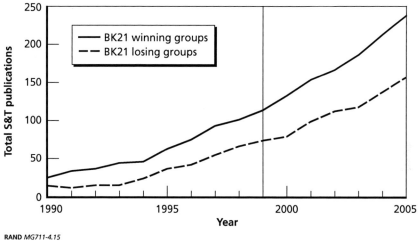

Figure 4.16
Phase I Trend in Log Publications in S&T: Winners Versus Losers

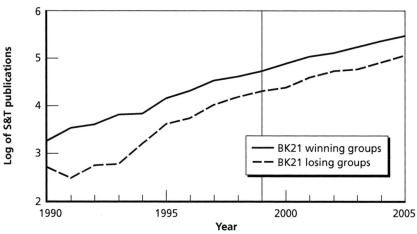

ients and nonrecipients had roughly similar levels of growth in their publications. These figures, while illustrative, do not demonstrate whether differences between recipients and nonrecipients before BK21 implementation were statistically significant. To test the significance of these differences we use

$$(publications)_{it} = \beta_0 + \beta_1 1(BK21)_{it} + \sum_{year} \gamma^Y \cdot 1(year = Y)_{it}$$

$$+ \sum_{year} \delta^Y \cdot \left(1(year = Y) \cdot 1(BK21)\right)_{it} + \varepsilon_{it}. \qquad (4.6)$$

This model includes a dummy variable for BK21 participation, a dummy for each year evaluated, and a full set of terms for interactions between BK21 participation and year of analysis. The δ coefficients on the interactions indicate whether, in a given year before or after BK21 implementation, the difference in number of publications for participants and nonparticipants exceeded the overall annual average difference between the two. We test for differing trends by comparing the δ coefficients across years. This is a weak test, as imperfect data can make identifying statistical differences more difficult. Although we cannot reject the equality of δ's over the years for the results in Column 1 of Table 4.4, we observe almost a 650 percent change from a coefficient of 11.44 in 1990 to a coefficient of 73.74 in 2005. This is suggestive (albeit not conclusive due to statistical imprecision) that there is a distinct trend for BK21 recipients even before BK21 Phase II.

We used Equation 4.6 to assess differences in trends in the natural logarithm of the number of publications for participants and nonparticipants by year, both before and after the program. Column 2 in Table 4.4 shows the results of this analysis of differences in the rate of change for the number of papers. This analysis reveals a much smaller change in coefficients: 250 percent over the years, also not statistically significant. These results confirm what Figure 4.16 suggested.

Combined, these analyses suggest that the semi-log fixed-effects specification is the most likely to be unbiased. We therefore use this model to analyze differences between eventual BK21 recipients from 1994,

Table 4.4
Testing for Common Trends in Pre-BK21 Phase II Data:
1990–2005

	S&T Publications (1)	Log of S&T Publications (2)
Pre-BK21		
BK21 x year 1990	11.44 (9.04)	0.70+ (0.40)
BK21 x year 1991	11.20** (3.79)	0.44+ (0.23)
BK21 x year 1992	10.37* (4.25)	0.28 (0.26)
BK21 x year 1993	20.30** (6.89)	0.54+ (0.29)
BK21 x year 1994	11.62+ (6.52)	−0.01 (0.31)
BK21 x year 1995	19.74+ (10.85)	−0.20 (0.32)
BK21 x year 1996	25.64* (12.35)	−0.12 (0.30)
BK21 x year 1997	28.09+ (16.56)	−0.27 (0.32)
BK21 x year 1998	27.15 (19.45)	-0.39 (0.37)
BK21 Phase I		
BK21 x year 1999	29.34 (22.38)	-0.39 (0.37)
BK21 x year 2000	44.84+ (24.20)	−0.26 (0.36)
BK21 x year 2001	45.62 (28.92)	−0.29 (0.37)
BK21 x year 2002	47.07 (31.97)	−0.45 (0.37)
BK21 x year 2003	63.31+ (34.46)	-0.28 (0.39)
BK21 x year 2004	70.72+ (39.91)	−0.31 (0.39)
BK21 x year 2005	73.74 (47.81)	−0.37 (0.39)
Observations	974	974

OLS regressions; standard errors clustered at the research group level. + p<0.10, * p<0.05, ** p<0.01. Standard errors are in parentheses. Also included (but not reported) are a full set of year dummies and a constant term.

or the period during which the assumption of common trends for the two groups appears to hold.

Another Possible Comparison Group: Nonapplicants

A weakness of using the losing applicants as a comparison group for the winning applicants is a failure to capture broader effects that the program may have had on both winners and losers by, for example, stimulating competition. One way to identify those effects would be to use nonapplicants as a comparison group for both winning and losing applicant groups. These nonapplicant groups, being less focused on research, are likely to differ from applicant groups in ways that we are unable to capture wholly using our measures, and so differences attributed to treatment in several methods we discussed above may in fact be due to unobserved characteristics.

Difference-in-differences estimation, as explained earlier, can be used to control for unobserved characteristics as long as the trend in the variable of interest between the observed groups is similar. To test this, we selected a pool of nonapplicant universities most likely to be similar in research to the applicant universities. (BK21 does not operate at the university level, but we did not have data on the departments in each nonapplicant university.) Among the top 50 institutions as ranked by the highest number of S&T publications for Korea in 1997, we identified 14 universities that did not apply for BK21 Phase I funding. (Other institutions included think tanks and overseas partner institutions.) As when comparing the winning and losing research groups, we here examine the number of publications for the various S&T research areas for each of these universities (using the matching method described above and shown in Table 4.3) for winning applicants, losing applicants, and nonapplicants. Figures 4.17 and 4.18 show the resulting trends.

Figure 4.17 indicates that the trend in absolute number of publications for nonapplicants diverges from those of both the winning and losing applicant groups. Figure 4.18 indicates the trend in the natural logarithm of the number of publications is roughly similar, meaning

Figure 4.17
Phase I Trend in Total Publications in S&T: Comparison with Nonapplicants

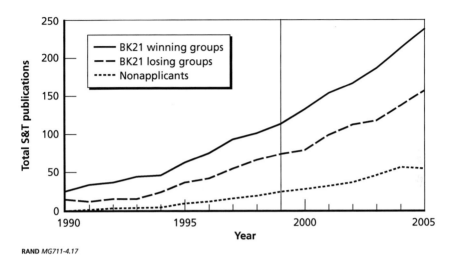

RAND *MG711-4.17*

Figure 4.18
Phase I Trend in Log Publications in S&T: Comparison with Nonapplicants

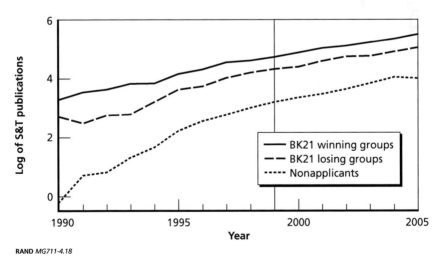

RAND *MG711-4.18*

that the trend in percentage growth in the number of publications is roughly similar. We test for these similarities using

$$
\begin{aligned}
\left(publications \right)_{it} &= \beta_0 + \beta_1 1\left(BK\,21\ winner \right)_{it} + \beta_2 1\left(BK\,21\ loser \right) \\
&+ \sum_{year} \gamma^Y \cdot 1\left(year = Y \right)_{it} + \sum_{year} \delta^Y \cdot \left[1\left(year = Y \right) \cdot 1\left(BK\,21\ winner \right) \right]_{it} \\
&+ \sum_{year} \delta^Y \cdot \left[1\left(year = Y \right) \cdot 1\left(BK\,21\ loser \right) \right]_{it} + \varepsilon_{it}.
\end{aligned}
\tag{4.7}
$$

The results of this test (because of its length) are shown in Appendix D, Table D.1. The estimates for differences in the absolute number of articles between nonapplicants and both groups of applicants are statistically significant throughout the time series (Appendix D, Table D.1, Column 1). Nevertheless, the differences between these groups in rate of growth for number of articles are not statistically significant (Column 2) except for a marginal case in 2002. We can, therefore, assume the trends in rate of growth of articles among all three groups are similar, and include nonapplicant universities as a comparison group.

Validation
In this subsection we demonstrate how the models work using sample data. In Table 4.5, we show estimates unadjusted for confounding factors (for contrast), difference-in-differences estimates, and fixed-effects estimates. For both difference-in-differences estimates and fixed-effects estimates, we used the semi-log specification and included publications from 1994 onward, given the results of our earlier tests (see Figure 4.16 and Table 4.4). Previous evaluations of BK21 have used quality-adjusted publications as the dependent variable. We used unadjusted publications for two reasons. First, we do not have the data to calculate quality-adjusted publications for both treatment and comparison research groups. Second, we consider separate measures of quantity and quality as more transparent and easier to interpret than a quality-adjusted estimate.

Table 4.5
Various Impact Estimates for BK21

| | Dependent Variable | | | | |
| | S&T Publications | | Log of S&T Publications | | |
Model	Winners vs. Losers (1)	Before vs. After (2)	Winners vs. Losers (3)	Before vs. After (4)	Difference in Differences (5)
Selected for BK21 Phase I	60.56+ (34.71)		0.38 (0.26)		0.46 (0.28)
1999 or later		95.42** (17.14)		0.94** (0.10)	1.03** (0.14)
(BK21 Phase I) x (1999 or later)					−0.08 (0.17)
Constant	112.17** (19.80)	77.31** (13.48)	4.19** (0.20)	3.62** (0.18)	3.16** (0.22)
R-squared	0.03	0.07	0.02	0.12	0.15
Years included	1999–2005	1994–2005	1999–2005	1994–2005	1994–2005
Observations	485	510	485	510	806
Median of dependent variable	94.00	76.00	4.54	4.33	4.13

+ p<0.10, * p<0.05, ** p<0.01. Standard errors are clustered at the level of the research group. Standard errors reported in parentheses.

To assess the relationship between BK21 participation and subsequent number of publications we use

$$\left(publications \right)_{it} = \beta_0 + \beta_1 \cdot \left(selected\ for\ BK\,21 \right)_{it} + \varepsilon_{it} . \qquad (4.8)$$

Our data indicate that, in this equation, $\hat{\beta}_1 = 60.6$. This means that, between 1999 and 2005, research groups selected for BK21 had about 61 more SCI publications each year than losing BK21 applicants did, a marginally significant result (Table 4.5, Column 1). Non-BK21 groups had about 112 publications each year, so the estimated impact of BK21 is an increase of more than 50 percent in publications. Moving on to use Equation 4.8 to assess differences between BK21 applicants and nonapplicants (as opposed to winners versus losers), we find that winning BK21 applicants had 132 more publications each year between 1999 and 2005 than nonapplicants had. Even losing applicants had 72 more publications each year than nonapplicants had. (These results are not reported in tables.) Though substantial, these differences likely cannot be attributed solely to applying for BK21 Phase I funding, as it is likely (and evident, from Figure 4.17 above), that there were major differences between applicants and nonapplicants before BK21. Indeed, some of the differences in numbers of publications are likely the result of differences between applicants and nonapplicants before implementation of BK21. The estimates using the natural logarithm of publications (Table 4.5, Column 3) are not statistically significant, indicating no significant differences in the rate of growth for the number of publications after BK21 implementation.

To assess the effect of BK21 implementation on number of publications before and after implementation (i.e., just comparing the BK21 winners to their own performance before the program), we use

$$\left(publications\right)_{it} = \beta_0 + \beta_1 1 \cdot \left(post\,BK\,21\right)_{it} + \varepsilon_{it}. \qquad (4.9)$$

Estimation of this equation indicates that the average annual number of publications by BK21 research groups more than doubled after BK21 implementation, from about 77 to 173, an increase of 123 percent (Table 4.5, Column 2). Similarly, estimation of this equation shows a large and significant change with BK21 implementation on the natural logarithm of the number of S&T publications by Korean universities (Table 4.5, Column 4). This indicates the rate of growth in the number of publications increased after BK21 implementation, although, again, given the rapid upward growth in publications before BK21, it is likely that not all this growth can be attributed to BK21 alone.

To focus more specifically on the difference in percentage increase in the number of publications for winning and losing BK21 applicants, we estimate the difference-in-differences equation earlier displayed as (4.2):

$$\ln\left(publications\right)_{it} = \beta_0 + \beta_1 1 \cdot \left(after\,1999\right)_{it}$$
$$+\beta_2 1 \cdot \left(BK\,21\,participation\right)_{it}$$
$$+\beta_3 1 \cdot \left(after\,1999\right)_{it} \times 1 \cdot \left(BK\,21\,participation\right)_{it} + \varepsilon_i. \qquad (4.10)$$

Here, $\hat{\beta}_3 = -0.08$ and is not statistically significant, with a 95 percent confidence interval ranging from −0.41 to 0.25. This suggests an impact of BK21 participation ranging from a 34 percent decrease in publications to a 29 percent increase in publications, hardly an insightful result (Table 4.5, Column 5).[6]

As discussed previously, BK21 likely has heterogeneous effects varying on the level of funding that a group receives. We therefore turn to fixed-effects equations showing a fixed-effect for each research group, as in

$$\ln\left(publications\right)_{it} = \alpha_i + \beta_1\left(BK\,21\,funding\right)_{it}$$
$$+\sum_y \gamma^Y \cdot 1\left(y = Year\right)_{it} + u_i + \varepsilon_{it}. \qquad (4.11)$$

Here, α_i is a research group–level fixed effect, $BK21$ *funding* is measured in millions of KRW,

$$\sum_y \gamma^Y \cdot 1\left(y = Year\right)_{it}$$

represents a full set of dummy variables for each year included in estimation, u_i is a research group–specific error term, and ε_{it} is the standard observation-level error term. We first consider results for all BK21 applicants. (We later show results for nonapplicants.) Fixed differences across research groups are shown by α_i and those by years are picked up by

---

[6] Although estimates from the semi-log regression ($\ln y = b * x$) can generally be interpreted as a one unit change in x implying a ($b * 100$) percent change in y, this is not true when x is a dummy variable (taking only a value of 0 or 1), in which case a change in x from 0 to 1 implies a change in y approximately equal to (($\exp(b)$–1) * 100) percent (Kennedy 2003, p. 123).

$$\sum_{y} \gamma^{Y} \cdot 1\big(y = Year\big)_{it}.$$

This leaves β_1 to capture the impact of an additional million won of BK21 funding.

Using data from Phase I BK21 S&T groups and applicants, we found no measurable effect from an additional million won of funding. The principal drawback of this specification is that it imposes linearity on the relationship between funding and publications, implying that the first million won of funding has the same impact as the hundredth million won of funding, which is unlikely to be the case.

To assess the likely nonlinear relationship between funding and publications, we replaced $\beta_1\big(BK21\,funding\big)_{it}$ in Equation 4.11 with a set of four dummy variables, one for each quartile of participant funding. (The omitted category is receiving no funding, which is true for all groups that applied for funding but did not receive it and for all groups previous to 1999.) Doing this, we found that groups in the bottom quartile of funding (receiving 1.3–3.8 billion KRW over Phase I), appear to have had a 34 percent increase in publications as a result of BK21. Groups in the top quartile (receiving more than 14.6 billion KRW over Phase I) appear to have had a 31 percent decrease in publications.[7] The effects for the middle quartiles are insignificant. This suggests that research groups receiving lesser amounts of funding most benefited by that funding, whereas the groups at the top of the funding ladder experienced a slowdown in publications.

We obtained a similar result when we omitted the research groups at the five largest schools, redefining the quartiles for each modified sample. Funding had a strong positive impact on groups in the lowest quartile. This suggests that BK21 has the strongest positive impact on groups that received the least funding, either because those groups have less access to other funds, meaning BK21 funding may have been more significant to them, or because groups that won funding at lower levels

---

[7]   Thirty-four percent stems from the coefficient estimate (0.29) entered into the following equation: $34 = 100 * (\exp(0.29) - 1)$. Likewise, 31 percent $= 100 * (\exp(-0.37) - 1)$.

were making an extra effort to win more BK21 funding in the future. By contrast, there appears to be virtually no relationship between funding quartile and the effects of the program on publications at the top universities.

There are several possible explanations for this surprising finding. First, for research groups at the top universities, other funding may have been crowded out (David, Hall, and Toole, 2000). These research groups may in general have more access to non-BK21 funding than other research groups. As a result, BK21 funding may have replaced other funding for these top research groups but may have represented a true funding increase for the groups outside the top universities that received lower levels of BK21 funding. Second, although the research groups at the top universities do not seem to have increased their number of publications as a result of BK21, they may have taken advantage of the increase in funding to invest in higher-quality research. Third, even independent of crowding-out, BK21 funding may represent a larger proportionate increase in funding for smaller research groups that received lower levels of funding. Finally, if the program increases the number of graduate students, top schools may be bringing in new graduate students with significantly lower qualifications than those already in the lab, actually hurting productivity. Alternatively, less-productive labs at less-prestigious schools may benefit from any increase in manpower. We do not have access to data to test these hypotheses, but some combination may explain this pattern of findings.

To capture the more general effects of competition in the BK21 program, we considered differences by funding quartile and by whether a university applied for BK21 funding. We found that applying for BK21 funding had a positive but statistically insignificant effect on the rate of growth in publications. This result is not precisely estimated and does not rule out a general impact of the BK21 funding; it is possible that using Phase II data would indicate a different result. The other results are broadly similar, with BK21 having a strong positive effect at the lowest levels of funding and with some evidence of negative impacts at the higher levels. Given no evidence that applying, in itself, had an effect on rate of growth in publications, we do not consider it in the following discussing of variations on the specification.

Variations on the Specification

We explored several potential variations in specification or interactions and how they might affect our findings. This included considering the potential for lagged effects, differential effects based on how well research groups implemented MoE reforms, differential effects on whether a group was at a private or public university, and separating effects for the top three universities (SNU, KAIST, and Korea University).

First, as discussed previously, funding may only have an impact after some time has elapsed. To assess this possibility, we used a variation of Equation 4.11 in which we regressed a given year's publications on the previous year's funding in one case and the current year's publications on funding in the previous two years in the second case. In both cases, the results are very similar to those above, that is, BK21 funding had the strongest positive impact on groups in the bottom quartile of funding. Despite limited variation in funding from year to year, we might expect the results to differ if BK21 impacts clearly did not set in until one or two years after the program initiation.

Second, at the time of BK21, educational institutions were encouraged to make certain reforms, such as improving the undergraduate admissions process, broadening the spectrum of undergraduate applicants, reducing the number of undergraduates, and centralizing the administration of research funding. In 2004, each research group received a score from the MoE indicating its performance on these reforms. We estimated the impact of BK21 on the natural logarithm of the number of publications (and the rate of growth in the number of publications) for research groups above and below the funding median. Because the reforms were concurrent with BK21, we cannot interpret the difference as causal. We also had incomplete data on reforms, so our sample size is smaller for this specific analysis than for others, leading us to estimate the effect of reforms on groups by whether they were above or below the funding median rather than by funding quartile. Our estimation results indicate a stark contrast between those schools that were successful in reform and others, with BK21 apparently having a positive effect on publications for schools at all funding levels that implemented reforms, a negative effect on schools receiving more funding but implementing fewer reforms, and virtually no effect on schools receiving little funding and implementing few reforms. Again, because BK21 funding may itself have affected these reforms, it is not clear how to interpret these results. Still, the contrast between reformers and nonreformers is striking.

Quality

These same estimation methods can be used to examine the effect of BK21 funding on other dependent variables, such as measures of publication quality. (We discuss potential measures of publication quality in detail in the next chapter.) As we note there, one might measure quality changes in journals (according to impact factor) from across all S&T journals and one might also use field-specific journals. Using both measures allows one to see whether research groups receiving BK21 funding are improving in quality in science journals both overall and in field-specific niches. For example, one might use "number of publications in the top 10 percent of all S&T journals" or "number of publications in the top 10 percent of journals in a given field" as outcome variables in the same fixed-effects regressions as above.

Figure 4.19 shows the number of Korean articles by year in the top decile and quintile of S&T publications as ranked by quality. Unfortunately, the public-use data on the ISI Web site are difficult to use, limiting our analyses; future analysts may wish to consider purchasing all these data, enabling more detailed and flexible analysis. The number of Korean articles in the top quintile is relatively small, limiting our ability to test the effects of BK21 on research quality.

The number of Korean articles in top journals of specific fields is also relatively low and therefore is not conducive to sophisticated tests for BK21 effects. Figure 4.20 presents data on the annual number of all Korean articles in all robotics journals or biochemistry journals at least one standard deviation above the mean journal impact factor (where the journal impact factor is the average number of citations for each article in the journal in 1997 and 1998).

Figure 4.19
All Korean Articles in S&T Publications

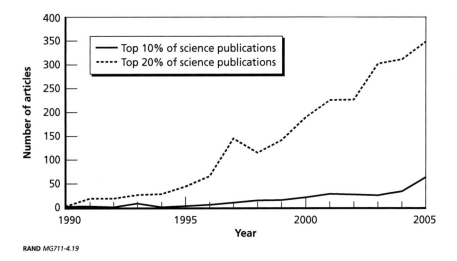

Figure 4.20
All Korean Articles in Robotics and Biochemistry Journals
(one standard deviation above mean)

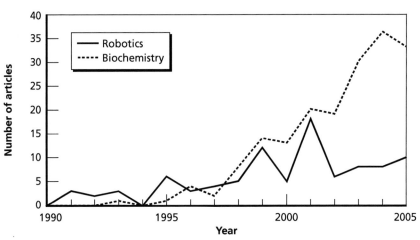

An additional limitation to our analysis, discussed previously, is our inability to link papers to specific departments. (The Korean government would be able to do this by using direct publication reports from applicant departments.) For example, our earlier matching method would not work for examining the top science publications, because it is based on the assumption, for example, that a paper in a biology journal is published by a biology professor and ignores the few high-level general-interest journals (such as *Science* and *Nature*). Direct data on publications from research groups would eliminate that problem.

Rather than providing empirical estimates, Table 4.6 lists hypothetical data, which might be collected at the research group level, for assessing the effect of BK21 on publication quality. Such data would allow analysts to assess the effect of BK21 on publication quality through a fixed-effects approach by research group:

$$\ln\left(\text{publications in top journals}\right)_{it} = \alpha_i + \beta_1\left(BK21\ funding\right)_{it}$$
$$+\sum_y \gamma^Y \cdot 1\left(y = Year\right)_{it} + u_i + \varepsilon_{it}. \tag{4.12}$$

The term $\beta_1\left(BK21\ funding\right)_{it}$ could also perhaps be replaced with indicators for funding quartiles or some other divisions similar to those we used in previous analyses exploring effects by groups of recipients.

Table 4.6
Example Data Format for Assessing BK21's Effect on Publication Quality: Korean IT Department Publications in the Top 20 Percent of IT Journals

	Selected for BK21?	1990	1991	1992	...	2010	2011	2012
SNU IT	Yes	0	5	4	...	32	40	37
KAIST IT	Yes	3	1	9	...	40	38	46
Korea University IT	Yes	0	0	1	...	15	17	24
Hanyang University IT	No	0	0	0	...	5	5	8
Yonsei University IT	No	0	0	0	...	10	12	9
...					...			

Social Science and Humanities

Science and engineering account for 85 percent of the BK21 research budget, with the remainder allocated to liberal arts, social science, and interdisciplinary fields. The goals for these areas are similar to the broader goals of BK21. Figures 4.21 and 4.22 show that Korean universities have had more publications in both social sciences and arts and humanities since the implementation of BK21. These trends could be analyzed further with the same quantitative models that we outline previously, separating BK21 research groups from non-BK21 research groups.

Other Aspects of the Logic Model

To this point, we have focused on the net effect of the program, examining the effect of BK21 on some output, such as publications. It is also important to understand the mechanisms by which a program has an effect. It is more challenging to identify the individual effect of the specific mechanisms, but there are ways to explore these relationships.

Figure 4.21
All Korean Social Science Publications, 1990–2005

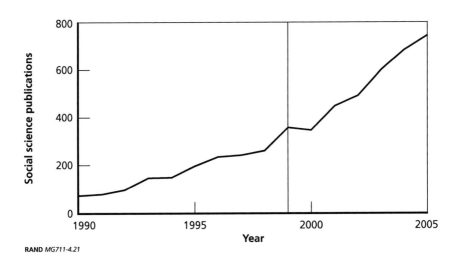

RAND MG711-4.21

Figure 4.22
All Korean Arts and Humanities Publications, 1990–2005

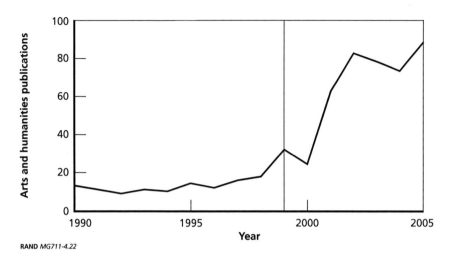

For example, suppose we have demonstrated a positive net effect of BK21 funding on a given output, such as human resource production or high-quality publications. The next step would be to understand whether this was a result of changes in program activities (for example, student stipends led to more-focused student work) or a change in individuals and institutions (such as changes to department composition resulting from BK21 activities). One way to examine this effect would be to control for variables such as funding and numbers of professors and PhD students by year (among others) in

$$\ln\left(publications\right)_{it} = \alpha + \beta_1\left(BK21\,funding\right)_{it}$$
$$+\beta_2\left(\#\,of\,professors\right)_{it} + \beta_3\left(\#\,of\,PhD\,students\right)_{it}$$
$$+\cdots+\sum_y \gamma^Y \cdot 1\left(y = Year\right)_{it} + u_i + \varepsilon_{it}\,. \qquad (4.13)$$

If the coefficient on BK21 funding (β_1) were to diminish significantly, it would suggest that the variation previously being explained by the BK21 funding measure is now being explained by its more direct causes (the compositional shifts). That implies that a significant portion of the effect of BK21 funding is through the compositional change in the department. One can perform the same test with another mechanism, such as a measure of student stipends. Such tests would help indicate which mechanisms are pivotal.

An important caveat to using such methods is that one must be sure that the covariate controlled for is the operative factor. For example, a decrease in the size of the BK21 funding coefficient could result from changing department composition or through *something correlated with department composition* but not included in the regression. One must therefore consider carefully what excluded covariates may be correlated and also responsible for the BK21 impact and therefore should be included in the equation.

Simultaneous Equations Methods

So far in this chapter, we have developed a single-equation model that could be applied to estimate the program effect on any quantitative output, including total publications, high-quality publications, or production of PhDs. The single-equation model, with the extensions described above, also can explore the mechanisms that produce the program effect. In addition to these methods, evaluators may want to consider multiple-equation methods for estimating program effects. We discuss two types of multiple-equation methods here: jointly determined outputs and endogenous or multistage processes.

In the case of jointly determined outputs, each possible output can have an estimated effect found through the single-equation model presented above. But we may be concerned that some pairs of outputs are, in fact, jointly determined in the *sa-up-dan*, and therefore the error terms in the two separately estimated equations are correlated. The standard approach to this situation is to use seemingly unrelated regression methods (with fixed effects as in the single-equation model) to produce more efficient estimates. The single-equation models would produce unbiased estimates (provided the conditions outlined earlier hold), but the seemingly unrelated regression estimates might be more efficient for some combinations of output variables.

In the case of a multistage process or endogenous variables, the *sa-up-dan*, for example, determines the number of graduate students based on some exogenous time-varying variables and fixed *sa-up-dan* effects. The *sa-up-dan* also determines the number of faculty members by a similar process. An output variable such as total publications is determined by the number of graduate students, number of faculty, fixed effects, and perhaps other exogenous time-varying variables. These three relationships define a system of three equations. Although the single-equation methods described earlier are appropriate for understanding the total (or *reduced form*) effect of BK21 on a given outcome, it might also be interesting to understand how the BK21 program affects total publications (or some other outcome) net of its effect on the number of faculty or graduate students. To do this, another estimation procedure is needed.

A standard way to estimate such a system of equations is with two-stage least squares estimation. To implement two-stage least squares estimation for this system, two instrumental variables (also called *instruments*) are required. One instrument must be correlated with the number of graduate students but not otherwise correlated with total publications (except through the effect of the graduate student variable). Similarly, the second instrument must be correlated with the number of faculty members but not otherwise correlated with the total publications (except through the effect of the faculty variable).

Sometimes it is possible to find suitable instrumental variables that meet these conditions in a dataset. If the instruments have a strong correlation with the number of graduate students and with the number of faculty members, respectively, the model can generate reliable estimates. If the correlation is weak, however, the model will fail to generate reliable estimates even if they technically meet the conditions. If suitable instruments cannot be identified, it is not possible to estimate the system of simultaneous equations. A common approach to finding suitable instruments is to identify some feature, such as geographical variation, that is not related to the output variable but is related to the intermediate or endogenous variables. In the absence of actual data on BK21 Phase II, we cannot say whether such instruments exist; but given our knowledge of the Korean education system we do not see any obvious candidates for instruments for a simultaneous system like this one. If the data turn out to contain such valid instruments, then the simultaneous equations method may yield additional insights beyond the single-equation model that we recommend as the primary estimation strategy. Since we expect that the instrumental variables procedure will not be successful for these reasons, the single-equation method of Equation 4.13 is likely to be the best way to estimate these process effects.

International Competitiveness

As noted previously, one of the goals of BK21 is to nurture globally competitive research universities. One measure of global competitiveness is international university rankings, such as the Shanghai Jia Tong university rankings and the *Times Higher Education Supplement* rankings. In this section, we discuss how some variables—such as SCI publications—that can be measured and controlled in regression equations can be tested for their effect on the BK21 goal of creating more globally competitive universities.

To see whether publications in BK21 research groups are enhancing international competitiveness, we recommend a broader measure of quality. The assessment must also distinguish between having a high impact across science journals generally and having a high impact in a particular field. Of the 25 top science journals as measured by ISI impact factor, all but four are medical or biology journals. An SNU research group in information technology may have a massive impact in computer science journals but no noticeable impact in the top 25 journals. We therefore recommend measures, which we discuss in more detail in the next chapter, for assessing the performance of a research group in the top journals in its field and in the top science journals overall.

Simulation: Ability to Precisely Estimate Effects at Phase II Funding Levels

We have demonstrated how to implement a fixed-effects quantitative model, using Phase I data as an illustration. Because the goal of this monograph is to assist in evaluating Phase II, we now use a simple simulation to indicate how much precision one might expect in estimating BK21 impacts at Phase II funding levels using this approach. Funding levels for Phase II are known, but the outputs, such as publications or PhDs graduated, are not yet known. Given that limitation, we use the following process to simulate estimation precision for Phase II.

We begin by taking the actual publication levels for the period during Phase I of BK21 (1999–2005) and *de-trend* them of estimated Phase I impacts. The purpose is to simulate what Phase I performance would have looked like in the absence of BK21 funding and then to simulate the impact of Phase II funding levels. To do this, we use the fixed-effects estimates for program winners and losers in all but the five largest universities and the data sample from that same regression as before. (It is straightforward to replicate this process for some other sample.) So, for example, we take the schools in the bottom quartile of funding in Phase I, for whom the estimated impact of BK21 was a 54 percent increase in publications, and we multiply actual publications by (1/1.54), eliminating the 54 percent increase and bringing the publication numbers to what one would have predicted in the absence of BK21 funding.

Then, using actual data on Phase II funding, we estimate the fixed-effects regression from before:

$$\ln\left(\textit{de-trended publications} + \textit{potential effect}\right)_{it}$$
$$+\textit{noise}_{it} = \alpha + \beta_1 1\left(\textit{top quartile of Phase II funding}\right)_{it}$$
$$+\cdots+\beta_4 1\left(\textit{bottom quartile of Phase II funding}\right)_{it}$$
$$+\sum_y \gamma^Y \cdot 1\left(y = \textit{Year}\right)_{it} + u_i + \varepsilon_{it}. \qquad (4.14)$$

The dependent variable here is the natural logarithm of the combined number of de-trended Phase I publications, plus a predicted potential effect of BK21 funding, plus some "noise" (resulting from introducing other effects into the measurement, whose values would have a normal distribution).

By experimenting with different potential effects and levels of noise, we can gauge how likely it will be to estimate effects precisely at Phase II levels of funding. Because the noise is drawn randomly each time, multiple iterations give a truer picture. For each effect and level of simulated noise, we run the regression 100 times and present the average coefficient and significance from across those 100 iterations.

We first run the simulation imagining that Phase II funding led to similar effects as Phase I: a 12 percent increase in publications for the top quartile of funding, a 16 percent increase for the second quartile, a 15 percent increase for the third, and a 54 percent increase for the bottom. We also add normally distributed noise with mean zero and—separately—with a standard deviation of 0.1 and 0.2. (A larger standard deviation presumes more variance in the outcome that is unexplained by variables in the model.) Under these parameters, we run Equation 4.14 100 times, generating the simulated results shown in Table 4.7. Under this scenario, we observe precisely estimated effects for the third quartile only (show in italics). The average p-value from that simulation is 0.06 under a standard deviation of 0.1, implying that we could detect an effect of BK21 funding statistically significantly different from zero with 94 percent confidence, and 0.10 under a standard deviation of 0.2, suggesting 90 percent confidence in such an effect.

Because Phase II funding is more evenly distributed than Phase I funding, one might expect a more even distribution of effects. To better assess the hypothetical effects of such a distribution, we reduce the estimated spread of effects from Phase I by 50 percent around the same mean, implying an average 20 percent increase in publications for the top quartile, a 22 percent increase in the second quartile, a 22 percent increase also in the third, and a 41 percent increase in the fourth. This yielded results shown in Table 4.8.

These estimates are necessarily very speculative. They depend on the expected size of impacts, among other variables. If these were

Table 4.7
Average Coefficient and Average p-Value from a Simulation
of Estimate Precision at Phase II Funding Levels

	Average Coefficient (for either level of noise)	SD = 0.1 p-value	SD = 0.2 p-value
Top quartile	0.00	0.90	0.81
Second quartile	0.21	0.20	0.25
Third quartile	*0.31*	*0.06*	*0.10*
Bottom quartile	0.20	0.30	0.33

SD = standard deviation.

Table 4.8
Average Coefficient and Average p-Value from a Simulation
of Estimate Precision at Phase II Funding Levels
(with narrower distribution of effects)

	Average Coefficient (for either level of noise)	SD = 0.1 p-value	SD = 0.2 p-value
Top quartile	0.07	0.78	0.74
Second quartile	0.26	*0.12*	0.16
Third quartile	0.37	*0.02*	*0.05*
Bottom quartile	0.12	0.56	0.57

already known, then no evaluation would be necessary. Yet this exercise suggests that, at certain levels of random noise, we can expect to precisely identify BK21 Phase II impacts for some groups.

Simulation: Outside Funding

Non-BK21 funding for these research groups is one important covariate we cannot control in our estimates because we lack sufficient data. As we noted above, BK21 may crowd out other funding, either because other government ministries give funds to groups not winning BK21 funding *or* because research groups winning BK21 funding spend less time seeking other, additional funding. It is also possible that BK21 funding, if it is seen as a signal of high-quality work for a group, would attract other funding to a group.

To test how well our model would control for the effects of outside funding, we perform a simple simulation using the same sample from the previous estimation (all applicant research groups except those from the top five universities), creating a variable called "other funding" (i.e., non-BK21 funding). For BK21 winners, we assume that other funding is equal to twice their average annual BK21 payout. (This is just a demonstration: It is not based on actual research group budgets because we do not have immediate access to that information.) For BK21 losers, we assume that other funding is equal to the *average* value of other funding for the BK21 winners.

We then run three regressions: The first assumes that other funding does not change in response to BK21 funding (i.e., when BK21 funding starts for winners in 1999, other funding does not change);[8] the second assumes that BK21 funding is a substitute for other funding (i.e., when BK21 funding begins, other funding falls for winners and rises for losers); and the third assumes that BK21 complements other funding (i.e., other funding rises for winners and falls for the losers).

If non-BK21 funding did not change in response to BK21 funding, then controlling for it would have no effect on the estimate of the impact of BK21. If non-BK21 funding did change in response to BK21 funding, then it would significantly reduce the size of the estimated BK21 effect, *regardless of whether it is a substitute or a complement*. This is very important: If changes in other funding are somehow correlated with BK21 funding (either through crowding out, signaling quality, or in some other way), then failing to control for that other funding leads to a significant overestimate of the impacts of BK21. This change in other funding can be seen as an important effect of BK21 as well; it merely is not a *direct* effect on research, competition, and research group composition. Controlling for the change is therefore essential to understanding the mechanisms by which BK21 funding affects outputs. When we control for the correlated other funding, the coefficients for the four quartiles of Phase I funding for groups outside the "Big 5," discussed above, all decrease (from 0.12 to 0.00 for the top quartile,

---

[8]   As a technical note, we added some normally distributed noise with mean zero and standard deviation of one to the "other funding" in the unrelated scenario. Otherwise, if "other funding" were to remain unchanged throughout the time series, it would have dropped out of the fixed-effects regression (which can only include variables that change in the course of the time series).

0.16 to 0.06 for the second, 0.15 to 0.06 for the third, and 0.54 to 0.46 for the bottom). This drop occurs regardless of whether other funding is correlated positively or negatively with BK21 funding. In both cases, the key is that analysts may attribute more of the change in outputs to BK21 than is due directly to it. This implies that gathering data on non-BK21 funding for all BK21 applicants is very important.

Implications for Data Collection

The methods reviewed here are appropriate for a broad range of quantitative measures including, among others, total publications, high-impact publications, faculty composition of research groups, PhD graduates, and patents.

Our analysis leads to several specific suggestions for database design. Evaluating Phase II differs from Phase I in one significant way: The Phase II evaluation must account for the fact that many BK21 participants have been receiving BK21 funding for six years. One way to account for this is to combine pre-BK21 data, Phase I data, and Phase II data, as in

$$
\begin{aligned}
\left(publications\right)_{it} &= \alpha_i + \beta_1 \left(BK21\,funding\right)_{it} + \beta_2 1 \cdot \left(Phase\,II\right)_t \\
&\times 1 \cdot \left(BK21\,funding\right)_{it} + \sum_y \gamma^Y \cdot 1\left(y = Year\right)_{it} + u_i + \varepsilon_{it}\,.
\end{aligned}
\qquad (4.15)
$$

In this model, β_1 shows the impact of BK21 funding in Phase I, $\beta_1 + \beta_2$ gives the impact of BK21 funding in Phase II, and β_2 (obviously) is the difference.[9] As in the validation exercise above, the simple linear indicator of BK21 funding could be replaced with nonlinear indicators, such as dividing the data into quartiles. An amendment to this model can capture heterogeneous impacts across department size, as in

---

[9] Note that we exclude the dummy for Phase II (except in the interaction with *BK*21 *funding*) because it is perfectly collinear to the linear combination of the year dummies for 2006–2012 and therefore would drop out.

$$\left(publications \right)_{it} = \alpha_i + \beta_1 \left(BK21\ funding \right)_{it}$$
$$+ \beta_2 1 \cdot \left(Phase\ II \right)_t \times 1 \cdot \left(BK21\ funding \right)_{it} + \sum_y \gamma^Y \cdot 1 \left(y = Year \right)_{it}$$
$$+ \beta_3 \left(BK21\ funding \right)_{it} \times \left(initial\ group\ size \right)_i$$
$$+ 1 \cdot \left(Phase\ II \right)_t \times 1 \cdot \left(BK21\ funding \right)_{it} \times \left(initial\ group\ size \right)_i$$
$$+ u_i + \varepsilon_{it} . \tag{4.16}$$

Note that we omit the level effect of the initial department size because it is collinear with the research group fixed effect.

To carry out this analysis, we need data on both winners and losers for three time periods: pre-BK21, Phase I of BK21, and Phase II of BK21. Data on non-BK21 funding is also very important. For many indicators, such as PhD graduates, faculty composition, and patents, the research groups and their departments may already have the relevant information in accessible form.

Summary

In this chapter, we have explored potential quantitative models for evaluating the impacts of BK21 Phase II. After examining each, we recommended a fixed-effects estimation strategy. We then discussed some of the caveats to using such a strategy and demonstrated its application with Phase I data. We also showed how the model can be adjusted to evaluate Phase II impacts, as well as to examine differential impacts by research area, lags in treatment effects, and nonlinear treatment effects. We demonstrated how the model could be used to assess the effect of BK21 on the number of science publications, but it may also be used to examine other quantitative outcomes, such as patents, private-sector collaboration, or publications in particular subsets of journals (as a way of examining the quality of research).

In the next chapter, we explore in more depth measurements that the MoE may wish to collect to assess the effects of Phase II.

CHAPTER FIVE

Metrics and Measurement for Program Evaluation

A firm embarking on a new business strategy would have a relatively easy time of tracking the success of its effort. It generally possesses a baseline of previous experience and expectations. It knows precisely what steps it has taken and has an implicit model of how those changes should affect existing processes under its control and perhaps, to some extent, important external variables that could affect success. Most importantly, it has available a series of indicators (e.g., return on investment, growth in net income, profit margin, and market share) that are directly related to success or failure and widely understood by those outside the firm evaluating its performance. And yet, as investors know, the complexity of the processes and the interaction among variables that could affect performance make it difficult to predict performance, measure actual performance, or attribute performance directly to the firm's strategies and actions.

The problem of evaluating the performance of Phase II of BK21 is greater than the simple case of the performance of a single firm operating within a market. Many institutions—government, academic and private-sector—are involved in producing the results of interest, and they do so at various levels of action. The products being directly created—knowledge, skill, capability, linkage, mastery—are less tangible than the outputs from an industrial firm. These outputs, in turn, are also used to generate other ultimate outcomes such as increased productivity, scientific leadership, and international recognition. The "production" process for these outcomes requires years or even decades, making it more difficult to trace cause and effect than it is for a business expecting results within a business quarter or a fiscal year.

In the previous chapter, we discussed a model for using selected quantitative measures to assess net program effects. In this chapter, we examine alternative specific measures to use with these models. We first discuss some of the problems with measuring BK21 performance. We then present and weigh several candidate measures for evaluating program performance.

Our work focuses on assessing the net effect of BK21, not evaluating the Korean higher education system. Nevertheless, it may prove to be a useful core around which an integrated evaluation system may be constructed. There are some measures that may be only indirectly related to BK21 but would be useful for other purposes besides evaluation of that program. These might be relatively easy to collect during the course of evaluating the BK21 program and so would represent opportunities for generating multipurpose data at little additional cost. This theme will be elaborated in Chapters Seven and Eight.

General Issues of Measurement

A measurement and evaluation system must distinguish between "metric" and "measure." The distinction is not just semantic. A "metric" is the ideal yardstick by which we would wish to evaluate BK21 program performance, observed periodically to assess progress toward the program's goals. A measure is the practical means we use to estimate the value of a metric.

An example of the difference is the metric of "prestige" attaching to specific Korean universities and departments as well as to Korean higher education as a whole. While BK21 goals include many that aim to improve the prestige of Korean universities, we cannot, as a practical matter, directly perceive prestige. Rather, we must select some measure by which we can assess the prestige attaching to Korean institutions. The measure we use to evaluate prestige might be one of several available international rankings of universities. In this example, prestige is the metric we wish to use to determine the degree of program success; rankings are the practical means—the measure or measurement tool—we use to estimate the value of that metric.

This example raises the issue of selecting the correct measurement tool. In the case of international university prestige rankings, there are several measurement options. The two most often cited are those of the *Times* [of London] *Higher Education Supplement* (THES) and the *Academic Ranking of World Universities* (ARWU) by the Shanghai Jiao Tong University. We could use either one to assess the metric we seek to estimate (prestige), or we could use a combination of the two or even propose alternative measures.

Several issues determine the choice of measure. We want the measures we use to be reliable and valid and wish to understand how directly we are measuring and at what cost. We review these issues below.

Reliability

A measure is reliable if it is consistent during the period of measurement. Concerns about reliability might arise if there are observation errors that affect the measurement results, particularly errors that are not constant from year to year. Reliability also becomes a concern if the measure is corrupted, that is, if it becomes skewed as a result of measurement. This might occur, for example, if knowledge of the use of the measure affects data reporting by those who are subject to measurement.[1]

Because the object of our evaluation is the performance of the program as a whole rather than of individual participants, this concern should be somewhat reduced, though still present. The major events of BK21 Phase II have already occurred: Research groups have been formed, applications have been prepared, and awards have been made. This means there is less concern that choosing particular measures to evaluate the program or the act of measurement itself will distort the

---

[1] This was a notorious problem during several nations' planned economy periods. If the performance by a factory that produced skiing equipment, for example, was evaluated on the basis of the number of pairs produced, the factory would produce too many children's skis since this economized on materials; if evaluated on weight of output, the result would be too many large adult sizes because this reduced processing costs.

behavior of participants. Further, while evaluating the output of individuals, departments, and universities is an important activity related to the task of assessing the outcomes of BK21 as a program, the two are not synonymous. There is little chance that the act of measurement will skew performance. Nevertheless, BK21 evaluators may wish to continually assess specific measures to ensure the measures themselves are not affecting participant behavior.

Validity

Continual assessment of measures is needed even more to ensure their validity, i.e., the extent to which inferences may be drawn from them about the metrics we seek to evaluate. Validity concerns how measurement results may be interpreted with reasonable assurance that the connection between the measure and the metric is a sound one.

Several issues may affect validity. For example, the prestige measures cited above are compound or integrated measures of several simpler measures, weighted and aggregated into an overall assessment result. Both the weighting and selection of measures raise questions about how likely it is that the measurement is accurate, as well as what lag might exist between occurrence of an effect and when that effect is observed. Merely assessing what changes occurred using a variety of metrics is not sufficient to demonstrate the value of BK21. Other variables and processes may affect the metrics we use to judge BK21 program performance. To truly assess performance, we must not only evaluate the metric of interest but also be able to attribute any change we observe to BK21 rather than to another, concurrent event.

The previous chapter dealt extensively with the issue of determining net effect. Many issues of validity can only be resolved during measurement. This suggests the value of both an ongoing effort of reappraisal and testing and a sufficiently large data gathering effort to evaluate varying measurement tools.

Direct and Indirect Measures

The issue of validity is ubiquitous, in part, because we may not have enough data available or may not be able to observe what we actually wish to examine. We may therefore consider proxy variables that we can observe and believe will respond in the same way as the variable we wish to observe. Here, too, there is a potential gap between the practical and the ideal that should be weighed and well understood when establishing an evaluation framework.

Cost Versus Benefit

The theme of practical choice raises the issue of cost of collecting data on a measure versus the benefit of the data that measure can offer. Measures and the measurement framework itself must be practicable. We need to be assured, for example, that the necessary data are and will be available and that the cost of data collection will not be prohibitive. At the same time, the measure itself must be valid. Sometimes we can enhance validity by spending more effort and resources on collecting data for a given measure. Hence, a better measure may cost more. How much one should spend on it depends on how much more validity would result from the expenditure and how important the specific measure and its corresponding metric are.

Gathering data on career paths for BK21 graduates illustrates the trade-off between cost and benefit. The less-costly but less-informative way to gather these data would be to survey a sample of graduates some time after they complete the program. The more-costly but more-informative way would be to do a periodic longitudinal survey of program graduates through at least the early stages of their career. Evaluators need to weigh this choice carefully beforehand, particularly given that it is rather easy to move from more-expensive to less-expensive methods once research has started, but it is often difficult to move from less-expensive to more-expensive ones.

For the balance of this chapter, we propose measures for evaluating the performance of BK21 and discuss their relative strengths and weaknesses. However, we lack the information necessary to make the cost-benefit trade-offs that are required to determine precisely which measures should be used. This is partly an issue of how crucial any particular measure is for evaluating its underlying metric. We suggest those measures that appear to us to be most salient for evaluating BK21, but we recognize that data availability, reliability, and cost—issues we cannot assess at this time—can affect their use. Therefore, the presentation that follows must necessarily be more in the nature of input to a decision process that must occur among the actual evaluators of BK21 in Korea.

Strategy for Framing Evaluation Measures

While BK21 is large in both scope and scale, it is a narrowly targeted investment program. For example, while it seeks to enhance Korea's capacity for R&D along many dimensions, BK21 targets human capital development, especially at the graduate and young researcher level, rather than the infrastructure required for the conduct of research. The latter, while clearly important, is left for future government initiatives. The principal idea behind BK21 is that targeting the crucial element of R&D manpower development will result in a large-scale shift in the R&D capacity of Korea's universities and institutes. The implication is that this, in turn, will lead to positive changes in the economic and social well-being of the country as a whole.

As a result, any evaluation of BK21 should be based on the intended goals of the program, i.e., the metrics used should directly illuminate the extent to which the envisioned purpose has been served. The evaluation must also look at different levels of action (individual, departmental, university and national) and clarify the degree to which BK21 has succeeded and through what means it has done so. The logic model in Chapter Three makes this concrete.

Metrics should include both *outputs* and *outcomes*. It might also be useful to define measures for intermediate indicators that, in turn, will yield measurable outputs. One measurable intermediate indicator might be changes in the number of students enrolled in advanced degree programs that have benefited from BK21 funding. These measures could shed light on questions regarding broader BK21 program effects. Where tracking intermediate indicators is possible, adding them to measures of outputs and outcomes provides three distinct sampling points and levels of action that may be useful in understanding the working of BK21.

Below we provide an integrated framework for identifying and selecting measures for evaluating BK21. This approach is inspired, in part, by the "Balanced Scorecard" used to evaluate organization performance (Kaplan and Norton, 1992, 1996). While originally conceived as a performance evaluation approach for business corporations, Balanced Scorecard methods can be useful in evaluating BK21. Although there are obvious differences between evaluating corporations and BK21, there are also several similarities. The central one is that evaluations should have multiple attributes. That is, because both types of institutions have multifaceted performance environments, the evaluation should be made along several dimensions rather than based on a single statistic. The Balanced Scorecard approach may permit better understanding of program outcomes along all its dimensions.

Matching Measures to Goals

We use the logic model presented in Chapter Three to match measures to goals. Rooting the discussion in this model is a crucial first step in applying Balanced Scorecard methods to BK21 program evaluation. As we noted previously, Phase II has three major goals:

1. To nurture and expand the next generation of Korean scientists and engineers as the future R&D workers for industry and universities
2. To enhance Korean university and departmental quality and world standing
3. To strengthen the ties of universities to their regions and to enhance industry-university ties to promote innovation.

Mapping outputs and outcomes to these goals provides a first-order listing of appropriate metrics for judging BK21 (see Table 5.1).[2]

---

[2]   Phase II may also yield unintended effects. If these secondary effects have a net influence on the ability of BK21 to meet its goals, they should be detectable by the measures we use to gather data on BK21 metrics. This would not, however, indicate unintended effects, either positive or negative, that BK21 may haven other Korean government goals not directly related to those of BK21.

Table 5.1
Principal Metrics and Inferred Major Goals for BK21 Phase II

Major BK21 Phase II program goals	1. Increase size and capability of research manpower pool	2. Foster globally competitive research universities	3. Strengthen local universities and enhance university-industry collaboration for innovation
Metrics			
Outputs	1. Human resource production	1. Improve graduate school infrastructure	1. University-industry linkages
	2. Research quantity and quality	2. Promote an environment for competition within and be-tween universities	2. Regional graduate school promotion
		3. Promote signaling for faculty and graduate students	
Outcomes	1. Employment of highly educated workforce	1. International university prestige	1. Industrial research quantity and quality
		2. National prestige	2. Labor productivity

Selecting Among Candidate Measures

Once metrics have been matched with goals, the next step is to devise the actual measures that will be used to assign values to the metrics. This is where practicalities may part company with the ideal, leaving latitude for selecting among possible measures. Table 5.2 presents a framework for selecting the performance metrics for BK21 Phase II. For each metric, we present several alternative measures, varying them by data requirements and procedures as well as by whether they are for intermediate, output, or outcome metrics.

Each metric has a unique three-part identifier. The first number identifies the goal it relates to, the second number indicates the relationship of that metric to intermediate products ("1"), outputs ("2"), or outcomes ("3"). The third number is unique to each metric within intermediate, output, or outcome groups for each goal. Therefore, the flow of human resources into the Korean research system by field, an intermediate metric for the first goal of increasing the size and capability of the research manpower pool, is given the identifier of 1.1.1.

Table 5.2
Measurement Framework for Evaluating BK21 Phase II Performance Metrics

Measure Number	Metric (Arranged according to BK21 goals, intermediate indicators, outputs, and outcomes)	Data Required	Notes on Procedures
	Goal 1. Increase size and capability of research manpower pool		
	1.1. Intermediate indicators		
1.1.1	Flow of human resources into graduate studies, by field		
1.1.1.1		Students enrolled in graduate programs in Korea	Actual numbers gathered annually
1.1.1.2		Students enrolled in graduate programs abroad	Actual numbers gathered annually
1.1.1.3		Research assistants in Korean departments	Actual numbers gathered annually
1.1.1.4		Research assistants abroad	Actual numbers gathered annually
	1.2. Outputs		
1.2.1	Human resource production		
1.2.1.1a		Placement in universities, Korea	New Masters and PhDs hired as teaching and research faculty
1.2.1.1b(i)		Placement in universities, Korea, quality weighted	New Masters and PhDs hired as teaching and research faculty; weighted per THES or ARWU
1.2.1.1b(ii)		Placement in universities, Korea, quality weighted	New Masters and PhDs hired as teaching and research faculty; weighted per 2.3.1.5
1.2.1.2		Placement in industry, Korea	New Masters and PhDs hired as R&D personnel in industry
1.2.1.3		Placement in other professional	New Masters and PhDs hired in non-R&D industry management, government R&D, senior government positions
1.2.1.4a		Placement in universities, abroad	New Masters and PhDs hired as teaching and research faculty
1.2.1.4b		Placement in universities, abroad, quality weighted	New Masters and PhDs hired as teaching and research faculty; weighted per ARWU or SJT (e.g., top 50; top 200; rest)
1.2.1.5		Placement in industry, abroad	New Masters and PhDs hired as R&D personnel in industry

Table 5.2—continued

Measure Number	Metric (Arranged according to BK21 goals, intermediate indicators, outputs, and outcomes)	Data Required	Notes on Procedures
1.2.2	Researcher quantity and quality, national level		
1.2.2.1a		Publication quality intensity measure	Total articles published in "top bin" journals divided by total Korean research workforce (domestic; could also be calculated to include Korean nationals abroad: use 1.2.2.4 as divisor)
1.2.2.1b(i)		Publication quality intensity measure, grouped	Number of Korean authored papers in top 10% of highly cited papers
1.2.2.1b(ii)		Publication quality intensity change measure	Distribution of Korean papers in top 10%, 1–25%, 25–50%, 50–100% of cited papers at different time intervals
1.2.2.1c		Publication quality intensity measure, weighted	Weighted score of total articles published divided by total Korean research workforce (domestic; could also be calculated to include Korean nationals abroad: use 1.2.2.4a or -b as divisor as appropriate)
1.2.2.2		Publication quantity intensity measure	Total articles in Science Citation Index-expanded (and where appropriate, Social Science Citation Index and Arts and Humanities Citation Index.) divided by Korean research workforce (domestic; could also be calculated to include Korean nationals abroad: use 1.2.2.4 as divisor)
1.2.2.3a		Subjective quality assessment, domestic	Quality of research staff: peer assessment survey, Korean respondents, pooled to view national trends
1.2.2.3b		Subjective quality assessment, foreign	Quality of research staff: peer assessment survey, non-Korean respondents, pooled to view national trends
1.2.2.4a		Size of Korean research workforce	Universities, industry, government
1.2.2.4b		Size of Korean research workforce, including abroad	As above, including Korean nationals abroad
1.3.1	**1.3. Outcomes** Employment balances for highly educated workforce		

Table 5.2—continued

Measure Number	Metric (Arranged according to BK21 goals, intermediate indicators, outputs, and outcomes)	Data Required	Notes on Procedures
1.3.1.1a		Survey of firms' opinions of 20 selected Korean universities	Qualitative judgment of type and nature of training of new research workers and other research inputs received by industry from university research departments
1.3.1.1b		Longitudinal survey of graduates	See discussion in text.
1.3.1.1c		Like 1.3.1.1b, including interviews with present employers of graduates	
	Goal 2. Globally competitive research universities		
	2.1. Intermediate indicators		
2.1.1	Change in rates of flow of human resources into graduate study, by field		
2.1.1.1		Change in share of graduate students who choose to study in Korea	
2.1.1.2		Change in share of students who pursue graduate studies	
	2.2. Outputs		
2.2.1	Graduate school infrastructure		
2.2.1.1	Libraries and computers	Total funding and amount per student, by university	Track sources of funding: government entitlement funding; government competitive funding; university central funding; private foundation funding; corporate funding, direct earnings from licenses and other intellectual property payments
2.2.1.2	Laboratories, special equipment, and in-kind support	Total funding and amount per student, by university, by department	Track sources of funding: government entitlement funding; government competitive funding; university central funding; private foundation funding; corporate funding, direct earnings from licenses and other intellectual property payments

Table 5.2—continued

Measure Number	Metric (Arranged according to BK21 goals, intermediate indicators, outputs, and outcomes)	Data Required	Notes on Procedures
2.2.1.3	General facilities	Total funding and amount per student, by university	Track sources of funding: government entitlement funding; government competitive funding; university central funding; private foundation funding; corporate funding, direct earnings from licenses and other intellectual property payments
2.2.1.4	Research project funding	Total and amount per student, by university, by department	Track sources of funding: government entitlement funding; government competitive funding; university central funding; private foundation funding; corporate funding, direct earnings from licenses and other intellectual property payments
2.2.2	**Competitive environment within and among universities**		
2.2.2.1		Relative share of funded research projects with foreign collaborators: number and value (KRW), by department	
2.2.2.2a		Papers authored with foreign collaborators, by department	
2.2.2.2b		Papers authored with foreign collaborators, by department, quality weighted	
2.2.2.3		Funded research projects with Korean collaborators: number and funding level, by department	"Collaborators" are Korean research workers coming from different universities
2.2.2.4a		Papers authored with Korean collaborators, by department	"Collaborators" are Korean research workers coming from different universities
2.2.2.4b		Papers authored with Korean collaborators, by department, quality weighted	"Collaborators" are Korean research workers coming from different universities
2.2.2.5a		Competitive funding to department, net of government BK21 funding (total; per faculty; per graduate student; relative to university size/funding)	Funding for facilities and research coming from private grants and contracts, foundation grants, or government competitive grants and contracts but not including the government funding received for BK21

Table 5.2—continued

Measure Number	Metric (Arranged according to BK21 goals, intermediate indicators, outputs, and outcomes)	Data Required	Notes on Procedures
2.2.2.5b		Competitive funding to department, net of government and private match BK21 funding (total; per faculty; per graduate student; relative to university size/funding)	Funding for facilities and research coming from private grants and contracts, foundation grants, or government competitive grants and contracts but including neither the government nor the corporate match funding received for BK21
2.2.3	Signaling for faculty and graduate students		
2.2.3.1		Change in enrollment/application ratio for domestic students, by department	
2.2.3.2		Faculty transfers between institutions	Movement patterns within the groups of BK21 and non-BK21 departments and between these groups.
2.2.3.3		Changes in faculty size, by department	
2.2.3.4		Changes in faculty size, by department, relative to university size	
2.2.3.5		Allocation among BK21 and non-BK21 departments of students who choose to enter graduate studies	
2.2.3.6		Research output profile, by department	Histogram analysis of published paper share by ISI category
2.3. Outcomes			
2.3.1	International prestige for Korean research groups and departments		Latent variable analysis (after Guarino et al., 2005)
2.3.1.1a		Weighted (binned) score of articles published (in field)	To distinguish the order of author affiliation, a weight of 100% is assigned for corresponding author affiliation, 50% for first author affiliation (second author affiliation if the first author affiliation is the same as corresponding author affiliation), 25% for the next author affiliation, and 10% for other author affiliations. Scores based on assigning linear weights based on bins defined by distance from mean ISI impact factor for journal of appearance.

Table 5.2—continued

Measure Number	Metric (Arranged according to BK21 goals, intermediate indicators, outputs, and outcomes)	Data Required	Notes on Procedures
2.3.1.1b		Weighted (smooth) score of articles published (in field)	To distinguish the order of author affiliation, a weight of 100% is assigned for corresponding author affiliation, 50% for first author affiliation (second author affiliation if the first author affiliation is the same as corresponding author affiliation), 25% for the next author affiliation, and 10% for other author affiliations. Scores based on assigning exponential weights defined by distance from mean ISI impact factor for journal of appearance.
2.3.1.2a		Weighted (binned) score of articles published (across fields)	To distinguish the order of author affiliation, a weight of 100% is assigned for corresponding author affiliation, 50% for first author affiliation (second author affiliation if the first author affiliation is the same as corresponding author affiliation), 25% for the next author affiliation, and 10% for other author affiliations. Scores based on assigning linear weights based on bins defined by distance from mean ISI impact factor for journal of appearance.
2.3.1.2b		Weighted (smooth) score of articles published (across fields)	To distinguish the order of author affiliation, a weight of 100% is assigned for corresponding author affiliation, 50% for first author affiliation (second author affiliation if the first author affiliation is the same as corresponding author affiliation), 25% for the next author affiliation, and 10% for other author affiliations. Scores based on assigning exponential weights defined by distance from mean ISI impact factor for journal of appearance.
2.3.1.3a		Number of Korean authored papers in each rank of highly cited papers	Using quartiles, quintiles, deciles, or nonuniform thresholds
2.3.1.3b		Share of total Korean authored papers in each rank of highly cited papers	Using quartiles, quintiles, deciles, or nonuniform thresholds
2.3.1.4a		Quality of research staff: peer assessment survey, Korean respondents	Results viewed at the level of the academic department
2.3.1.4b		Quality of research staff: peer assessment survey, non-Korean respondents	Results viewed at the level of the academic department

Table 5.2—continued

Measure Number	Metric (Arranged according to BK21 goals, intermediate indicators, outputs, and outcomes)	Data Required	Notes on Procedures
2.3.1.5		Academic performance and quality of education	Composite measure derived from information obtained from anonymous reviewers of dissertations; from industry surveys and interviews suggested in connection with other metrics; from post-graduate longitudinal and research output quality assessments; and from department and research group descriptions of dissertation processes and requirements. (Weights derived from applying the methods in Guarino et al., 2005.)
2.3.1.6		Academic performance and quality of education with respect to the size of an institution	Weighted scores of the above indicators divided by the number of full-time equivalent academic staff
2.3.1.7a		Foreign students attending Korean departments	
2.3.1.7b		Foreign students attending Korean departments, quality weighted	Weighted by student's undergraduate institution
2.3.2	National prestige for Korean research groups and departments		May also use measures gathered under 2.3.1
	Goal 3. Enhance university-industry collaboration		
	3.1. Intermediate outcomes		
3.1.1	Formal indicators of university-industry collaboration		
3.1.1.1		Number of industry-laboratory cooperative contracts	Total
3.1.1.2		Value (KRW) of industry-laboratory cooperative contracts	Total
	3.2. Outputs		
3.2.1	University-industry linkages		

Table 5.2—continued

Measure Number	Metric (Arranged according to BK21 goals, intermediate indicators, outputs, and outcomes)	Data Required	Notes on Procedures
3.2.1.1a		Patents by department	May be broken down into total patents, domestic patents, and patents granted in the U.S., EU, or Japan
3.2.1.1b		Patents by department from cooperative contract	Would include patents where either the university or the industrial partner is the patent holder. May be broken down into total patents, domestic patents, and patents granted in the U.S., EU, or Japan
3.2.1.2		Value (KRW) of license fees and other intellectual property payments, by department	
3.2.1.3a		Number of new products from cooperative contract	
3.2.1.3b		Value (KRW) of new products from cooperative contract	
3.2.1.4		Share of new products from cooperative contracts in total industry output	
3.2.1.5		Numbers and ledger of industry-department contacts	Non-financial contacts with business and industry including: sabbatical exchanges, guest lecture exchanges, internship exchanges, seminars on specific industry-department collaborations
3.2.1.6		Histogram breakdown of industrial collaborators	The industry partners of formal cooperative contracts and other contacts with university departments to be assessed by type of contact, volume of contact, industrial sector and size of firm
3.2.2	Regional graduate school promotion		
3.2.2.1		Number of industry–university laboratory cooperative contracts by department	Must be consistent with placement of variables
3.2.2.2		Value of industry–university laboratory cooperative contracts by department	

Table 5.2—continued

Measure Number	Metric (Arranged according to BK21 goals, intermediate indicators, outputs, and outcomes) Data Required	Notes on Procedures
3.2.2.3	Proximity of industry–university laboratory cooperative contracts	Distance in kilometers between industry headquarters and cooperating laboratory and between industry R&D facility and cooperating laboratory
3.2.2.4	Intensity of non-Hub industry–university laboratory cooperative contracts (number)	Number of cooperative contracts between firms not located in Seoul or other areas defined as major industrial hubs and non-Hub laboratories divided by total number and value
3.2.2.5	Intensity of non-Hub industry–university laboratory cooperative contracts (value)	Value of cooperative contracts between firms not located in Seoul or other areas defined as major industrial hubs and non-Hub laboratories divided by total number and value
3.2.2.6	Number of Hub industry–non-Hub university laboratory cooperative contracts	Number of cooperative contracts between Hub-based firms and non-Hub-based laboratories
3.2.2.7	Value of Hub industry–non-Hub university laboratory cooperative contracts	Value of cooperative contracts between Hub-based firms and non-Hub-based laboratories
3.2.2.8	Number of Hub industry–non-Hub university laboratory cooperative contracts	Number of cooperative contracts between Hub-based firms and non-Hub-based laboratories divided by total number and value
3.2.2.9	Value of Hub industry–non-Hub university laboratory cooperative contracts	Value of cooperative contracts between Hub-based firms and non-Hub-based laboratories divided by total number and value
3.2.2.10	Numbers and ledger of university–community cultural contacts	Analogous to 3.2.1.5 and 3.2.2.1 for departments and fields where industry collaboration would not apply
3.2.2.11	Proximity of university–community cultural contacts	Analogous to 3.2.1.5 and 3.2.2.1 for departments and fields where industry collaboration would not apply
3.2.2.12	Intensity of non-"Top 3 (5)" university production of MAs and PhDs	Number of higher degrees awarded by universities not included in top 3 (or 5) schools as ranked by ARWU and THES divided by total number of higher degrees awarded by all similar departments (absolute number and normalized by department size)

Table 5.2—continued

Measure Number	Metric (Arranged according to BK21 goals, intermediate indicators, outputs, and outcomes)	Data Required	Notes on Procedures
	3.3. Outcomes		
3.3.1	Industrial research quantity and quality		
3.3.1.1		Patents (foreign) by industrial sector	
3.3.1.2		Patents by industrial sector	
3.3.1.3		Number of new products by industrial sector	
3.3.1.4		Value of new products by industrial sector	
3.3.1.5		Share of new products by industrial sector	
3.3.1.6		Delphi-type survey among industry R&D directors	Consider range of responses on past situation, current situation, and expected future situation (i.e., direction of change) in several important outcome-based categories
3.3.2	Labor productivity		
3.3.2.1		Labor productivity	Use existing national data series

The fourth number is unique to each candidate measure proposed for a metric. For example, for metric 1.1.1 we propose measures 1.1.1.1, students enrolled in Korean graduate programs; 1.1.1.2, students enrolled in graduate programs abroad; 1.1.1.3, research assistants in Korean departments; and 1.1.1.4, research assistants abroad. Measures with appended letters (e.g., 1.2.1.4a and 1.2.1.4b) denote similar measures with varying costs. Those with appended Roman numerals (e.g., 1.2.1.1b(i) and 1.2.1.1b(ii)) vary slightly in method of calculation. In the remainder of this chapter we examine some of the larger concepts and issues underlying the framework of Table 5.2. This integrated presentation will make it easier for Phase II evaluators to make the judgments necessary to frame the actual measurement strategy they choose.

Our system of evaluation measures, set within a formal framework, also addresses the concern that the evaluators not use too many measures but rather a small number that may be readily comprehended. This is an admirable goal but one we do not feel is attainable at this stage. While a small number of ideal measures might suffice in theory, the practical problems with data collection and measurement make it prudent not to rely on the accuracy of any given measure or a small number of measures. Reliability and validity issues suggest it may take multiple measures to provide a valid inference regarding a metric or construct of interest. Multiple measures for a given metric will better ensure that complete information is gathered on a metric. For example, the metric for improving graduate school infrastructures (2.2.1) has four measures attached to it, each measuring a different aspect of infrastructure important to meeting the larger goals of BK21 Phase II. BK21 is a complex program designed to achieve a number of related but different objectives, many of which are complicated and whose processes and outcomes may not be easy to detect. A number of diverse measures will be needed to capture these.

Having fewer measures can help make the results informative, parsimonious, and efficient. Multiple measures can raise problems of interpretation. Our matrix approach provides a partial solution to the need for ease of comprehension by making clear what any particular measure is designed to achieve and illustrating how measures relate to one another. Using a series of measures rather than only a few simple ones to assess BK21 requires an explanation of why evaluators should seek these data and how they should understand them. The discussion of the measurement framework in Table 5.2 will aid this purpose.

The intent of this framework is to provide a structure within which the BK21 program evaluators can develop the actual measurement strategy. Ultimately, the evaluators must decide which measures to select among those presented. We do recommend that each metric should have at least one measure to match it. Ideally, the metric and the measure would be congruent or nearly so. The metric of improving Korea's labor productivity, for example, can be measured directly from statistics already collected by the government. In other cases, however, the measure will be only an approximation of, or related indirectly to, the metric itself. In such cases, it would be useful to have several measures, each capturing some aspect of the underlying metric. This approach provides greater assurance that the measurements capture the essence of the metric of interest.

A framework containing measures that overlap to some extent can provide the opportunity for gaining different perspectives on a metric. Different measures may yield conflicting data. Using a framework of overlapping measures enables evaluators to conduct ongoing validity studies to monitor the quality of the inferences from the measures and to determine which measures are most suitable for ongoing evaluation. We recommend adopting an ongoing audit and validation mechanism as part of the evaluation process. Collecting data to support several measures from the outset provides the possibility of changing measurement options at a later date.

There is also a practical aspect to choice of measures. Some measures may require data obtainable at greater cost and difficulty than would others. For the metrics that truly lie at the heart of the BK21 program framers' intent, this is a cost that the evaluators might choose to bear willingly. For those metrics less central to the perceived core goals of the program, evaluators might decide that the benefits are not worth the costs. It will ultimately be their choice to determine the value of greater or lesser detail with respect to any given metric and its measurement alternatives.

Generally speaking, when choosing between less-challenging and more-challenging measures for a given metric, the choices to be made will depend on either the level of aggregation or the amount of effort required to make the measurement. Table 5.2 illustrates many instances of "nested measures." Evaluators will need to choose the level for aggregation. In the example of infrastructure development, we could achieve more detail by looking within the large aggregate categories "libraries" and "laboratories": The evaluators could assess changes in particular types of library or laboratory. Although we do not recommend this particular disaggregation of data because improvement in physical infrastructure is incidental to the BK21 program's main goals, it still shows how disaggregation can provide more detailed insights. Here, "physics laboratory" nests within the larger concept of "laboratory," while "laser and optics laboratory" would nest within the concept of "physics laboratory." The choice between alternatives becomes more challenging when measures are not nested. Here, the choice usually comes down most clearly to one of cost—that is, between more or less resource-intensive alternatives, as discussed previously.

Some of the measures in Table 5.2 are "composite" measures in which two or more different measures are combined into a single measure, usually through differential weighting of the individual components. The "league table" rankings of world universities by the THES and the Shanghai Jiao Tong University's ARWU are constructed by creating composite measures. There are relatively few such measures in our framework. Composite measures can be helpful when seeking to compare heterogeneous situations—for example, universities that follow the U.S. liberal education model with those adhering to the more typically European faculty tracking model. Composite measures are particularly helpful when there is a need for a single, all-encompassing metric, as in the case of university rankings.

Neither of these constraints holds true in the case of Korea and BK21. Korean universities, faculties, laboratories, and the conditions under which R&D workers perform in both industry and universities are more similar to each other than they are different. Furthermore, BK21 seeks, especially in Phase II, to fulfill myriad purposes. Single summary statistics on these purposes would ignore or bury considerable information that could provide a more nuanced and accurate insight into the workings of the program and its results. Thus, composite measures are not suitable for BK21 program evaluation.

Below, we discuss in more depth the measures that may be used to evaluate BK21. The measures are grouped by metrics (the three-digit level of classification) they are designed to inform. While the discussion loosely follows the order in Table 5.2, it is most efficient to group several metrics together when they are thematically linked. In addition, not every metrics-based grouping receives the same level of treatment. The discussion concentrates on those that are the most problematic. It should help guide evaluators in choosing among measures and evaluating them.

Adding to Korea's Research Manpower Pool (1.1.1; 1.2.1; 1.2.2)

The first group of measures in Table 5.2 relates to the first broad goal of BK21: Increasing the size of the pool of trained research workers in Korea by increasing the production and retention of such workers. The focus of these measures is on change at the national level of aggregation.

Most of the suggested measures for assessing the metric of human resource production (1.2.1) are simply a national tally of the numbers of trained personnel who enter the sectors of the economy and society related to research, development, and production. Intermediate indicators, such as the number of new graduate students (1.1.1), can also assist in measuring the effect of BK21 on the outputs and outcomes of interest.

Two concepts incorporated in these measures merit comment. The first is that placement of graduates both in Korea and abroad should be tracked. This is an instance in which data useful for interpreting the effect of BK21 may also be of use to inform policy in other areas that affect Korea. BK21 seeks to increase the size and quality of the domestic pool of knowledge workers, but it is not clear that those who pursue their professional careers abroad represent a loss to the nation or even a wholly negative phenomenon from the perspective of achieving BK21 goals. Those who take first and even successive positions abroad may return, providing a useful input of external knowledge and practice. The phenomenon of return becomes more likely as Korea becomes a more attractive venue for knowledge creation. Even those who do not return may act as bridges between their domestic Korean colleagues and the larger world of knowledge creation and commerce in ideas. Tracking changes in the rates of domestic and foreign career development for Korean advanced graduates would provide data for better understanding the balance between loss and gain over time through job placements in Korea or abroad.

The other concept worth comment is how to assess the careers of those who leave the R&D field. Should those who receive advanced technical training but then choose other careers not directly involving R&D be considered losses from the pool of skilled labor the program seeks to increase? In the narrowest sense of how innovative activity occurs, they may appear to represent a loss of potential. A broader view, however, would hold that the innovative enterprise takes place within a larger structure of a national innovation system that encompasses not only R&D labs but a wider institutional base, both formal and informal, which supports the activities of the R&D community. If this institutional base is insufficient or does not pay enough attention to supporting innovation, much R&D effort may be wasted. Having technically trained persons take managerial or other nontechnical positions may therefore still prove valuable to the efforts BK21 seeks to support more directly. Tracking non-R&D future career paths of participants in BK21 could illuminate how much the success of Korea's knowledge creation activities depends on having technically sophisticated managers and administrators.

The suggested quality measures (1.2.2) for the first goal are derived from those that we recommend for assessing efforts to attain BK21's second major goal, improving the standing and quality of Korean research faculties. We discuss these in more detail when we consider metrics focused on department-level rather than national quality assessment (1.2.2; 2.3.1; 2.3.2). To help distinguish between quantity and quality effects, the national *quality intensity* measures are normalized by the size of the pool of Korean research workers—that is, those effects that are due to a larger manpower pool and those that attest to enhanced quality of research performance by the average member of that pool.

Highly Educated Workforce Employment (1.3.1)

The true effect of BK21 in improving the size and quality of the pool of knowledge workers in Korea will become apparent only over time. Nevertheless, it is helpful to observe this evolution as it occurs. The measures we suggest regarding employment balances can help provide insight on this outcome.

The choice of specific measures here depends heavily on the willingness to undertake the data collection burden. Among measures with the lowest relative costs, surveys of employers could take successive snapshots of the size, composition, and subjective assessment of the Korean R&D workforce. Other measures are more expensive but also potentially more useful. The MoE or another appropriate body may wish to consider, for example, a longitudinal survey of those receiving advanced degrees from Korean institutions or who have obtained degrees abroad and now are employed within Korea. This would help not only in assessing BK21 but could also have a broader policy impact beyond evaluation of just one program. Unlike the employer survey, which samples information on the demand for R&D workers, a longitudinal survey would provide a more detailed view of the professional life course of individuals from the supply side.

One example of a longitudinal survey such as those the MoE may wish to consider is the biennial survey the U.S. National Science Foundation conducts of individuals who have obtained doctoral degrees in a science, engineering, or health field from a U.S. institution. The Survey of Doctorate Recipients (SDR) follows these individuals until age 76 and includes variables such as educational history, employment status, family and citizenship status, and work-related training (National Science Foundation, 2006). Such a survey, designed to meet the particular needs of Korea, could be one of the best ways to gain better understanding on many topics of interest to BK21's administrators and evaluators. A longitudinal survey might also include limited interviewing of various categories of employers for additional insights on the career paths of BK21 graduates. The interview component could be conducted less frequently than the longitudinal survey. It could usefully be carried out at the beginning and end of each phase of BK21.

High-Quality Globally Competitive Research (1.2.2; 2.3.1; 2.3.2)

The second main goal of BK21 is to enhance the creation of globally competitive research departments and universities. This goal rests on developing the means to produce superior research. Unlike the first group of measures, which were national in scope, the focus here is on individual departments. The prestige and international stature enjoyed by Korean universities will depend almost entirely on the perceived excellence of individual departments and their research groups. This brings into focus the work performed by department members— faculty, research associates, and graduate students.[3]

Measuring Quality of Research Output

The quality of preparation received by advanced students and the quality of the research work that they and their more senior colleagues produce is perhaps the most important metric for assessing the effect of BK21. Framing a suitable measure for research quality is challenging. We proceed from the view that the impartial perception of peers constitutes the best measure of the quality of research by Korean university departments. There are accepted norms for recognition of substantial contributions in the world of science and knowledge creation,

---

[3] As noted previously, most international ranking systems operate at the university level. This is not the appropriate level for the BK21 evaluators to assess. As a practical matter, it is not worthwhile to reproduce efforts being carried out elsewhere. Beyond that, it is unlikely that university-level rankings would reflect much movement in the relevant time period. A focus on departments is therefore more useful in assessing BK21 goals.

one of which is the creation and citation of foundational research work. Therefore, the frequency with which a research paper is cited as an important contribution and precursor in the work of others is an indicator of the paper's quality.

Phase II evaluators may choose to measure the impact of individual papers directly by weighting each paper by the number of citations it receives in works later published by other researchers.[4] This approach has been adopted in several measurement schemes used in other countries. Indeed, we later propose a variation of this approach for assessing relative research quality. Such a measure could serve several useful purposes.

The great advantage of the direct citation measure is its connection with the underlying metric we wish to evaluate. The principal drawback is one of time and particular purpose: Can useful measures be derived in the time relevant to the evaluation of BK21 Phase II?

Many papers in some research fields have "immediate" impact as measured by citations in other works. Others normally require time to produce such an effect. Establishing a baseline against which change due to BK21 Phase II may be assessed could therefore require different lengths of time for different fields and would not in any case be instantaneous. Even the relatively rapid citation impact of a major paper will take many months to yield its first citation. In some fields, a period of several years might be more likely. We therefore propose an alternative measurement basis for BK21 program evaluation.

Weighting papers by the measurable impact of journals on their fields is an indirect measure compared with the direct citation-based measures. The relationship this measure bears to a direct citation index is somewhat analogous to the relationship between a futures price for a commodity and the spot price that actually prevails when that future period becomes the present. In science, prestige derives from such influence. Editors of journals with greater measured impact—that is, a high average number of citations per paper—can generally be more selective than those of journals with a more limited supply of papers

---

[4]   The weighting could be either by raw number or made analogous to either of the two derived weighting schemes discussed later in this chapter.

for consideration. Therefore, we may approximate quality by assigning weights to individual published papers based on the average impact of the journals in which they appear.[5]

The value of such a measurement for BK21 program evaluation is that this indirect but independent assessment of the likely perceived influence of any given paper is more or less instantaneous. Though based on the judgments of an editorial board rather than an actual test in the larger market place for ideas, it provides a strong indicator of how a paper is likely to be received in its field. This impact factor–based method for constructing measures will yield a baseline for assessing change as soon as the first period data are assessed. Meaningful change may be observed as early as the next data collection period.

Although we suggest a measure for research quality based on a journal's impact, we recognize that a direct citation index might still be useful. Such an index would enable BK21 program evaluators to perform useful crosschecks on their data and validate them on an ongoing basis. It would also allow evaluators to later determine whether one method is truly superior to the other or whether the redundancy is useful.

In assessing the effect of BK21, we are principally interested in change. The absolute values of the results from any particular measure in any given period are of less interest than assessing the change that has taken place between periods. Therefore, even if there are known problems or unavoidable measurement errors associated with any particular measure, the measure will serve its intended purpose as long as those problems are known and, more importantly, the evaluators have reason to believe that they will remain consistent throughout the measurement period. This also means that interpreting the absolute value of such measures in any given period should only be done with care.

---

[5]   ISI assesses journal impact by counting the number of references to articles appearing in that journal that are cited in papers published in other journals. A journal's impact factor for a given year is equal to the number of citations attributed to that journal during the year divided by the total number of articles published in the journal in the prior two years. ISI calculates another factor, the immediacy index, based on citations that occur within one year of publication.

Consistent Measures of Quality Within Fields

Direct or, especially, weighted citation indices can vary across fields because differing fields have differing numbers of journals, as well as differing levels of impact. This makes the interpretation of such measures fraught with challenges.

Table 5.3, based on data obtained from the ISI Web of Science Journal Citation Reports database, helps illustrate the problem. "Robotics" and "Biochemistry and Molecular Biology" are both hierarchical field categories at the same level within the database structure of the Journal Citation Reports index. Nevertheless, the two fields are far from quantitatively equivalent. There are nearly 25 times as many journals in biochemistry and molecular biology as in robotics. This clearly has an effect on impact, as measured by ISI. While journals may vary in size, frequency of publication, and editorial policies, there are presently physical limits on the number of articles they can publish within a given year or volume.[6] Thus, articles published in fields with many more journals are likely to have greater impact by virtue of the size of those fields. More journals mean more opportunities for citation of any given article.[7] Indeed, the ratio between the impact factors of the most prestigious journal in each of the two exemplar fields is not much different from the ratio of numbers of publications in those two fields.

Of course, the mere fact of citation does not indicate why one research paper has been cited in another. In recent years, certain research projects and their products have become notorious or even scandalous and therefore widely noted. This, however, is a relatively rare phenomenon.

Practical implementation of measures using journal prestige as a proxy for quality could take several forms. If we wish to use a single measure within fields that may also be used for comparisons across fields, disparity in field size would lead us to avoid measures that weight research paper quality by ISI impact factors. A simple

---

[6]   This may be subject to change if Web-only journals become more prevalent.

[7]   This effect will be diluted in the opposite direction if many more articles make claims on the attention of peers in such fields.

Table 5.3
Comparison of Journal Impact Factor Values and Statistics Between Two ISI Fields of Science Classification

	Robotics	Biochemistry and Molecular Biology
Number of journals in ISI-defined field	11	256[a]
Range of journal impact factor values		
Minimum	0.198	0.097[b]
Maximum	1.486	33.456
Mean impact factor value	0.663	3.574
Standard deviation (SD)	0.442	4.144
Threshold I (1.0 SD from mean)	1.105	7.718
Number of journals exceeding threshold	3	22
Percentage of journals exceeding threshold	27.3%	8.6%
Threshold II (1.5 SD from mean)	1.326	9.790
Number of journals exceeding threshold	1	15
Percentage of journals exceeding threshold	9.1%	5.9%
Threshold III (2 SD from mean)	1.547	11.861
Number of journals exceeding threshold	0	10
Percentage of journals exceeding threshold	0.0%	3.9%

[a] ISI reports 261 journals, of which five are too new to calculate impact factors using the ISI methodology.

[b] Japanese language journal; lowest ranked English language journal has an impact of 0.199.

alternative approach would be to use the raw impact measures to place journals within quality "bins."

How to construct those bins is more of a conceptual issue than a technical one. It rests on understanding what we are trying to capture through our measure. One view is that there ought not be a direct comparison between an excellent paper in the field of robotics with one in biochemistry: In what meaningful sense is the latter more important or of greater innate quality than the former? This suggests using some standard means to rank journals by quality within a field and to bin them accordingly.

Consistent with the field-specific view of measurement, one method requires calculating the mean and standard deviation of impact factors in a defined field. Table 5.3 shows the results for calculating mean impact factors and their standard deviations for robotics and biochemistry.[8] These statistics can be used to define quality bins for journals within a field. In our example, establishing a bin one standard deviation above the mean impact factor values would place 27.3 percent of robotics journals in the top bin and 8.3 percent of biochemistry and molecular biology journals in the same bin. More bins could be constructed: establishing a bin 1.5 standard deviations above the mean would include 9.1 percent of robotics journals and 5.9 percent of biochemistry and molecular biology journals.[9]

The next step would be to assign appropriate weights for papers in each quality bin. It is fairly standard practice to assign proportions of values to individual researchers according to their contribution to a paper. The THES, for example, uses a scheme whereby a weight of 100 percent is assigned for corresponding author affiliation, 50 percent for first author affiliation (second author affiliation if the first author affiliation is the same as corresponding author affiliation), 25 percent for the next author affiliation, and 10 percent for other author affiliations. But

---

[8] Logically, if one were to calculate a mean impact factor for journals in an ISI field, it would be best to calculate a weighted mean. With weighting, the impact factor of a journal that publishes 10 percent of a field's total papers during a given year would have more effect on the actual mean value than that of one that publishes less than 1 percent. In the case of robotics, for example, where the top-rated journal also publishes more papers than others, this weighted mean journal impact factor would be 0.722, about 9 percent higher than the simple arithmetic mean shown in Table 5.3. The standard deviation, 0.471, would be about 6 percent higher. To keep our illustrations simple, we use simple rather than weighted means and standard deviations in our discussion.

[9] In our example, the distributions of impact factor values in the two fields differ. This causes the greater winnowing effect seen in setting a higher threshold in robotics. It is conceivable that SD-based thresholds can be set individually for each field using a calculation based upon the various higher moments (skewness, kurtosis, etc.) describing the shape of the underlying distribution. This would reduce the anomalies evident in Table 5.3, where similar thresholds based on fixed standard deviation displacements from the mean lead to dissimilar sized bins for different fields. The net effect of this, however, would be to engage in a complicated pathway to achieve the same practical result as arbitrary bin thresholds (e.g., "top 10 percent," "next 20 percent") could achieve.

what of the weighted value assigned to the paper itself from which relative contribution by authors and co-authors may be assigned?

There are two broad choices for assigning such values while still keeping within the conceptual framework of using distance from mean journal impact value as the basis for measurement. The first is to note the obvious—namely, that setting thresholds at, for example, 1 and 1.5 standard deviations to establish quality bins is arbitrary. This is not necessarily a drawback. It means that BK21 evaluators can tune these thresholds and set them either on a per-field basis or as a single standard across fields to conform to their best understanding of the comparisons they wish to make. In this case, the weights assigned to bins can be equally arbitrary. Some multiplicative factor (e.g., 1 for papers published in peer-reviewed journals, 2 for papers appearing in journals binned above the first threshold, 4 for papers appearing in journals binned above the second threshold, and so forth) might then be simply assigned. The arbitrariness of this standard is lessened to the extent that the resulting measurements are used to assess relative changes over time and not taken as absolute measures in themselves. In fact, these multiplicative factors may be adjusted retrospectively in light of future experience. Once the raw data have been collected, evaluators may transform measurements as they wish as long as they do so consistently and in a way that makes net changes apparent.

A similar approach, based on distance from mean journal impact value, may help evaluators avoid entirely the need to bin journals. This measure would implicitly suggest that the impact of papers published in increasingly prestigious journals is not linear but exponential.[10] It would highly reward papers that appear in more prestigious journals while not excessively penalizing those appearing in peer-reviewed journals of lesser caliber. In this case, evaluators select a fixed tuning factor, T. For each paper being assessed, this factor is raised by an exponent, d, whose value is equal to the distance, in standard deviations, of the

---

[10] This is one reason both the THES and ARWU ranking systems use publication in *Nature* and *Science* as an indicator. We do not advocate this measure for BK21 evaluation because it is too restrictive and would provide limited information. These data are also already available in the raw data series from which the THES and ARWU rankings are derived.

impact factor of the publication journal from the mean impact value for journals in that field,[11] as in

$$\text{Weighted value of paper} = T^d \qquad (5.1)$$

BK21 evaluators may choose the tuning factor, a single number, based on the valuation they wish to place on increasing quality. Setting $T = 2$, for example, would mean that a paper appearing in a journal two standard deviations above the mean value would be given a weight four times that of a paper whose journal had the mean impact value.

The principal value of this tuning approach is that once the distance from the mean is decided on as a standard, at least one arbitrary decision is removed, namely, where thresholds should be placed (thereby removing the concept of bins). It also recognizes that one significant paper may be worth a number of more ordinary ones. At the same time, removing the concept of bins or the decision of where to place thresholds removes an option for evaluators who might want to examine publication impact by groups of journals. Furthermore, this method begins to stress the conceptual expedient of using journal impact as a proxy for quality. Even in *Science* and *Nature*, not all papers have equal impact. Indeed, it can be shown clearly that in both those journals that relatively few papers account for the bulk of the observable impact effect.

A final issue to consider in comparing quality across fields is how to regard publishing outside an author's primary field of specialty. How, for example, should evaluators consider a robotics paper appearing in a more widely read journal of mechanical or electrical engineering? What if it were to appear in a journal whose raw impact value is greater than that of even the highest journal in the robotics field, but in a bin

---

[11] For papers appearing in journals whose impact score is greater than the mean, d would take on positive values. For those whose impact is less than the mean the value of d would be negative.

in another ISI field category that is not much different from the mean value in that field?[12]

Conceptually, the answer is clear. In this instance, the paper's authors have "captured" the higher impact-valued journal for the purpose of publishing their paper on robotics. In doing so, they have brought it to the attention of a wider audience. The journal's actual impact value should be used but placed within the bin defined by robotics journals. This most often will mean that such an extra-field paper would fall in a notional bin that would be yet one threshold beyond the highest-threshold bin that already has been constructed for journals in that particular field. If evaluators were to use the tuning approach rather than bins, then the researchers would be credited with an impact score calculated from the difference between the impact factor of the journal of publication and that of the mean journal in the field of robotics.

Practically, however, it is more difficult to measure the impact of publication outside the field of one's specialty. Making the required calculations for each paper can be quite burdensome. And there are conceptual problems as well. The presumption is that a researcher working in the field of robotics will publish only research relevant to that field. This will not always be the case. If, for example, a robotics researcher were to publish a paper of general interest but only average quality in an average-impact electrical engineering journal, it would be an error to, in effect, give this paper an additional quality rating that it would not otherwise merit by treating it as a robotics paper and employing one of the methods discussed above. In this view, the reasoning would be that a journal editor is looking for appropriate content for that journal. The paper in question should be viewed as being in competition with the other papers appearing, or vying to appear, in that journal and not with those papers that actually were submitted to and appeared in other journals. In this view, the problem of evaluating papers outside

---

[12] To make this concrete with an example, suppose the article appears in a non-robotics journal whose impact is 4.5, approximately triple that of the highest-impact journal in robotics but in a field whose mean journal impact value is also 4.5. Rather than appearing in a higher-threshold bin, as it would have had it appeared in a top-prestige robotics journal, it will appear in a lower-prestige grouping, albeit with higher journal impact.

the primary field should be addressed by only measuring the differential impact value of the journal with that of others in the field where it has been placed. We recommend that the BK21 evaluators take the latter view as well.

Measures of Quality Across All Fields

Our discussion of quality measurement has so far focused on measures that can be used within a field to assess changes in the quality of reported research that also provides for uniform observation across fields. Another approach is to view impact the same way, regardless of field, and measure quality for all publications similarly. In taking such an approach evaluators would assume that truly seminal papers in such fields as robotics are more likely to be published in journals with wider coverage and recognition, such as those in general mechanical or electrical engineering. This assumption therefore reduces the arguments about field disparity and suggests there is a more equal standing across fields than might be inferred just by looking at the relatively few specialist journals.

Both interpretations of the role of quality changes for evaluating the BK21 program's performance are important. In keeping with our general approach that multiple and possibly overlapping measures can help ensure that all relevant effects are being observed, we recommend using two types of measures. Each should encompass a choice of measures to assess these two different concepts of quality.

One type should be the field-specific impact measure as discussed above. This would guard against the possibility that choice of measure may inadvertently skew the very behavior one seeks to assess. In this case, it would not benefit Korea to signal to graduate students and research fellows unintentionally that they should avoid less crowded fields where potentially large and important findings await discovery. The relatively lower level of competition in such fields could also lead to Korean researchers making greater strides and achieving greater recognition in them.[13]

---

[13] This is perhaps a greater concern in such fields as robotics, where there is likely to be more immediate application for research findings than in more theoretical fields. The third set of

To measure more-general scientific and technical impacts, irrespective of field, evaluators could, as described above, use a binning approach or one based on a tuning factor. In the binning approach, evaluators would establish impact weights across the full range of scientific journals and not be limited to journals in the author's field. They may set thresholds either by calculating standard deviations or fixed percentages. If the thresholds were set at the top decile, quartile, and half, for example, it might be useful to measure both the actual number and the share of Korean-authored research papers that are published during different periods of time as Phase II progresses. Evaluators could also use such measures retrospectively to assess the period before the beginning of BK21.

Using a tuning factor across fields also relies on Equation 5.1. With choice of the tuning factor, T, evaluators may calibrate this measure to provide a desired impact-based rating for those publications appearing in the most highly rated journals. The general skewing of the distribution of journal impact factors toward those with higher impact means that this method assigns a bonus to papers appearing in high-impact journals while not severely penalizing those that do not.

Using the data on biochemistry and molecular biology as an example,[14] we note if the tuning factor were set to $T = 1.33$, then, applying Equation 5.1, a paper published in the highest-impact journal would receive a weight of 10 compared to a weight of 1 assigned to a paper appearing in the lowest-impact journal. This method would have the same benefits and deficiencies noted with the field-specific method discussed above.

---

measures in Table 5.2, relating to the third major goal for BK21, on enhancing university-industry collaboration, is designed to capture these effects. This offsets the risk of possibly downplaying these crucially important activities in measures related to the second program goal of enhancing academic stature.

[14] While this discussion is intended to apply to measures across fields, using the data on this one field is a useful illustration. This list includes many of the journals appearing in the list of 20 highest-impact journals across all fields but also some journals with impact factors that are among the lowest. It therefore represents in microcosm the same issues evaluators would face when expanding the measure to all journals.

Relative Research Quality Measures

Using only the two sets of different impact-weighted quality measures would leave unanswered the question of what improvements in research quality could be ascribed to BK21 as distinguished from other influences within Korea, the research fields themselves, the nature of scientific publishing, or still other changes taking place elsewhere in the world. We therefore suggest additional measures of relative research quality.

One method involves tabulating the number of papers authored or co-authored by Koreans that appear among the top-cited papers in the world during the measurement period. This would provide some insight on the degree to which change has occurred within Korea specifically or in the world more generally. If it is the former, for example, one would expect to see a change in the share of Korean-authored papers among those falling into the top 10 percent of most-cited papers. An increase in the latter, on the other hand, would suggest that Korea's relative standing in research had shifted.

It would also be useful to assess the distribution of research papers from a given department or research group along the full range of all ten deciles. Other aggregations, such as quintiles or quartiles, may also be used. In fact, the groupings need not necessarily be uniform, but they should be constant across evaluation periods. Once raw data are collected, evaluators may redefine the groupings at a later date to assess constant categories across years.

Changes to University/Department Infrastructure (2.2.1)

BK21 is focused on investment in and development of human capital. Other investment programs address the adequacy of physical infrastructure and nonhuman research resources. Although the two issues may not be directly related, there is clearly a need to ensure adequate infrastructure to get the most value from human capital investment. The differentiation, specialization, and signaling that BK21 seeks to enhance may also become evident in the flow of nonhuman resources to different universities, departments, and research groups.

The actual influence of BK21 investments on nonhuman capital building is not necessarily clear. Such funding may change the pattern of allocation by universities and other funding sources, similar to the crowding-out effects discussed in the previous chapter. As a result, BK21 could substitute for, rather than supplement, other sources of funding. While this would make more resources generally available to university departments as a whole, it would also mean that BK21 would not have the desired effect of leveraging funds to help the most-capable research groups grow even more.

The measures we have proposed for this metric are intended to provide insight into the relationship between BK21 funding and more-general funding as well as how much other funding for facilities may follow in the wake of BK21 funds. These measures look at various aspects of R&D infrastructure as well as the funding of research itself. The changes over time in the volume and sources of funding will help BK21 evaluators understand the overall effect of the program. As with many measures, it will be more difficult to gather detailed data on non-BK21 departments and research groups, but such information may be gradually acquired from other sources.

Fostering a Competitive Environment Within Korea (2.2.2; 2.2.3)

Our discussions with Korean scholars revealed an uneasiness about the standardization of Korean higher education and a tendency toward equal distribution as a governing norm. They point principally to the presence in almost every university of the same departments and programs, faculty promotions that sometimes are granted as a result of longevity rather than qualitative assessment of individual contributions, and university governance systems that do not support strong leadership. As a result, it is sometimes difficult to truly distinguish where quality work is being done, to assess how priorities for further investment should be assigned, and to develop new departments and fields that may better reflect emerging trends in S&T.

BK21 is not designed to address all issues associated with the nature and strength of signals and indicators in the higher education system in Korea. Nevertheless, it is important to understand the extent to which focused investments such as those of BK21 may change the strength of signals within the system, how these signals are received, and what effect they have on competitive aspects that would lead to greater differentiation and specialization. These effects may result either from the cumulative effect of many individual decisions or from organization-level decisions to make departments and universities more competitive for BK21 funding.

Much of BK21 is designed to modify behavior by young students making career decisions, faculty and research workers seeking the most profitable application of their skills, and administrators of institutions. Such behavior is difficult to observe directly. The measures we suggest for this metric emphasize understanding behavior through the revealed choices of individuals and institutions. No single measure will suffice for this, but a collection may help yield the insights sought by BK21 evaluators.

We assume that a change toward more competitive behavior will be reflected, in part, by measures of international collaboration. As with research quality measures, the production of formal papers is a useful indirect indicator of standing among departments. Papers that result from collaboration with non-Korean authors are a partial indicator of a change in competitive standing. As with goods exports, the international market for knowledge is demanding; potential non-Korean collaborators will choose to work with those Korean collaborators who can contribute most. Such collaboration may also reflect behavioral decisions of the Korean authors, with those having the greatest competitive standing engaging in the costly effort of searching for potential international collaborators. In Korea as elsewhere, the nature and degree of the external network to which the individual researcher (and the department's total research staff) belongs is an important determinant of standing and focus of specialization.

It would be useful to know if increased international collaboration comes at the expense of domestic collaboration with researchers working in the same or complementary fields of study. A negative effect on domestic collaboration might indicate a secondary effect not fully intended by the BK21 program's framers. We therefore recommend a domestic measure of collaboration paralleling the international collaboration measure to better understand the full implications of both types of collaboration.

Multiple measures could also help indicate whether greater collaboration is indeed improving quality. For example, it is possible that an increase in foreign collaboration could mark a move away from quality and toward an effort to boost overall research and paper output. Evaluators could weight all the measures, both foreign and domestic, by quality to verify that collaboration is leading to greater quality.

There is a further value in measuring collaboration. While measures based on publication of papers will prove useful over time, research paper production remains a relatively long process whose length varies by field. In applied fields, the relative importance of formal papers might also be less than in basic research. Both the prolonged publication process for some papers and the varying importance of papers by field would reduce the ability of the measures we propose to assess international collaboration. We therefore suggest similar measures of collaboration for research projects.

Evaluators may also develop several measures to assess whether and to what extent behavioral changes produce more specialization across departments and universities. Among the simplest measures is one based on the choices of both graduate students and faculty in selecting one department over another. In particular, comparing the number of Korean applicants for graduate education to the number of domestic students actually accepted for study may begin to show greater differentiation among departments.[15] Tracking the movement of staff researchers and professors from one department to another may

---

[15] Departments tend to have fixed numbers of places open for domestic students. Often, foreign students are admitted as a way of filling places left unclaimed by Korean graduate students.

also prove useful. Such movement may not occur until other changes in policy and institutions are put in place. Nevertheless, developing a baseline would help understand how and to what extent such migration occurs when it becomes more common.

Evaluators could use the same data series gathered to assess changes in research output quality to construct a field profile of the research activity of departments as a whole. Determining the ISI fields in which a department's faculty and staff publish journal articles could provide a "fingerprint" or "spectrum" for each department. Here, again, a baseline would prove helpful. Once a baseline is established, evaluators could assess the extent to which departments specialize or generalize over time. This measure would have many of the same general problems of journal-based methods: Some departments have more subfields and outlets for publication than others, and truly important papers may appear in general rather than specialized journals. Nevertheless, the measure is worth constructing given that the data for it will be available and the result could prove useful to improve understanding. Measures of specialization showing departments are not distinguishable would make measurements of quality even more valuable in determining which departments are more likely to provide significant future leadership within a field. Measures of specialization showing departments are becoming more distinguishable in their research would provide evidence of changing behavior in the direction of niche development.

Other Measures of Prestigious and Competitive Graduate Research (2.1.1; 2.3.1; 2.3.2)

Our approaches for measuring quality of Korean research and competitiveness of Korean researchers described above have two drawbacks. First, the proposed measures, based on journal publication, are only proxies of the underlying metric we wish to evaluate. Second, there are many components to the intangible property of quality, only some of which contribute directly to the journal-based measures we suggest.

One way to assess other components of quality is through qualitative peer assessment of research quality and prestige. Such assessment could also help address some of the concerns raised above regarding practical measurement issues.

We suggest that BK21 evaluators consider at least one of two possible qualitative measures. The first is a survey of department heads, recognized researchers, and relevant industry representatives in Korea about department and research team quality. The second would be a survey of department quality of similar persons outside Korea.

Such surveys could include ordinal rankings, in which respondents either bin departments or research teams by quartiles, quintiles, or another division that evaluators choose or assign a qualitative measure to each department or research team in the relevant field. It would also be particularly helpful to go beyond questions of relative standing among departments in Korea and ask respondents the extent to which individual departments, research groups, and entire fields of Korean research are improving their standing internationally. Additional questions could yield more information that would help in comparing departments and research groups, but they would also require a trade-off with response rates: As the number of questions increases, the number of surveys completed, and the amount of valid information they yield, will decrease. More questions would also entail more processing.

There are clear practical difficulties associated with surveying international respondents. Such a survey would have the benefit of providing an additional, external perspective of changes in Korea's S&T enterprise. Conversely, international respondents are less likely to detect changes within Korea until they become large and palpable. Nevertheless, such a measure could still help verify both the international standing of Korean institutions and researchers as well as the findings of a domestic survey.

The effect of BK21 on the quality of graduate education is also clearly of interest for overall program performance, but it is quite difficult to assess. One approach used to determine the value of undergraduate education has been the College Learning Assessment test developed by the Council for Aid to Education in the United States, but it is difficult to apply this to graduate education. Its focus on measuring growth in the skills of communication and reasoning is suitable for assessing undergraduate education but less so for graduate education, which is designed to train persons already skilled in general reasoning or communication to acquire particular classes of knowledge and skill. Put another way, college graduates in both literature and science can be assessed for their basic skills before entering graduate studies, but PhDs in literature and chemistry have little in common that can be measured by a single instrument.

We propose a composite approach for assessing the effects of BK21 on graduate education, based largely on data that may be gleaned from other data series but on some new variables as well. Evaluators should be mindful of the peculiarities of graduate education by field when choosing the components of this measure.

One source of data for this composite approach could be anonymous reviews of the quality of completed dissertations. This would provide direct, field- and specialty-specific data on changes in quality over time, by department, and on the extent to which specialization is occurring. If gathered for both BK21 participating and nonparticipating departments, such data might offer insight on the qualifications of Korean graduates that would be difficult to obtain by other means.

Several sources of data could also indicate how well graduates are prepared to be research workers. One source is industry surveys and interviews suggested above. Another is longitudinal surveys of graduates in their careers. Evaluators may combine these with still other measures.

Evaluators might also ask departments to formally describe their graduate study and dissertation systems. This would permit them to independently assess changes instituted over time, including the degree and nature of change, and the likelihood that the change occurred as a result of BK21 (e.g., How have core courses been changed? What is the role of external readers or dissertation committee members?)

Evaluators might assess these data streams individually or, as we suggest, in a composite measure where heterogeneous data are weighted to yield a single measure. This would make quantification more tractable and provide a more comprehensive measure than would a series of individual measures. It would also demonstrate that change can be realized in many ways, thus increasing specialization. Composite measures such as we suggest are at the core of global university ranking systems, such as those of THES and ARWU. They do have two principal problems. The first is how to assign appropriate weights among multiple data series, including how to decide which one should have the most influence or if all should have equal influence. The second is that such approaches yield measures designed not to be interpreted in absolute terms but rather to provide a relative assessment. This makes it difficult to interpret the meaning of differences. Is a department that receives a value 1 percent or 10 percent greater than another necessarily qualitatively different from the department that receives a lower grade? Guarino et al. (2005) address these shortcomings in their latent variable analytic approach for measuring ordinal differences, an approach BK21 evaluators may wish to consider if composite measures are chosen for evaluation.

A further set of measures to help assess how changes may be occurring in academia is to determine how those eligible for graduate school are deciding whether and where to go. These measures could be constructed from statistics on Korean students applying to Korean universities. As individual departments become more attractive and more highly regarded research centers, the numbers of applicants should increase. Similar measures based on matriculation of foreign students at Korea's universities are more problematic. While foreign students might be considered a good indicator of a department's international standing, often Korean departments are less selective when it comes to admitting such students for several reasons.[16] Therefore, using a foreign attendance measure should also involve a weighting of foreign students by the quality of their undergraduate institutions as ranked by THES or ARWU.

---

[16] The principal reason is that such students are often a source of net revenue to the university and so frequently do not affect caps that may be in place for Korean students limiting the number of places available.

Measuring Enhanced University-Industry Collaboration (3.1.1; 3.2.1)

Previously, we demonstrated that application of common measures, such as those based on number and quality of papers, may not work as well in applied science fields, such as robotics, as in fields of basic science or even the arts and humanities. A similar problem is evident in assessing BK21's third goal, enhancing the communication and partnership between researchers in private firms and those at Korean universities. Presumably, these formal and informal ties would not only enhance the degree of support that industrial firms inside and outside the Seoul area may derive from academic research activities but would also provide another source by which universities and research departments at regional universities could become fuller participants in innovative activities at a higher level of competence. This, too, is part of a strategy to enhance the standing of Korean universities internationally and of regional universities within Korea.

The measures we propose to assess the metrics associated with collaboration are more straightforward than those for assessing quality. Nevertheless, they, too, involve the use of proxies rather than direct measures. The proxies derive from being able to track and enumerate two conditions for which data may prove elusive.

The first proxy requires tracking formal instruments of collaboration between industrial research and product development teams and academic research teams or departments. Instruments like this are only a rough means for tracking such interactions. In some cases, interactions may be well along before they are formalized in a manner that would be detectable by outside evaluators. In others, formal agreements may be entered into but remain inactive, falling far short of the original intentions of the parties to the agreement. Still, a time series of collected data for this measure would provide an approximate measure of change in the system, assuming that the errors would likely remain constant over time.

The second proxy would more closely reflect BK21 desires for the goal of industry-university collaboration but perhaps be more challenging to measure. This is tallying the number and value of new products or product improvements that might be claimed as a result of identified collaborations. It is not uncommon for industrial firms, particularly those involved in areas of production that rely on leading-edge innovation, to track and identify new products or improvements[17] as a means of assessing their own performance and also as a signal to investors, customers, and potential partners. Some companies explicitly mandate that a specified share of total production come from new products.

Such measures are, of course, subject to various types of measurement errors. However, it is the change over time, particularly the change that may be attributed to Phase II, that is of interest for program evaluation. Again, consistent rather than precise measurements are most important.

Gathering data for these measures may be less challenging than it first appears. Since 2001, special organizations within each university have overseen each school's formal contracting with industry. Although these organizations gather data for the university as a whole rather than by individual department, it may still be possible to use these data for information on departments that are not participating in BK21. These data can be made part of the standard data call for participants. BK21 already collects data on commercial spin-offs and commercial revenue streams (such as license income) for departments and research groups receiving BK21 funding.

Beyond cooperation contracts, patents, license fees, and other direct payments for intellectual property goods, other contacts could exist between industry and the academy. Industry, for example, needs access to information on where specialized expertise may be found within academia. Universities and their departments are required to find funds to partially match the funding they receive from the government under BK21. Both of these needs lead to greater active contact between industry and academia. Informal contacts are also required at the personal professional level before formal arrangements can be made.

---

[17] The Organization for Economic Co-operation and Development (OECD) (2005) refers to innovative products and processes (IPP) and defines them. For the purpose of framing this measure, we distinguish IPPs from other types of innovations, such as those in organization or marketing. BK21 evaluators may wish also to consider these in their work.

It would be helpful to gain more information on the level of routine contacts between industry and BK21 recipients. Establishing a baseline for and tracking changes in such data would have value beyond BK21. Evaluators might gather such data in a narrative fashion rather than by using strict numerical tallies, although these, too, would be useful where feasible. Most important in early stages is maintaining records of such contacts for future planning purposes and raising awareness on the part of both prospective partners to an industrial-academic cooperative relationship of the importance and value of these exchanges.

Just as all collaborations are not alike, so firms may differ in the goods or services they offer and their culture and managerial style. One of the biggest differences among firms is the one between large firms (as defined in terms appropriate for each country as well as on an absolute scale that is important for global competition) and small or medium-sized enterprises (SMEs). A healthy, innovative, and efficient industrial structure generally requires a mix among firms. In some countries, SMEs provide the greatest innovation, but, because of their size, they may have difficulties obtaining information and resources to compete with larger firms. This is another area in which BK21 concerns overlap those of other government initiatives. It would therefore be useful to gain insight into differing behaviors by firms of varying sizes in their contacts with universities.

Qualitative assessment tools, such as the employer surveys, interviews, and site visits that we suggested above, can also be used to assess the university-industry link. Listening to responses from industry and university people in their own words would be a standard way of assessing the university-industry link qualitatively. Again, data gathering through these tools would be in a narrative fashion rather than by using strict numerical tallies.

Measuring Enhanced Regional University Standing and Industry Linkage (3.2.2)

So far, we have discussed measures that would either be aggregated across the country or developed for individual academic departments or *sa-up-dan*. Nevertheless, from these same data series we could derive measures of intermediate activities regarding the capabilities and academic stature of regional universities outside traditional development hubs like Seoul and a few other such areas. Regional measures could provide a more nuanced view of changes in industry-university collaboration, specifically by showing where changes are occurring geographically. Such measures may also offer insight on how innovative processes may be fostered nationally.

This potential application of such measures is based on a particular view of innovation in the context of increased globalization. In this view, the particular features of each locality are crucial in determining the success of local innovation. Innovation is a social, interpersonal activity because only a fraction of the knowledge that innovators possess is codifiable.

The importance of locality is even greater on the leading edge of technology. Successful innovators are usually technically well-trained persons who also have intuition based on their experience and use an inductive logic that is sometimes difficult to communicate or describe. This practicality makes innovation a social phenomenon of communication requiring both a "sender" and a sophisticated "receiver" who can recognize the value of the information being articulated. When industry hires science and engineering graduates, it does so not only for what they know but for what they can learn. Their specific local activities give them the familiarity and experience to make use of the richness of what is happening outside academia. In this sense, all innovation is local.[18]

This perspective suggests that a practical strategy to enhance innovation will focus on (1) identifying local assets that can build local advantage, (2) recognizing the advantage of proximity in accelerating innovation, and (3) making a disciplined effort to acquire external assets, especially knowledge assets, for local use. All these elements are inherent in the Phase II goals.

---

[18] See, for example, many of the papers and presentations from the Accelerating Innovation conference, October 2005.

We propose several measures to illuminate how well linkages are formed between regional universities and industry. One measure is the geographical distance between regional universities and their industry partners in collaboration agreements. Applying such a measure requires care. Industrial activities are concentrated in certain areas—Seoul and its vicinity, Inchon, and others. Some regions, such as Kangwon, have no industrial base except tourism. Some, such as Chulla-do, have a smaller industrial base than others, such as Kyunsang-do. Nevertheless, collecting regional data could prove useful not only for BK21 evaluation but also for other purposes.

We propose several other measures to assess the share of cooperative agreements between industrial partners outside traditional hubs, such as Seoul, and corresponding local research teams and academic departments. One measure of particular interest would be to assess the number and value of agreements between industrial partners based in Seoul and other development hubs and research teams and academic departments outside the hubs. Such measures could supplement survey instruments designed to assess change in industry-university collaboration.

One survey instrument BK21 program evaluators may wish to consider is a Delphi-type study among industrial R&D managers about collaboration.[19] Managers could weight issues of concern to them in the study, with participants indicating over rounds of the study whether conditions are improving, worsening, or remaining the same. This technique would capture how perceptions about the nature, degree, and usefulness of contributions by academic teams to industrial R&D efforts change over time.

Finally, while the focus of BK21 has been on basic and applied areas of science and engineering, the program has also sought to strengthen

---

[19] The traditional Delphi study is used to achieve consensus within a group of experts by asking questions iteratively, allowing individuals to examine the anonymous replies to the first round and to change their response for subsequent rounds. It is useful because it permits substantive interaction while limiting the influence of social dynamics that would be present in the case of direct interaction among experts. Issues of rank, influence, obligation, and personality do not skew the result. Further, it is often impractical to have group consultative sessions in real time. The Delphi method supports asynchronous interaction.

local collaborations in arts and the humanities. This includes boosting regional centers outside traditional hubs, encouraging specialization to enhance excellence and efficient use of resources, and cooperating with regional institutions, including local cultural and educational institutions. These collaborations are more difficult to measure because they are usually less formal than agreements or contracts in science and engineering. Information from arts and humanities teams and departments not participating in BK21 may be especially difficult to acquire. Nevertheless, BK21 evaluators should recognize the importance and stature of such collaboration, including establishing an appropriate standard for enumerating those contacts. Here is surely an instance where the possibility of measurement affecting behavior should be welcomed if it makes the knowledge contained in Korea's universities more widely available to the communities in which they are situated.

Industrial Research Quantity, Quality, and National Labor Productivity (3.3.1; 3.3.2)

Measures of industrial research and national labor productivity can also be constructed from data that have already been collected. For example, the Delphi survey discussed above would also apply to understanding these outcome metrics. The measures recommended for these metrics do not represent departures from those commonly used to assess industry capabilities. The techniques discussed in the previous chapter can make them relevant for BK21 evaluation as well.

CHAPTER SIX

Database Design to Support BK21 Program Evaluation and Measurement

So far, we have explored the goals for BK21 and provided a logic model for understanding its process, a model for determining the net effect of Phase II, and an extensive list of measures by which evaluators may judge its success. In this chapter, we consider how to prioritize candidate evaluation measures and then propose a general database structure for measurement and evaluation, including detailed identification of the necessary data time series and mapping of these series onto the suggested measures.

Priority Among Proposed Measures

In previous chapters, we noted the practical bases for evaluating how well Phase II is fulfilling its goals, and we highlighted trade-offs and design decisions so that BK21 evaluators can understand and implement the evaluation framework. The actual application of this framework will depend on practical considerations of time, resources, and the importance of a given measure and its variables. We have presented a range of choices while indicating which metric each measure seeks to quantify and how that measure relates to other candidate measures.

Not all candidate measures are equally important in assessing BK21 program metrics. Choices must be made if the evaluation design is to become practical. Evaluators or even program sponsors may consider some to be essential to measuring program success; others may be considered more peripheral. There is probably a hierarchy of importance among the metrics themselves. Some program outputs and outcomes clearly must be seen as having improved if BK21 is to be deemed a success and worthy of continuation. Lack of achievement for some of the more peripheral aspects of the program, however, would more likely lead to fine-tuning than to abandoning the program as a whole.

In this sense, the first step in determining priority among measures is in the realm of policy. An important step for assigning this priority will be for evaluators, or the policymakers to whom they ultimately must answer, to assign priorities to the metrics the measures are intended to support. The policy decision, therefore, is to determine what must be demonstrated to present credible evidence for judging BK21 a success.

After the policy decision about metrics has been made, determining priority among candidate *measures* requires two tasks. First, the evaluator must assign a relative raw importance to the measures, such as designating measures as *core* or *additional*, the former indicating a measure that is more important for evaluating BK21 than the latter. Table 6.1 suggests which measures may be considered in these two categories. Second is the practical issue of finding, generating, and processing the necessary data. These data may vary by the difficulty or time involved in gathering them. We cannot make this judgment from afar; the assessment is entirely practical and circumstantial. For example, several of the candidate measures defined in the previous chapter (3.3.1.3a, 3.3.1.3b, and 3.3.1.4) would require information on the number of new and innovative products or processes introduced in Korean industry during a given period. It would be feasible for BK21 evaluators to consider these data in their measures if they have already been collected and made available by others. If not, the costly effort to collect these data will likely mean these measures are not a feasible part of the evaluation architecture.

Table 6.1 shows how evaluators might prioritize selection of measures. It suggests that priority is a product of the inherent value of a candidate measure and the practicality of obtaining the necessary data. We consider some measures of core importance because they are directly related to a metric that is itself considered by the evaluators to

Table 6.1
Hierarchy for Determining Priority Among Candidate Measures

Importance of Measure for Evaluating BK21 Performance Metrics	Difficulty or Cost of Obtaining Necessary Data	
	Low	High
Core	I	II
Additional	III	IV

be crucial. If the needed data are relatively easy to acquire, the measures would be classified as priority I. Other candidate measures might be determined to be useful but not necessarily key to understanding BK21 processes or results. Among this second group those that also required considerable cost or effort in obtaining data would be classified as priority IV.

It is also likely that those measures that have been classified as priority III by this means would be worth considering. The data would already exist or be relatively easy to obtain and the resulting measures would provide some illumination. They receive a lower priority than class II, however, which would have been judged more important for understanding central elements of BK21. Class II measures would require careful consideration. The ultimate decision whether to include them in the BK21 evaluation process would depend on actual resource expenditures, the amount of total resources available, and a variety of other practical considerations based on actual circumstances.

The system shown in Table 6.1 is notional and simplified. Decisions about difficulty or cost of measures for assessing metrics may not fit neatly into one of the four categories. Classification will depend on evaluators' best judgment. The categorization of the importance of a measure can only partially be derived on theoretical grounds and in isolation from other measures. Some measures thought to be peripheral may become more important if the ideal core measures are found to be impractical. A measure's importance may also vary by whether it is used to construct still other measures meant to amplify it. A measure may become relatively more valuable if others linked to it are also included in the evaluation measurement regime; less valuable, if it alone is selected. Additionally, as shown below, some data series may be used as input, along with other data, to form as many as a half dozen or more individual measures. This possibility would presumably enhance the benefit of expending the resources to obtain these data and so change the priority assessment of the measures on which they depend as well. The categorization in Table 6.1 is only an initial point for assessing what measures to include in the evaluation.

Ideally, BK21 evaluators will need similar data from universities and departments that received funding through the program, from those that applied but did not receive awards, and from those that never applied. Gathering some of the data would present no difficulty because they are readily available from common sources. Gathering other data, however, presents more of a challenge. Evaluators could require BK21 recipients to provide information of a type that has not been collected previously in Korea, but they would not have the same degree of leverage with nonparticipants and nonapplicants. The data gathered from institutions outside the BK21 regime might also be in different formats and not entirely parallel with those collected from BK21 participants. This would raise issues about consistency for any measures constructed with these data and would also raise questions of measure validity as a result.

The additional effort and cost of gaining data from nonrecipients and nonapplicants may lead evaluators to shy away from measures that depended on these data. It is for this reason that the measure-data combinations falling into class II in Table 6.1 take precedence over those in class III. Careful consideration should be given before excluding a measure classed as being of core importance from the evaluation regime. Before determining that the difficulty or cost in obtaining certain data may be too great for the associated measures to be included in the evaluation, evaluators must give some thought to the intrinsic value of these data as well. Not only may difficult-to-obtain data be important for measuring the performance of BK21, they might also be valuable for other planning and strategic uses.

In addition to a hierarchy of priorities among measures, evaluators should establish a hierarchy of procedures for implementing the measures themselves. Some of the proposed measures merely require application of data that are currently collected and for which there is a historical time series. If this is not the case, modified forms of the measures should be considered. So, for example, if the necessary data have not been collected but can be obtained from both BK21 recipients and nonrecipients, the measure could still be assessed from the time that the necessary data can be made available rather from the ideal starting point of Phase II's inception. If data are more easily obtainable—or are only obtainable—from recipient institutions, consideration should be given to whether the measure's core importance warrants beginning with this smaller sample with a view toward expanding it later. Although a truly controlled evaluation should determine changes equally in recipient and nonrecipient institutions, an examination of the former alone may still be valuable if that is the only reasonable course. If data are available in some fields and not others, the opportunity for insight should not be sacrificed to the ideal of universal coverage. The measures could be applied to those fields where information exists. For example, the desire to measure change in the number of funded research projects that have either non-Korean collaborators or Korean collaborators from different institutions (measures 2.2.2.1 and 2.2.2.3) might prove laborious to realize for all Korean institutions across all fields. Doing so for several fields of particular interest, however, would be entirely tractable.

Should universal coverage not be practicable for some measures, the evaluators may wish to consider a small-scale case study on a local level to illuminate trends that would be difficult to assess on an aggregate level and to pioneer data collection and assessment techniques that could be applied to other regions. For this reason, BK21 evaluators may wish to consider establishing a funding competition for doctoral dissertations relevant to BK21 assessment and analysis. These types of analytical tasks lend themselves well to dissertations in public policy and other related fields—the studies themselves would require precisely the type of intelligent, dedicated effort that graduate students provide. This would be a way to increase coverage, provide greater analytical depth, and leverage assets available for assessing BK21—while at the same time developing researchers who can apply these analytical skills to issues Korean policymakers must consider as they develop other programs similar to BK21.

Database Design and Content

The database for the measures identified in the previous chapter may be conceived of as a large spreadsheet workbook computer file. Each individual dataset or time series necessary for one or more of the measurements is a worksheet in that file. A directory worksheet lists all data series in the file and their locations, including special notes on usage or characteristics peculiar to individual data series and a mapping of these data to the evaluation measure or measures they support.

Table 6.2, which largely replicates Table 5.2, presents a notional database structure and its components. It shows metrics and their measures but notes whether each measure is of "core" importance or an "additional" variable to be considered. The last column of this table also presents the data series that each measure would require. The data series appear in four appendixes to this monograph. Appendix E shows series for research data, covering university and academic department activities focusing on scientific and academic inquiry by field. Individual data series numbers in this grouping are preceded by the letter "R." Appendix F shows data series covering the educational activities of universities and departments. Individual series in this grouping are preceded by the letter "E." Appendix G shows series for industry data, covering information on innovation and R&D within industries as well as industry structure and interactions with academic researchers. Individual series in this grouping are preceded by the letter "I." Appendix H shows series for other general data, including those on the Korean economy, geographical information, and other information not fitting under the other three groupings but necessary for some candidate measures. Individual series in this grouping are preceded by the letter "G." Again, our format is only notional; BK21 evaluators may choose another format better suited to their purpose.

Table 6.2
Candidate Measures with Required Data Series and Suggested Priority

Measure Number	Metric (Arranged according to BK21 goals, intermediate indicators, outputs, and outcomes)	Measure Importance	Measure Nature of Data Required	Data Series Required
	Goal 1. Increase size and capability of research manpower pool	—		
	1.1. Intermediate indicators			
1.1.1	Flow of human resources into graduate studies, by field	—		
1.1.1.1		Core	Students enrolled in graduate programs in Korea	E-2; E-4
1.1.1.2		Core	Students enrolled in graduate programs abroad	E-6
1.1.1.3		Additional	Research assistants in Korean departments	E-9; E-10
1.1.1.4		Additional	Research assistants abroad	E-11
	1.2. Outputs			
1.2.1	Human resource production			
1.2.1.1a		Core	Placement in universities, Korea	E-12; E-13
1.2.1.1b(i)		Additional	Placement in universities, Korea, quality weighted	E-12; E-13; E-22
1.2.1.1b(ii)		Additional	Placement in universities, Korea, quality weighted	E-12; E-13; E-40; E-39; I-25; R-38; I-24; E-38; R-36; R-37; E-41
1.2.1.2		Core	Placement in industry, Korea	I-1
1.2.1.3		Core	Placement in other professional	E-12; E-13; E-21; E-15; I-1; I-2; ; E-14
1.2.1.4a		Core	Placement in universities, abroad	E-15
1.2.1.4b		Additional	Placement in universities, abroad, quality weighted	E-15; E-22
1.2.1.5		Additional	Placement in industry, abroad	I-2
1.2.2	Researcher quantity and quality, national level			
1.2.2.1a		Core	Publication quality intensity measure	R-31; R-32; R-34; I-12; E-18; E-19; R-27; R-28
1.2.2.1b(i)		[One of these three should be selected as Core]	Publication quality intensity measure, grouped	R-31; R-32; R-35
1.2.2.1b(ii)			Publication quality intensity change measure	R-31; R-32; R-35
1.2.2.1c			Publication quality intensity measure, weighted	R-31; R-32; R-34; I-12; E-18; E-19; R-27; R-28

Table 6.2—continued

Measure Number	Metric (Arranged according to BK21 goals, intermediate indicators, outputs, and outcomes)	Measure		
		Importance	Nature of Data Required	Data Series Required
1.2.2.2		Core	Publication quantity intensity measure	R-31; R-32; I-12; E-18; E-19; R-27; R-28
1.2.2.3a		Additional	Subjective quality assessment, domestic	R-36
1.2.2.3b		Additional	Subjective quality assessment, foreign	R-37
1.2.2.4a		Core	Size of Korean research workforce	I-12; E-18; E-19; R-27; R-28
1.2.2.4b		Additional	Size of Korean research workforce, including abroad	I-12; E-18; E-19; R-27; R-28; I-13; E-20; R-29; R-30
1.3.	**1.3. Outcomes**			
1.3.1	Employment balances for highly educated workforce			
1.3.1.1a		Core	Survey of firms' opinions of 20 selected Korean universities	I-24
1.3.1.1b		Core	Longitudinal survey of graduates	E-38
1.3.1.1c		Additional	Like 1.3.1.1b, combined with interviews with present employers of graduates	E-38; I-25; R-38; E-39
	Goal 2. Globally competitive research universities			
	2.1. Intermediate indicators			
2.1.1	Change in rates of flow of human resources into graduate study, by field			
2.1.1.1		Core	Change in share of graduate students who choose to study in Korea	E-2; E-4; E-6
2.1.1.2		Core	Change in share of students who pursue graduate studies	E-2; E-4; E-6; E-1
2.2.	**2.2. Outputs**			
2.2.1	Graduate school infrastructure			
2.2.1.1	Libraries and computers	Additional	Total and amount per student, by university	E-23; E-24; E-25; E-26; E-27; E-28
2.2.1.2	Laboratories, special equipment, and in-kind support	Additional	Total and amount per student, by university, by department	R-1; R-2; R-3; R-4; R-5; R-6; R-7; R-8; R-9; R-10; R-11; R-12

Table 6.2—continued

Measure Number	Metric (Arranged according to BK21 goals, intermediate indicators, outputs, and outcomes)	Measure		Data Series Required
		Importance	Nature of Data Required	
2.2.1.3	General facilities	Additional	Total and amount per student, by university	E-29; E-30; E-31; E-32; E-33; E-34
2.2.1.4	Research project funding	Core	Total and amount per student, by university, by department	R-13; R-14; R-15; R-16; R-17; R-18; R-19; R-20; R-21; R-22; R-23; R-24
2.2.2	Competitive environment within and among universities			
2.2.2.1		Additional	Relative share of funded research projects with foreign collaborators: number and value (KRW), by department	R-13; R-14; R-15; R-16; R-17; R-18; R-19; R-20; R-21; R-22; R-23; R-24; R-25; R-26
2.2.2.2a		Core	Papers authored with foreign collaborators, by department	R-31; R-32; R-33
2.2.2.2b		Additional	Papers authored with foreign collaborators, by department, quality weighted	R-31; R-32; R-33; R-34
2.2.2.3		Additional	Funded research projects with Korean collaborators: number and volume (KRW), by department	R-13; R-14; R-15; R-16; R-17; R-18; R-19; R-20; R-21; R-22; R-23; R-24; R-25; R-26
2.2.2.4a		Core	Papers authored with Korean collaborators, by department	R-31; R-32
2.2.2.4b		Additional	Papers authored with Korean collaborators, by department, quality weighted	R-31; R-32; R-34
2.2.2.5a		Additional	Competitive funding to department, net of government BK21 funding (total; per faculty; per graduate student; relative to university size/funding)	R-2; R-4; R-5; R-8; R-10; R-11; R-14; R-16; R-17; R-20; R-22; R-23
2.2.2.5b		Core	Competitive funding to department, net of government and private match BK21 funding (total; per faculty; per graduate student; relative to university size and funding)	R-2; R-4; R-5; R-8; R-10; R-11; R-14; R-16; R-17; R-20; R-22; R-23
2.2.3	Signaling for faculty and graduate students			
2.2.3.1		Core	Change in enrollment/application ratio for domestic students, by department	E-2; E-3; E-4; E-5
2.2.3.2		Core	Faculty transfers between institutions	E-16; E-17; ; E-12; E-13

Table 6.2—continued

Measure Number	Metric (Arranged according to BK21 goals, intermediate indicators, outputs, and outcomes)	Importance	Measure: Nature of Data Required	Measure: Data Series Required
2.2.3.3		Core	Changes in faculty size, by department	E-16; E-17; E-12; E-13
2.2.3.4		Core	Changes in faculty size, by department, relative to university size	E-16; E-17; E-12; E-13
2.2.3.5		Core	Allocation among BK21 and non-BK21 departments of students who choose to enter graduate studies	E-2; E-4
2.2.3.6		Additional	Research output profile, by department	R-31; R-32
	2.3. Outcomes			
2.3.1	International prestige for Korean research groups and departments			
2.3.1.1a		[One should be chosen as Core]	Weighted (binned) score of articles published (in field)	R-31; R-32; R-34
2.3.1.1b			Weighted (smooth) score of articles published (in field)	R-31; R-32; R-34
2.3.1.2a		[One should be chosen as Core]	Weighted (binned) score of articles published (across fields)	R-31; R-32; R-34
2.3.1.2b			Weighted (smooth) score of articles published (across fields)	R-31; R-32; R-34
2.3.1.3a		Core	Number of Korean authored papers in each rank of highly cited papers	R-31; R-32; R-35
2.3.1.3b		Additional	Share of total Korean authored papers in each rank of highly cited papers	R-31; R-32; R-35
2.3.1.4a		Additional	Quality of research staff: peer assessment survey, Korean respondents	R-36
2.3.1.4b		Additional	Quality of research staff: peer assessment survey, non-Korean respondents	R-37
2.3.1.5		[One should be chosen as Core]	Academic performance and quality of education	E-40; E-39; I-25; R-38; I-24; E-38; R-36; R-37; E-41
2.3.1.6			Academic performance and quality of education with respect to the size of an institution	E-40; E-39; I-25; R-38; I-24; E-38; R-36; R-37; E-18; E-19; E-41
2.3.1.7a		Additional	Foreign students attending Korean departments	E-8
2.3.1.7b		Additional	Foreign students attending Korean departments, quality weighted	E-8; E-22

Table 6.2—continued

Measure Number	Metric (Arranged according to BK21 goals, intermediate indicators, outputs, and outcomes)	Measure		
		Importance	Nature of Data Required	Data Series Required
2.3.2	National prestige for Korean research groups and departments			
	Goal 3. Enhance university-industry collaboration			
	3.1. Intermediate indicators			
3.1.1	Formal indicators of university-industry collaboration			
3.1.1.1		Core	Number of industry-laboratory cooperative contracts	I-3; I-4
3.1.1.2		Additional	Value (KRW) of industry-laboratory cooperative contracts	I-5; I-6
3.2. Outputs				
3.2.1	University-industry linkages			
3.2.1.1a		Core	Patents by department	I-14; I-15; I-16; I-17
3.2.1.1b		Additional	Patents by department from cooperative contracts	I-3; I-4; I-9; I-10; I-14; I-15; I-16; I-17
3.2.1.2		Core	Value (KRW) of license fees and other intellectual property payments, by department	I-19; I-20
3.2.1.3a		Additional	Number of new products from cooperative contracts	I-3; I-4; I-7
3.2.1.3b		Additional	Value (KRW) of new products from cooperative contracts	I-3; I-4; I-8
3.2.1.4		Additional	Share of new products from cooperative contracts in total industry output	I-3; I-4; I-8; G-2
3.2.1.5		Core	Numbers and ledger of industry-department contacts	I-22; I-23
3.2.1.6		Additional	Histogram breakdown of industrial collaborators	I-21; I-3; I-4; I-5; I-6
3.2.2	Regional graduate school promotion			
3.2.2.1		Core	Number of industry-university laboratory cooperative contracts	I-3; I-4
3.2.2.2		Additional	Value of industry-university laboratory cooperative contracts	I-5; I-6
3.2.2.3		Core	Proximity of industry-university laboratory cooperative contracts	I-3; I-4; I-18; E-35

Table 6.2—continued

Measure Number	Metric (Arranged according to BK21 goals, intermediate indicators, outputs, and outcomes)	Measure		
		Importance	Nature of Data Required	Data Series Required
3.2.2.4–5		Core	Intensity of non-Hub industry–university laboratory cooperative contracts	I-3; I-4; I-5; I-6; I-18; E-35
3.2.2.6–7		Core	Number and value of Hub industry–non-Hub university laboratory cooperative contracts	I-3; I-4; I-5; I-6; I-18; E-35
3.2.2.8–9		Core	Intensity of Hub industry–non-Hub university laboratory cooperative contracts	I-3; I-4; I-5; I-6; I-18; E-35
3.2.2.10		Core	Numbers and ledger of university-community cultural contacts	E-36; E-37
3.2.2.11		Core	Proximity of university-community cultural contacts	E-36; E-37; G-3; E-35
3.2.2.12		Core	Intensity of non–"Top 3 (5)" university production of MAs and PhDs	E-21; E-22
3.3.	**Outcomes**			
3.3.1	Industrial research quantity and quality			
3.3.1.1		Core	Patents (foreign) by industrial sector	I-9
3.3.1.2		Core	Patents by industrial sector	I-10
3.3.1.3		Additional	Number of new products by industrial sector	I-
3.3.1.4		Additional	Value of new products by industrial sector	I-8
3.3.1.5		Additional	Share of new products by industrial sector	I-8; I-11
3.3.1.6		Core	Delphi-type survey among industry R&D directors	R-39
3.3.2	Labor productivity			
3.3.2.1		Core	Labor productivity	G-1

Format of Database Design Entries

Each of the four area worksheets (See Appendixes E–H) that make up the database design workbook has the same structure. Table 6.3 shows this generalized structure. Each row in a worksheet represents and describes the details of an individual data series. The leftmost column provides a unique identifier (e.g., "E-11", "G-3", "R-20") for data in a row. The second column gives name of the data series. The remaining columns provide more information on each data series.

Difficulty is the relative difficulty with which the necessary data may be obtained. RAND researchers are not able to make this assessment without reference to available data series; therefore, in most worksheet rows, this cell is blank. Nevertheless, as noted earlier, this is a crucial variable to consider in prioritizing data collection. Hence, we include it in our recommended database format.

Time interval is the period between the observations needed for each time series. Here, too, the evaluators must choose the appropriate length of time, compromising between the ideal and the practical. In most cases, this compromise will result in annual observations. Some less-quantitative data requirements, such as those requiring surveys, would be less frequent. Others, such as those requiring geographic analyses, would require a one-time effort with only occasional maintenance in succeeding years.

Some data series will be substantively identical but vary by source. For example, evaluators may need data on a given topic from both BK21 participants and nonparticipants and find those data easier to gather from participants. The *type* column designates the most salient characteristic of not only the data but the data providers as well. The indication for data coming from universities and departments that are BK21 recipients is "R" and from nonrecipients is "N". Other types of identifiers may be used to show further disaggregation—to distinguish, for example, between nonrecipients who applied for funding and those who did not or among classes of recipients. Differentiating data by type can help in assessing their priority. Because data may be more or less easily available, evaluators may choose to begin with what is available

Table 6.3
General Layout of Each Database Area Worksheet

Identifier	Data Series	Difficulty	Time Interval	Type	Level	Measures	Source	Notes

and then later seek data from additional sources. Such decisions will, of course, affect the interpretation of the resulting measures.

Data may also vary by the level at which they are gathered. In many cases, evaluators may find it best to collect data at the academic department level. While the basic unit of BK21 is the *sa-up-dan* working group, in many cases it may be difficult to distinguish the *sa-up-dan* from the department that houses it. Many BK21 goals, such as encouraging greater distinctiveness among departments, also make the department a better level of analysis. Nevertheless, in some cases evaluators may require data at the *sa-up-dan* level. For some data series, the appropriate level is the university itself. Industrial data likely to be of most interest are at an aggregate level, and are likely to be already available from government agencies (e.g., two-digit International Standard Industrial Classification codes). Evaluators may also find data on academic and industrial collaborations available from academic partners.[1]

The *measures* column lists measures for which each individual data series is an input. Some series will be an input to only a single measure; others may be used for multiple candidate measures.[2] These lists are intended to be inclusive. For example, determining the size of the total Korean research and development workforce requires several data series, with this measure in turn serving as an input to several additional measures. In this case, individual data series used to determine the R&D workforce will also appear as inputs to the subsequent measures. This level of detail allows BK21 evaluators to have the fullest information on the role each data series has in the evaluation process and to determine how to allocate data collection and management resources.

The *source* and *notes* columns provide further clarification and detail where possible and appropriate. The discussion of possible sources can guide the initial investigation of data availability and access. It also

---

[1] Details on ISIC Revision 3.1 may be found in United Nations, 2007.

[2] Note that the nomenclature used in identifying individual measures is the same as that used in Table 5.2. Each such identifier is unique to one measure just as each data series identifier is unique. Neither should be changed until the final decisions are made on evaluation metrics and their data requirements.

provides further insight on recommended data. The final notes column conveys insights on issues that are relevant for the data series in a given row. Evaluators with more-intimate knowledge of the available data sources may wish to add information to these columns before allocating resources for collection.

The database design presented in this monograph indicates only the types and characteristics of the data required for the candidate evaluation measures. Actual construction of the measures from these data will also vary in degree of difficulty. Some data may be used directly with no further treatment. Others will serve as necessary raw material but will require considerable further processing to create the desired measures. Evaluators may be able to determine priority among measures only after the extent of effort and available resources become clear.

CHAPTER SEVEN

Future Development of BK21 and University Research in Korea

We now turn to an examination of possible future directions for BK21 and the university research system in Korea. As the sponsor requested, we offer guidance on several topics related to BK21 and the research university system in Korea, including

- concentrating the funding on a limited number of research groups
- using the research group (*sa-up-dan*) as the unit of support
- establishing a minimum number of participating professors for a research group
- evaluating methods to determine recipients, including ranking scientific merit
- sub-programs to support professional schools, schools outside Seoul, and research groups smaller than the minimum requirement
- the optimal scale and optimal number of research universities in Korea
- minimum qualifications for research universities and suggestions for helping Korean institutions reach these qualifications.

Many of these topics extend beyond the present or likely future dimensions of the BK21 program and take a holistic view of the Korean university research system. We base our analysis of these topics on our understanding of the BK21 program, the findings presented in this monograph, and other studies on research and education systems, particularly those in the United States. To analyze these topics, we first synthesize the research findings concerning a good model for allocating research resources, including funding and human resources. Then we apply that model to Korea, allowing for possible adjustments to suit the Korean situation and policy priorities.

A Good Model for an Allocation System

Outstanding scientific research and education require an interrelated set of resources: research projects, faculty, graduate students, other personnel, facilities, and infrastructure. The likely effects of Korean policies, including BK21, on each of these resources is a useful guide to considering optimal policies for Korea.

In general, competition for funding spurs participants to strive for excellence; safe, uncompetitive funding diminishes those incentives. Of course, other effects are possible, even likely. For instance, reliable funding can help researchers build a stable base from which to do research and work with graduate students.

Previous research in the United States points to what might be a good system that balances the benefits of competition against reliability in funding (Goldman and Massy, 2001; Goldman et al., 2000; and Brewer, Gates, and Goldman, 2002). Components of such a system include

- competition for research project funding at the project level, with decisions made on the basis of scientific merit
- graduate student funding through portable fellowships that pay the student a stipend and pay the student's institution an allowance toward education (either as a credit toward tuition or in lieu of all tuition)
- efficient market financing (such as tax-free bonds) for universities to invest in long-term infrastructure costs
- recovery of the cost of capital investments and financing through overhead reimbursement on research project grants

- infrastructure grants awarded on the basis of departmental merit (until capital markets provide efficient financing to universities).

We recommend these features as a good way to organize the research funding and allocation system. This model has a number of likely effects on the system, however. The competitive system (and other institutional features) in the United States promotes concentration of research activity at a relatively small number of institutions. It also rewards up-and-coming institutions that specialize in particular subfields to build excellence rather than distributing their limited investment capital across many fields. At the institutional level, the system tends to be stable, but institutions can build excellence (slowly) over time and join the ranks of research universities. Observers including those cited above have identified these features of the U.S. system as good ways to raise performance of the research system in general.

Some governments may recognize the features of the good system for allocating research funding but deviate from it in order to achieve other public purposes besides efficiency in research output and training. A common reason to deviate from the purely competitive allocation model is to promote research in specific types of institutions, specific regions of the country, or specific fields.

Applying the Model to Korea

We now consider how to apply the model to Korea. As we stated previously, this analysis applies to the entire university research funding system. Some portions of the analysis apply to BK21 as it is presently organized or might be organized in the future. Other portions apply to the rest of the university research system and its funding sources.

Research Project Funding

As stated above, a competitive award mechanism to allocate research project funding is recognized widely as the best approach to promote excellence. In Korea, one difficulty in adopting this model is the small size of the research community. Peer review is difficult in Korea because the pool of peer reviewers considerably overlaps that of potential applicants. Korea would therefore need international reviewers to supplement national review panels when evaluating individual proposals.

BK21 is not a program for funding research projects; it reserves most of its funding for graduate student fellowships. But BK21 faces a similar challenge in how to allocate its awards to the research community. BK21 addressed the challenge of Korea's relatively small size by awarding funding based on the *sa-up-dan*, a large group of researchers. The *sa-up-dan* allows clearer but less competitive judgments even when the pool of reviewers overlaps the pool of recipients.[1]

The *sa-up-dan* is not an optimal unit of support because it aggregates researchers who likely vary in quality and productivity. Therefore, the *sa-up-dan* approach does not promote full competition at the project level. There are valid reasons for this system as a transition strategy to promote improvement in graduate research training and prepare the way for a future system of competitive project funding. The concerns expressed here apply more to agencies that fund project activities rather than BK21. Nevertheless, if the research group structure were retained in future phases of Bk21 or other funding systems, we would recommend smaller groups to increase the competition both among and within universities.

All good systems must balance competition and stability in funding. Competition promotes excellence but may undermine long-term planning that benefits from stability in funding. Therefore, it is best for project funding mechanisms, including size and length of funding, to balance competition and stability and serve possibly different needs of individual research fields. In some fields it may be appropriate to award funds for up to five years, with new competition after that time. Ideally, new awards would be made every year and last for several years, giving faculty with losing proposals the opportunity to revise them and obtain funding in a subsequent year.

We recommend allocating awards based on scientific merit. To implement that recommendation, policymakers need an objective and

---

[1] The *sa-up-dan* became the unit of support in Phase II for other reasons also. Policymakers see it as encouraging academic specialization within recipient universities.

reliable method of selecting the best applications. U.S. research programs generally use a peer review panel to evaluate applications. Members of the panel excuse themselves from considering applications in which they have an interest. Because of Korea's smaller size, it may not be as feasible to use this approach. In certain fields, the number of researchers available to staff panels may be limited and may overlap significantly with the applicant pool. One option for addressing this problem may be to use international scientists as members of the selection panels.

In this analysis, we address many parts of the Korean research and education funding system. We do not suggest that BK21 should shift its focus away from graduate student support to fund project work and professors. Decisions on the target for each funding stream should be made in accordance with the principles we explain here and should be coordinated across the agencies that fund university research. Some agencies may focus on project funding including some support for professors. Other agencies or programs may concentrate on supporting graduate students, which we discuss next.

Portable Student Fellowships

There are some concerns with using project funding as the only allocation mechanism in a research funding system. Goldman and Massy (2001) demonstrate the difficulties in the United States with relying only on project funding to cover both faculty and graduate student costs. They strongly recommend that graduate student support be provided separately in the form of portable fellowships. In fact, the U.S. National Science Foundation offers generous graduate research fellowships (GRFs) to encourage the most talented undergraduates to go on to PhD programs rather than to work or to master's programs. The GRF provides a living stipend to students and pays their tuition at universities. Selection of students is based on undergraduate achievement as well as general and subject-specific standardized tests. The top students in each field receive the awards and may attend any research university PhD program that accepts the conditions of participation.

BK21 already addresses this concern by reserving most of its funding for graduate student fellowships. To shift to a portable fellowship system, the Korean government would need a national selection process that can fairly rank all applicants in order to select the best for fellowship awards. Such a system could include a weighted evaluation of standardized test scores, undergraduate transcripts, faculty recommendations, and a personal statement of research interests.

Facilities and Infrastructure Funding

Funding for projects, students, and faculty is not enough for a world-class system, however. Universities also need facilities and infrastructure. None of the funding mechanisms we have discussed so far is well suited to providing these. In the United States, financial markets allow universities to raise funds for capital investments. Governments (federal, state, local) and other research funders then reimburse an overhead percentage on each research project to allow universities to recover their capital outlay and service their debt.[2] The federal government has established elaborate rules on the costs that can be included in overhead rates (Goldman et al., 2001). The system is based on costs that universities show they are incurring, both operating and capital, for research facilities and administration. Instruction costs are excluded from overhead rates.

Korea does not now have the legal, institutional, and financial structure to support a similar system. In the 1960s, the U.S. National Science Foundation faced similar market imperfections and established a major program of infrastructure grants for a limited period of time. Once the financial markets could serve university needs, these grants were largely discontinued, although some continued to be awarded in competitions among departments and centers and were targeted to the highest-priority fields of research. Korea could adopt such grants (which might or might not be part of BK21) as a strategy to promote scientific infrastructure. In the longer term, Korea could also pursue

---

2 Most universities have access to tax-free bonds, which carry lower interest rates and thereby save money for universities and governments that reimburse overhead costs. Taxpayers subsidize the interest cost on these bonds, so the savings actually come at the expense of government tax collections. The tax-free feature is not a necessary element of the financing system. What is essential is that universities can borrow at reasonable interest rates over the life of facilities and equipment and then be reimbursed over time from overhead payments.

the market financing and overhead reimbursement approach if the necessary legal and institutional supports can be established.

Promotion of Specific Regions or Fields

Because of Korea's concern with promoting development outside the Seoul metropolitan area, it has favored universities in other regions for some portion of Phase II funding. Governments often make such deviations from pure competition to promote an objective other than efficiency in current research output and training. They can achieve many of the positive effects of competition by using competitive principles within a preference system—for example, by restricting a portion of funding to institutions in specified regions and using competitive awards within that pool. Another way is to allow all institutions to compete for the same funding pool but to give extra preference to institutions in the specified region. Similar approaches could be used for fields to which policymakers wish to give preference.

BK21 Program Management

Researchers seeking funding from an allocation system may fear that decisions are made on the basis of administrative priorities rather than scientific principles. To promote the use of scientific principles, the U.S. National Science Foundation uses limited-term rotating appointments, drawn from a pool of practicing university scientists, for a portion of its staff. This ensures that the national research program management has a continuing flow of new personnel with knowledge of the latest scientific advances and thinking. BK21 already uses a similar system to benefit from the latest thinking in the Korean research community.

Requirements for University and Department Governance

Many of the market mechanisms we recommend depend on the governance of universities and departments for their desired effects. Universities and departments must be able to reallocate resources based on the signals from the markets for research funding, student support, and infrastructure funding. If universities are rigid and unable to allocate resources efficiently, the market signals that should promote excellence will not result in changes that improve research quality and productivity. The Korean government may wish to encourage universities to adopt more flexible and responsive governance systems with these considerations in mind. By using the *sa-up-dan* to allocate awards, BK21 was designed, in part, to promote restructuring and responsiveness of university departments. As competitive pressure increases in the system in the future, BK21 and other programs can choose between direct and more-indirect mechanisms to encourage responsiveness.

Changing the Korean System

Although Korea is not presently operating in accord with our recommendations based on the model presented above, it could move toward that model in the next phase of BK21 in coordination with other research funding programs.

Several of the ideas we recommend require certain preconditions to have beneficial effects. For instance, overhead reimbursement requires a market financing arrangement that universities can access efficiently. Until such financing is widely available, Korea may wish to adopt another system, such as infrastructure grants.

Similarly, awarding large numbers of portable student fellowships will require institutions that can process and evaluate applications on the basis of merit. To make management easier and smooth the effects on universities, it might be desirable to begin by putting a small percentage of the budget into portable fellowships and gradually increase the percentage over time.

Awarding research funding through multiyear project grants may take less preparation since this system has already been used in Korea for some programs. Still, it may be desirable to shift funding toward multiyear projects gradually, to avoid causing sharp changes in support for faculty members and departments currently receiving funds.

During the transition, the Korean government may wish to provide assistance and financial incentives to universities that undertake reforms to make themselves more flexible in reallocating resources in response to market forces. Because Korea funds research through several programs and agencies, it is important to that policies be coordinated across agencies to maximize the beneficial effects.

Most likely, even with substantial political commitment, it would take a number of years and several coordinated policy changes to eventually implement all the features of the system that we describe here. Until the full set of recommendations is realized, transition arrangements and incentives will be important to promote more responsiveness and limit the effect of abrupt shocks.

Appropriate Scale and Number of Research Universities

BK21 is intended to promote the development of university research in Korea. This goal leads us to consider several questions: What are the characteristics of a research university? What is the appropriate scale of such universities? How many research universities can Korea plausibly aim to support?

We begin our discussion by referring to analyses of the U.S. system, which is widely regarded as the international model for modern research universities. Using U.S. data as a starting point, we adjust for key differences between the United States and Korea. We then consider ways that Korean policymakers can use the tools proposed in this monograph to manage such a system and make continuing adjustments as the system develops.

Analogy to the U.S. System

According to conventional definitions, research universities require substantial size, significant doctoral-level education, and a large amount of funding for research activity. The United States offers some points of comparison for Korea.

The widely used 2005 Carnegie Classifications (Carnegie Foundation, 2007a, b) consider "research universities" to be those that award at least 20 research doctorates per year. This group is divided into three categories defined by the total amount of research activity (R&D expenditures) and other variables. The top two research university groups are those with "high" and "very high" research activity; they include 199 institutions. An additional 83 universities that grant 20 or more research doctorates are identified as research universities having "low" research activity. The overall size of universities tends to vary by category. The average number of total students enrolled per university is about 25,000 in the very high research activity group, 16,000 in the high research activity group, and 10,000 in the low research activity group.

The current estimated population of Korea, 49 million, is about 16 percent of the United States population, 301 million (U.S. Census Bureau, 2006). Two considerations cause us to conclude that even with an American-style system, Korea could support a smaller than proportional (16 percent) number of research universities. First, Korean fertility is much lower than U.S. fertility. As a result, the Korean college-age population will shrink over time, likely forcing closure or consolidation of Korean universities and implying fewer graduate students to enroll and perform research.

A second consideration is the substantial fraction of U.S. science and engineering graduate students and faculty who come from overseas. In many fields, the foreign student population represents over half of the doctoral degrees awarded (Table 7.1). Goldman and Massy (2001) calculate that the proportion of enrolled foreign graduate students is even higher than proportion of doctorate degrees awarded; thus, the proportion of foreign graduate students is much greater than half in many fields. Many new faculty members are foreign citizens as well. Thus, American research universities are drawing from a worldwide talent pool. Because Korea draws primarily from a domestic talent pool, we would expect it to support fewer research universities than its proportion of the United States population suggests. Coupled with the likely decrease in the student-age population noted above, we suggest that Korea could support about half of the proportional number of research universities if it adopted an American-style funding and institutional structure. Thus Korea could support about 8 percent of the 199 research universities in the United States, or about 16 research universities.

To estimate the funding required to support research university activity, we compiled 2005 data on U.S. research expenditures grouped

Table 7.1
Research Doctorates Awarded in the United States by Broad Field of Science and Citizenship, 2005

	U.S. Citizens and Permanent Residents	Temporary Residents	Percent Temporary Residents
Engineering	2,284	3,754	62
Physical sciences	1,900	1,550	45
Geosciences	442	233	35
Math and computer sciences	1,014	1,201	54
Life sciences	6,236	2,480	28

SOURCE: Authors' tabulations from NSF (2007).
NOTE: Only science fields shown; those with unknown citizenship omitted.

by research activity level. For universities with very high research activity, the median research expenditures per institution were about $300 million per year (Table 7.2). Because price and wage levels in Korea are lower than those in the United States—the International Monetary Fund (2007) indicates that gross domestic product (GDP) per capita in Korea is 36 percent that of the United States—less money would be required to finance similar levels of activity. To be sure, though Korean GDP is lower than that in the United States, some goods used in research are internationally traded and therefore are likely to have similar prices in both countries. In addition, wages in the university sector may be somewhat closer to those in the United States than other Korean wages, but they are about half of U.S. wages in absolute terms. As a result, we estimate that Korean institutions would require about 50 percent of the funding that U.S. institutions do for similar levels of research activity.

To examine the concentration in research funding, we need to consider all universities that might receive research funding. Among the total of 2,577 U.S. four-year institutions, 144 (5.6 percent) account for 90 percent of all research expenditures; 194 (7.5 percent) account for 95 percent of all research expenditures. Research funding in the United States is thus highly concentrated.

Table 7.2
Median and Average Research Expenditures by Research Activity Level, 2005

Research Activity Level	No.	Research Expenditures ($ millions)	
		Median	Average
Very High	92	308	358
High	37	91	99
Low	83	18	30

SOURCE: Authors' tabulations from NSF (2007).

Korea appears to have a somewhat broad distribution of funds while still providing some institutions a scale of research activity comparable with that of some U.S. universities (Table 7.3). Considering that approximately half the U.S. level of funding is required to maintain a similar activity level, all Korean universities in the top ten have funding that would correspond to research universities with "high" activity; a few can support the "very high" level. In terms of concentration, the top ten universities account for only 43 percent of total funding; comparable data shows 86 percent of total funding goes to a similar fraction of U.S. research universities.[3]

Korean policy goals and operating conditions vary from those in the United States on several dimensions. Thus, these comparisons should be considered cautiously—indicating broad policy goals and directions for Korea that should be tempered by local conditions and goals. The comparisons can help Korean policymakers set broad goals for the number of research universities they intend the funding system to support, the approximate scale of the largest research universities, the average scale for large research universities, and the concentration of funding among the top universities.

---

[3]   The "similar fraction" in the United States is 10/16, representing the share that ten Korean research universities represent out of the 16 estimated number that Korea could support.

Table 7.3
Largest University Research Expenditures in Korea, 2005

Rank	Institution Name	KRW (billions)	Dollars (millions)
1	SNU	246.5	266.2
2	Yonsei University	123.0	132.8
3	KAIST	108.3	116.9
4	Hanyang University	100.0	108.0
5	Sungkyun Kwan University	86.8	93.7
6	Korea University	86.7	93.6
7	Chonnam National University	81.4	87.9
8	POSTECH	77.2	83.4
9	KyungPook National University	59.0	63.7
10	Inha University	57.5	62.1
	Total	1,026.3	1,108.4
	Total for all universities	2,375.4	2,565.4

SOURCE: MoE (2006d).
NOTE: There were 216 four-year universities in Korea in 2005.

One example of applying these guidelines relates to the concentration and distribution of funding. Our analysis of the U.S. model indicates that a more competitive research funding system in Korea may increase concentration, which often drives research quality higher. Ultimately, however, Korean policymakers have to decide if this sort of concentration compromises any other national interest in favor of more even distribution of research activity. In that case, Korean policymakers may have to accept some trade-off in overall quality in order to advance another national goal (such as even distribution).

Applying the Proposed Measurement Tools

Implementing changes in the research funding system will likely take years and the outcomes may not be apparent for decades. Setting general long-range goals, perhaps motivated by the considerations in the previous section, is an important first step. As the system evolves, however, policymakers and program managers would benefit from a set of operational metrics drawn from the indicators proposed in Chapter Five.

Chapters Five and Six presented a large selection of measurement tools, but these tools are designed specifically for assessing the performance of BK21 and of the university research system toward BK21's goals. The measurements we propose can, however, also be used to help answer some broader questions for Korean education.

The optimal answer to the policy question of number and scale of research universities and of the departments within those universities is ultimately driven by the outcomes that different configurations of the system can produce. If a smaller number of large universities can increase the volume and quality of research outcomes, then the best answer is fewer large universities. If a larger number of small research universities is needed to increase performance, then that may be the right answer. The ultimate answer may not be obvious now and will depend on forces that shape Korea's universities and economy as well as international conditions.

The BK21 program is intended to provide a dynamic push for changes that will ultimately enhance the excellence of the Korean education and research system. Program designers told us that BK21 is designed to stimulate forces that will lead to greater differentiation between universities and departments, to subsequent specialization of capabilities, and to academic excellence that researchers and graduate students will reinforce through the choices they make. The proposed indicators for tracking signaling within the system may also provide useful insights for those who are seeking to fine-tune the institutional structure of Korea's academic research.

Chapter Five presented a series of measures to assess the competitive environment within and among universities and departments (measure 2.2.2 in Table 5.2) and signaling for faculty and graduate students (measure 2.2.3). These same measures can help address scale and distribution questions. The trend in these measures will indicate, in part, whether similar departments in different universities are separating into qualitatively distinguishable groups.

For instance, measure 2.2.3.6, the histogram "fingerprint" of publication specialization, can detect the extent to which departments are differentiated from each other in terms of research specialization. If separation into groups does occur, this measure can be used as a check to determine whether the separation is due to, or a result of, purposeful specialization. Specialization might occur with different groups that are all at reasonably high levels of quality. If quality and other indicators are satisfactory for the members of different department groups, it would indicate that forcing consolidation and reducing the number of departments or groups would reduce overall quality and therefore would not be desirable. If, on the other hand, output quality seems to vary across departments with similar patterns of specialization, it argues in favor of consolidating departments or groups that are covering similar research fields in order to promote the highest quality in the field. In that case, resources could be directed to the most productive performers in each field without fear that an important subfield will be deprived of funding, because there is little specialization across universities.

Almost certainly, departments will progress at differing rates across the range of indicators. Planners should monitor change over time as well as relative and absolute comparisons. That is, a department that lags the leading institutions in Korea but still achieves measurable absolute gains in its performance may be worth supporting because it is serving an important function in the system, such as promoting regional development in a part of the country not traditionally considered to be an industrial or economic leader. Other measures, such as university-industry collaboration (3.1.1) can also serve as markers of progress in domains other than merely overall quality. To the extent that policymakers value these other domains, they may wish to support such activities through the funding system. Departments that display no growth or are losing ground against comparison departments may be candidates for consolidation or closure.

Summary

Funding for advanced research and education is a complex matter, and policy choices are likely to have significant impact on the development of the university research sector. Excellence in university research depends on the availability and quality of research projects, faculty, graduate students, other personnel, facilities, and infrastructure. Based on an analysis of the U.S. model, we make policy recommendations to enhance these required factors. Our analysis applies to the entire Korean university research funding system, not just to the BK21 program.

We recommend that the role of merit-based competition for funding be increased and that funds be awarded based on individual projects. The *sa-up-dan* is not an optimal unit for support, even for graduate fellowships, because it does not promote full competition at the project and individual level. While there are valid reasons for using this system as a transitional strategy to improving academic and research capabilities, we recommend using smaller groups or individual projects to increase competition both among and within universities. Project funding mechanisms, including size and length of funding, should be adapted to different fields of science.

Although competition is important, it is also desirable to give researchers some stability in funding so that they can plan their programs. Awarding funding based on merit yet allowing the best researchers to obtain grants of up to five years in duration is a good way to balance competition and stability. Similarly, granting portable fellowships for individuals to pursue graduate study will further increase competition and promote excellence.

To finance infrastructure and facilities, Korea may wish to promote the development of an efficient financing market where universities can borrow for construction. These loans would be repaid from overhead recovery on future projects performed in the new facilities. Until the required financial markets can operate effectively, Korea may prefer to use a competitive system of grants to spur development of university research facilities and infrastructure.

The U.S. system also offers some lessons to help more Korean universities attain research university status. The largest Korean universities currently have research expenditures on a scale similar to that of American research universities, but there is room for more Korean universities to reach this level. Given differences in the American and Korean economies, as well as in the composition of their populations, we estimate that Korea could support about 16 major research universities comparable to those in this category in the United States. Korean university research can be stimulated further through a combination of competitive awards for project funding, fellowships for graduate students to select their universities, and university access to capital to construct research facilities.

It may take a number of years to implement all these changes. Until that time, transition arrangements may be appropriate to encourage the university research system to become more responsive without producing abrupt shocks and dislocations.

CHAPTER EIGHT

Conclusions

The BK21 Phase I program coincided with a period of improvement in the quality and productivity in Korean higher education and research capabilities. Previous evaluations of the Phase I program, however, could not identify the net contributions of Phase I funding to this general trend.

In this study, we have discussed ways to estimate the net effect of Phase II. We presented a logic model of program goals and missions, including how these are affected by program inputs and in turn affect program outputs; reviewed a quantitative method for identifying the impact of the program; suggested metrics and measures needed for program evaluation; and discussed how Korea may wish to allocate funding so as to best develop its research universities. Our findings and policy recommendations are summarized as below.

Directions for a Phase II Evaluation System

In proposing an evaluation system for BK21 Phase II, we suggest three specific directions. First, the evaluation should address accountability questions, allowing an objective assessment of the extent to which BK21 is achieving its goals and identifying the program's net effect. Second, evaluators should develop a set of metrics that reflect the goals of the program and the paths that lead to achieving them. Third, evaluators should establish a database that will facilitate objective assessment of program performance and monitoring. The database should contain data on recipients and nonrecipients as well as general data on research and development, human resource development, and higher education in Korea.

Phase II Program Goals and Characteristics Identified by the Logic Model

The goals of the Phase II program are (1) developing research manpower and (2) strengthening graduate programs and research universities to be globally competitive. The Phase II program, while operating through department-level research groups, seeks improvement far beyond them, both for Korean universities generally and among individuals who make up the R&D workforce. Much of BK21 is designed to modify the behavior of young graduate students making career decisions, faculty and research workers seeking the most profitable application of their skills, and administrators of institutions.

BK21 is a narrowly targeted investment program with broad goals. For example, although it seeks to enhance Korea's capacity for R&D along many dimensions, it targets human capital development, especially at the graduate and young researcher level, rather than the infrastructure required for the conduct of research. While the latter is clearly important, it is left to future government initiatives. The principal concept behind BK21 is that targeting the crucial element of R&D manpower development will result in a large-scale shift in the research and development capacity of Korea's universities and technical institutes. The implication is that this, in turn, will lead to positive changes in the economic and social well-being of the country as a whole.

Quantitative Model and Data Requirements

We explored several quantitative models for evaluating the impacts of BK21 Phase II. After examining each, we recommended a fixed-effects estimation model. We then discussed some of the caveats for using that model and demonstrated its application with Phase I data. We also showed how the model can be adjusted to evaluate the effect of

Phase II, as well as to examine differential effects by research area, lags in treatment effects, and nonlinear treatment effects. We demonstrated how the model could be used not only to assess how BK21 affects the number of papers published by Korean researchers, but also to examine other quantitative outputs and outcomes, such as collaboration with the private sector, number of patents, or number of publications in particular subsets of journals (a way of assessing the quality of the research).

To implement the quantitative model, evaluators need to collect data from universities and departments that received funding through the program, from those that applied but did not receive awards, and from those that never applied over the periods of pre-BK21, Phase I of BK21, and Phase II of BK21. The data requirements are broader than the scope of data compiled in previous evaluations in Korea. In particular, gathering data from nonrecipients and nonapplicants would involve greater effort and cost than doing so only from those who participated in BK21.

Metrics, Measures, and Database to Assess Program Effects and to Monitor Progress

We suggested relevant metrics and measures that allow both quantitative and qualitative assessment of the program effect.

Our proposed assessment model can incorporate measures varying in importance. Put another way, it allows evaluators to identify which measures and metrics are most important to them and gives them a framework for prioritizing measures by importance and ease of data collection. We recognizes that it may be difficult to gather data from nonparticipants and suggest that case studies may be appropriate in some instances to assess the effects of a given variable. BK21 evaluators may also wish to fund doctoral research on assessing and analyzing program effects. Finally, we provide a database format that evaluators may wish to use in gathering information on measurements to choose among them.

The measurement methods we have proposed in this monograph can assess not only the progress of the BK21 program but also the health and development of the Korean university research system as a whole. These measures offer policymakers and planners ways to look at the quality and quantity of training and output, specialization and differentiation in departments, changes in the Korean university research system, and the rate of progress toward the goals of BK21.

The BK21 program is intended to provide a dynamic push for changes that will ultimately enhance the excellence of the Korean education and research system. Program designers told us that BK21 is designed to stimulate forces that will lead to greater differentiation among universities and departments, to subsequent specialization of capabilities, and to other indicators of excellence that will be reinforced through the actions of researchers and graduate students. The proposed indicators for tracking signaling within the system may also provide useful insights to those who are seeking to fine-tune the institutional structure of Korea's academic research.

Chapter Five of this study, for example, presents a series of measures to assess the competitive environment within and among universities and departments (2.2.2 in Table 5.2) and signaling for faculty and graduate students (2.2.3). The trends in these measures should indicate, in part, whether similar departments in different universities are separating into qualitatively distinguishable groups.

For instance, the histogram "fingerprint" of publication specialization for measure 2.2.3.6 can detect the extent to which departments become differentiated from each other in terms of research specialization. If separation into groups does occur, this measure can be used as a check to determine whether that separation is due to, or a result of, purposeful specialization. Specialization might occur with different groups that are all at reasonably high levels of quality. If quality and other indicators are satisfactory for the members of different department groups, it would be an indication that forcing consolidation and reducing the number of departments or groups would reduce overall quality and therefore not be desirable. If, on the other hand, output quality seems to vary across departments with similar patterns of specialization, it would be better to consolidate departments or groups that are covering similar research fields to promote higher quality. In that case, resources could be directed to the most productive performers in each field without fear that an important subfield would be deprived of funding, because there is little specialization across universities.

Almost certainly, departments will progress at differing rates across the range of indicators. Planners should monitor change over time as well as relative and absolute comparisons. For example, a department that lags the leading institutions in Korea but still achieves measurable absolute gains in its performance may be worth supporting because it is serving an important function in the system, such as regional development in a part of the country not traditionally considered to be an industrial or economic leader. Other measures, such as university-industry collaboration (3.1.1), can also serve as markers of progress in domains other than overall quality. To the extent that policymakers value these other domains, they may wish to support such activities through the funding system.

With significant additions to cover other domains, the system proposed here could also serve as the core of a larger measurement system that would offer a comprehensive way to assess the health of university teaching, research, and community linkages.

Assessing the Quality of Program Outputs and Outcomes

Quality of Research

The quality of preparation received by advanced students and the quality of the research work that they and their more senior colleagues produce is perhaps the most important metric for assessing the effect of BK21. Framing a suitable measure for research quality is especially important and challenging. In our view, the impartial perception of peers is the best indicator of quality research. Citation of foundational research work is a central focus in all fields of scientific and technical knowledge dissemination. Therefore, the measure of a research paper's quality should rest on the degree to which it is cited by other researchers.

Weighting papers by the "impact" of the journals in which they appear—that is, the average number of citations a paper in that journal receives—is a more indirect proxy than counting actual citations for each paper would be. For BK21 program evaluation, however, the value of the measure is that it provides a strong indicator of how that paper is *likely* to be received by those in its field. Assessing actual citations, while important and useful for many purposes, would entail a lag of several years, whereas the indirect measure provides a baseline as soon as the first-period data are assessed.

There are two ways to weight papers and measure their quality: within individual fields and across all fields. Again, there are two methods for weighting papers based on calculating means and standard deviations: the "bin" approach and the "smooth" approach. Chapter Five contains a detailed discussion of quality evaluation schemes.

However, a truly complete assessment of quality requires more than weighting paper citations. Surveys of research quality by peers both inside and outside of Korea would considerably amplify the value of the quantitative measures and would provide a richer source of information.

Quality of the Highly Educated Workforce

The true effect of BK21 in improving the size and quality of the pool of knowledge workers in Korea will become apparent only over time. Nevertheless, it is helpful to observe this evolution as it occurs. The measures we suggest regarding the workforce can help provide insight on this outcome.

The choice of specific measures here depends heavily on the willingness to undertake extensive data collection. Among the measures with the lowest relative costs, surveys of employers could provide successive snapshots of the size, composition, and subjective assessment of the Korean R&D workforce. Other measures are more expensive but also potentially more useful. The MoE or another appropriate body may wish to consider, for example, a longitudinal survey of those receiving advanced degrees from Korean institutions or who have obtained degrees from abroad and now are employed within Korea. This would help not only in assessing BK21 but could also have a broader policy impact beyond evaluation of just one program. Unlike an employer survey, which provides information on the demand for R&D workers, a longitudinal survey would give a more detailed view of the professional life course of individuals from the supply side.

One example of a longitudinal survey such as those the MoE may wish to consider is the biennial Survey of Doctorate Recipients that the U.S. National Science Foundation conducts of individuals who have obtained a doctoral degree in a science, engineering, or health field from a U.S. institution. The SDR follows these individuals until age 76 and includes such variables as educational history, employment status, family and citizenship status, and work-related training (National Science Foundation, 2006). Such a survey could be designed to meet the particular needs of Korea, providing one of the best ways to gain better understanding on many topics of interest to BK21's administrators and evaluators. A longitudinal survey might also include limited interviewing of various categories of employers for additional insights on the career paths of BK21 graduates. The interview component could be conducted less frequently than the longitudinal survey. It could usefully be carried out at the beginning and end of each phase of the BK21 program.

Concentration Strategy and Competition Rule

The strategy of concentration appears to be a natural option, given the limited resources of BK21 and the large-scale investment needed for a graduate school to become globally competitive. Brewer, Gates, and Goldman (2002) show that universities successfully seeking to gain prestige use the concentration strategy, whereas already prestigious universities tend to distribute resources more evenly.

Although Korean universities appear to have somewhat broad distribution of funds, some Korean institutions maintain research activity on a scale comparable to that of some U.S. universities (Table 7.3). In Korea, the top ten universities (4.6 percent of a total of 216) accounted for only 43 percent of total university research expenditures in 2005. In contrast, university research funding in the United States is highly concentrated in top research universities. The top 4.6 percent of all 2,577 four-year universities in the United States accounted for 85 percent of all university research expenditure in 2005.

Our analysis of the U.S. model indicates that a more competitive research funding system in Korea may increase funding concentration. Although concentration is often a hallmark of competition that drives research quality higher, Korean policymakers will ultimately have to decide if this sort of concentration compromises any other national interest in favor of a more even distribution of research activity. In that case, Korean policymakers might have to accept some trade-off in overall quality in order to advance another national goal (such as even distribution).

Suggestions for Long-Term Changes in the Korean Scientific Research and Education System

Outstanding research and education require an interrelated set of resources: research projects, faculty, graduate students and other personnel, facilities, and infrastructure. Based on experiences in the United States and our understanding of Korean university research sector, we make policy recommendations to enhance these required factors. The recommendations apply to the entire Korean university research funding system, not just to the BK21 program.

Balancing Competition and Stability in Funding

We recommend that Korea increase the role of merit-based competition in funding and award funds on an individual project basis. The *sa-up-dan* is not an optimal unit for support, even for graduate fellowships, because it does not promote full competition at the project and individual level. While there are valid reasons for using the *sa-up-dan* as a transitional strategy for improving academic and research capabilities, we recommend using smaller groups or individual projects to increase competition both between and within universities. Project funding mechanisms, including size and length of funding, should be adapted to different fields of science. Although competition is important to promote excellence, it is also desirable to give researchers some stability in funding so that they can plan their programs. In some fields it may be appropriate to award funds for up to five years, with new competition after that time. Ideally, new awards would be made every year and last for several years, giving faculty with losing proposals the opportunity to revise and obtain funding for them in a subsequent next year.

Portable Student Fellowships

Goldman and Massy (2001) demonstrate the difficulties in the United States with relying on project funding alone to cover both faculty and graduate student costs. They strongly recommend that graduate student support be provided separately by means of portable fellowships.

In fact, the U.S. National Science Foundation offers generous graduate research fellowships to encourage the most talented undergraduates to go to PhD programs rather than to work or to master's programs. The GRF provides a living stipend to students and pays their tuition at universities. Selection of students is on undergraduate achievement as well as general and subject-specific standardized tests. The top students in each field receive the awards and may attend any research university PhD program that accepts the conditions of participation.

BK21 already addresses this concern by reserving most of its funding for graduate student fellowships. In order to shift to a portable fellowship system in Korea, the government would need a national selection process that can fairly rank all applicants to select the best for fellowship awards. Such a system could include a weighted evaluation of standardized test scores, undergraduate transcripts, faculty recommendations, and a personal statement of research interests.

Infrastructure Funding

In the United States, financial markets allow universities to raise funds for capital investments. Governments (federal, state, local) and other funders then reimburse an overhead percentage on each research project to allow universities to recover the capital outlay and service their debt. The federal government has established elaborate rules on costs that can be included in overhead rates (Goldman et al., 2001). The system is based on costs that universities show they are incurring, both operating and capital, for research facilities and administration. Instruction costs are excluded from overhead rates.

Korea does not now have the legal, institutional, and financial structure to support a similar system. In the 1960s, the U.S. National Science Foundation faced similar market imperfections and established a major program of infrastructure grants for a limited. Once the financial markets could serve university needs, these grants were largely discontinued, although some continued to be awarded in competitions among departments and centers and were targeted to the highest-priority research fields. Korea could adopt infrastructure grants (which might or might not be part of BK21) as a strategy to promote scientific infrastructure. In the longer term, Korea could pursue the market financing and overhead reimbursement approach, if the necessary legal and institutional supports could be established.

Improving University and Department Governance

Many of the market mechanisms we recommend depend on the governance of universities and departments for their desired effects. Universities and departments must be able to reallocate resources for research funding, student support, and infrastructure funding based on signals from the markets. If universities are rigid and unable to reallocate resources efficiently, the market signals that should promote excellence will not result in changes that improve research quality and productivity. The Korean government may wish to encourage universities to adopt more flexible and responsive governance systems with these considerations in mind. By using the *sa-up-dan* to allocate awards, BK21 was designed, in part, to promote restructuring and responsiveness of university departments. As competitive pressure increases in the future, BK21 and other programs can choose between direct and more-indirect mechanisms to encourage responsiveness in the system.

Preconditions for the Proposed Changes

Several of the ideas we recommend require certain preconditions. For instance, overhead reimbursement requires efficient market financing arrangements, such as tax-free bonds, so that universities can invest in long-term infrastructure costs. Until such financing is widely available, Korea may wish to adopt another system, such as infrastructure grants. Similarly, awarding large amounts of portable student fellowships will require institutions that can process and evaluate applications on the basis of merit. To make management easier and to smooth the effects on universities, it might be desirable to begin with a small percentage of the budget in portable fellowships and gradually increase the percentage over time. Awarding research funding by multiyear project grants may take less preparation since this system is already in use in Korea for some programs. Still, it may be desirable to shift funding toward multiyear projects gradually, to avoid causing sharp changes in support for faculty members and departments currently receiving funds. During the transition, the Korean government might wish to provide assistance and financial incentives to universities that undertake reforms that make them more flexible in reallocating resources in response to market forces. Because Korea funds the system through several programs and agencies, it is important that policies be coordinated across agencies to maximize the beneficial effects on the university research system.

Most likely, even with substantial political commitment, it will take a number of years and several coordinated policy changes to eventually implement all the features of the system that we describe here. Until the full set of recommendations is realized, transition arrangements and incentives will be important to promote more responsiveness and limit the effect of abrupt shocks.

Enhancing Program Evaluation and Management Capabilities

BK21 is under the jurisdiction of MoE, which determines its core elements and operational mechanisms in consultation with the Human Resource Development Council (MoE's highest-ranking decisionmaking body). The MoE entrusts the administration of the program to the Korea Research Foundation; within the KRF, the BK21 Program Management Committee, created to manage Phase II, has day-to-day

206 Brain Korea 21 Phase II: A New Evaluation Model

responsibility for it. Members of the BK21 Program Management Committee, who include experts from universities, industry, think tanks, and government, supervise Phase II management and evaluation, assisted by full-time experts who analyze the program performance and develop new evaluation tools.

To implement the new evaluation model and policy recommendations that we have suggested, the capabilities and institutional infrastructure of the BK21 program evaluation and management body needs to be strengthened, especially in the area of data compilation and database management. As we suggested in the monograph, the data include both quantitative (e.g. statistics) and qualitative data (e.g. survey results) on recipients, nonrecipients, the university sector in general, and relevant national-level data over time.

The evaluation and management body must ensure that the data compilation activity addresses questions of public accountability, such as how well the program is progressing toward its goal of assessing the net contributions of BK21. The database will be also useful during the process of selecting awardees, and as analytical support for enforcing the concentration strategy.

Performance Evaluation Metrics Used in Previous Evaluations of Phase I

Areas of Evaluation	Performance Indicators
R&D capability	Total BK21 funding to the research group
	Number of SCI papers per unit of funding
	Number of SCI papers per faculty member
	Sum of impact factors of SCI papers by faculty
	Impact factor per faculty[a]
	Impact factor per paper
	Number of SCI papers by graduate students
	Impact factors of SCI papers by graduate students
	Comparison with the benchmark university in number of faculty, number of SCI papers, and sum of impact factors[b]
	Number of patents—domestic and international
	Number of patents per faculty
Human resource development	Number of faculty members, graduate students, postdoctoral researchers, and contract-based researchers participating in BK21
	Number of entering master's students and PhD students in the department that houses the research group
	Number of graduate students receiving a scholarship
	Number of PhDs obtained by graduate students supported by BK21
	Number of master's degrees obtained by graduate students supported by BK21
	Career choices of BK21 graduates: PhD program in Korea, PhD program abroad, postdoctoral program, faculty, research institute, industry, other
University-industry collaboration	Number of technology transfers to industry
	Amount of research funds from industry
	Number of projects from industry

Areas of Evaluation	Performance Indicators
	Cases of technical guidance provided to industry
	Cases of commercialization
	Number of start-up companies incubated
	Number of faculty members who participated in each type of industry linkage listed above
Research and education infrastructure	Teaching hours per week per faculty member participating in BK21
	Investment in research equipment, facilities, and buildings in support of the BK21 research group
	Investment in education equipment, facilities, and buildings in support of the BK21 research group
	Student-faculty ratio
Institutional reform	Improvement in undergraduate admission system
	Reduction in undergraduate enrollments
	Simplifying organizational structure of undergraduate schools and departments
	Percentage of graduate students who did undergraduate studies in other schools
	Improvement in faculty performance evaluation system
	Central management system of R&D funding
International exchanges	Number of master's and PhD students who participated in long-term overseas training
	Number of graduate students, faculty members, postdoctoral researchers, and contract-based researchers who participated in short-term overseas training
	Frequency of overseas training
	Frequency of inviting foreign scholars to the research group
	Number of foreign postdoctoral researchers hired
	Number of papers authored with foreign institutions
Other	Graduate students' satisfaction with education and research conditions

[a] *Impact factor* is defined as the number of references to an article appearing in one journal in papers published in other journals divided by the total number of articles published in the first journal. The impact factor counts citations 2–3 years after initial publication.

[b] BK21 recipient universities are supposed to find a benchmark university against which to evaluate their progress.

Interview Guides for Representatives of Participants, Policymakers, and Users Related to the University Research and Education System

We prepared interview guides for each respondent group. These guides are reproduced in the first section below. We also sent some specific questions based on the guides to respondents in advance. These specific questions are reproduced in the second section.

Interview Guides

MoE and BK-NURI

1. What is the policy intention behind "More research universities in Korea"?
   a. To promote national academic champions in Korea to be global champions or regional (Asia Pacific) champions?
      - The first phase of BK21 was designed, by inference, to take a national academic champion, Seoul National University, and create an international academic center of excellence.
      - Phase II seeks to bolster the international standing of several Korean academic institutions.
   b. To strengthen Korean graduate school system in general?
      - Level of research activities
      - Quality of research
      - Quality of graduate education

    c. To compete for, maintain, and recruit high-quality labor from all over the world by creating a global center of excellence?
- Foreign students and postdoctoral fellows are not encouraged to become BK21 recipients
- There are other challenges to overcome to compete for high-quality labor in the world
- Language barrier
- Career opportunities
- Living environments

    d. To provide opportunities for local universities to become national academic champions?
- 25 percent of the Phase II funding is allocated to universities located outside metropolitan Seoul

2. Intention of the HRD mission and goals of BK21?
    a. A greater supply of technically skilled workers by subsidizing the cost of obtaining advanced degrees?
    b. Improving quality of workforce in Korea through more education and better research experiences?
- To move the workforce up the value chain to work in more skilled and more productive tasks

    c. Promoting more locally conducted research by having more PhDs and MAs in Korea?
- For this purpose, does Korea want to retain high-quality students in Korea instead of sending them abroad?

    d. Alleviating the mismatch between the demand and supply of S&T workforce?
- Would locally trained MAs and PhDs be a better fit for jobs in industry in Korea? (70 percent of BK21 recipients go to industry after graduation)

    e. Contributing to industrial R&D through university-industry link?

SNU and Loser-Winner Universities

1. Dynamics of the program effects

a. Changes in incentives of graduate students, young researchers, and professors?
   - Lower cost of obtaining advanced degrees
   - Income stability in the transition from graduate school to permanent jobs
   - More abundant labor for laboratory activities and research
b. Changes in behavior and decisionmaking of individuals, departments, and universities?
   - Choice of graduate schools by undergraduates (signaling effects)
   - Quality of graduate students
   - Research activities
   - Teaching activities
   - Research infrastructure
   - Industry link
   - International cooperation: foreign co-authors, global networking activities
   - Changes in research funds distribution
   - Among universities
   - Among departments with universities
   - Among the faculty members within departments
   - Between members of the faculty and the students
   - Changes in institutional structure, governance, and strategies in universities
   - Changes in faculty compensation schemes and levels: rewards for productive faculty
c. Changes in outputs?
   - Production of PhDs and MAs
   - Quantity
   - Quality
   - Fitness/suitability
   - Research productivity
   - University-industry collaboration
   - Competitive environment

    d. How do these changes differ between recipients and non-recipients of BK21 funds?

    e. What obstacles did nonrecipients face?
- Motivation of professors and students
- Research performance
- Recruiting students and faculty
- Fund-raising for research
- Industry link
- International networking

    f. To be eligible to BK21 Phase II, what extra efforts did the Phase I nonrecipients make that would not have happened without BK21?

    g. Complements or substitutes?
- BK21 funding vs. other funding to universities
- Crowding-out effect?
- Research and teaching

    h. Do the dynamics of Phase I program effects predict the future program effects of Phase II?

    i. If not, how would the program effect dynamics be different for the Phase II program?

    j. What are your expectations of the BK21 Phase II outcomes?
- Desired outcome of Phase II
- Intended/unintended by-products of Phase II

    k. Suggestions for BK21 evaluation system?

    l. Suggestions for BK21 program management system?

Industry

1. From a business point of view, what changes did the BK21 Phase I program make?

    a. Research capability of universities

    b. University-industry collaboration

    c. Producing PhDs and MAs suitable for industry needs

    d. More PhDs and MAs available (cheaper to hire PhDs and MAs)

    e. Better quality PhDs and MAs available

    f. Contribution to industrial research
    g. Quantity
    h. Quality

2. Would your answers to the above question change in 2012 when the BK21 Phase II ends? If yes, how will your answers different and why?

3. What were the criteria for selecting universities to support their research and/or to have industry-university partnership?
    a. Were the same criteria applied in selecting BK21 research groups (*sa-up-dan*) to be provided with matching funds?
    b. If not, how different they were and why?

4. What are the desired benefits of the university-industry partnership?
    a. Recruiting better-quality manpower
    b. Improving corporate image
    c. Improving the mismatch in demand and supply of S&T work force: Help universities to produce better-suited manpower for the industry
    d. Complementing internal research capability of the company
    e. Enhancing applied research activities in the universities for long-term benefit to industry

5. Evaluate actual benefit from the corporate matching funds to BK21 Phase I recipient universities. If there is a gap between the desired benefit and the actual benefit, what are the drivers of the gap?

6. What are the reasons behind the declining trend in share of corporate funding in university R&D? For example, has the increasing internal R&D capability of firms reduced the usefulness of university research? Will this trend be continued?

7. From the industry point of view, are you satisfied with the goals of the BK21 program? If not, how can the goals of the BK21 be improved in the future?

8. Suggestions for BK21 evaluation system?
   a. Suggestions for BK21 program management system?

Specific Questions

BK-NURI Committee and Program Staff

1. Objectives and desired outcomes of the BK21 program: faculty members' own opinions regarding the objectives and expected outcomes of the BK21 program, independent of what has been stated in BK21 planning guides and in MoE documents.

2. Positive and negative effects of Phase I on universities: its effects on academic research; change in incentive structures for the researchers; the distribution of research funds among universities, among departments within universities, among the faculty members within departments, and between members of the faculty and the students; increase in student research capabilities; any change in application patterns to graduate schools, etc.

3. Problems with outcome evaluation and administrative system that BK21 is facing, and opinions about possible solutions.

Seoul National University (SNU)

1. Positive and negative effects of BK21 program from SNU's point of view.

2. Effects of BK21 on SNU's R&D capabilities: for instance, the before–and-after changes in the following: quantity and quality of research, ways of conducting research, incentives for the faculty, incentives for the students, research funding, the distribution of funding (among departments, within departments, among faculty members, and between faculty and students.)

3. Effects of BK21 on SNU's ability to produce capable graduates: before-and-after changes in the aptitudes of graduate students, and if so, whether the change is related to BK21 program.

4. Whether BK21 program constituted an additional contributing factor with regard to SNU's research funding: for instance, whether BK21 had a multiplicative effect on research funding by attracting even more funding from other sources or whether funding from other sources decreased because of BK21.

5. Other changes in SNU that can be attributed to BK21.

Loser-Winner Universities

1. Expected upsides and downsides of being excluded from Phase I.

2. Whether there have been differences in research output compared with the universities that participated in Phase I, and if so, how they affected the decision to participate in Phase II.

3. Effects of BK21 on the university's reputation in terms of students' decision to apply.

4. Types of policy changes tried in order to be selected for Phase II, and the actual changes that occurred as a result.

5. Changes to the university expected to be brought about by Phase II.

Industry

1. Effects of Phase I from the business point of view: whether there have been changes due to BK21 in universities' research capabilities, industry-university partnerships, and in educating graduates with skills in demand by firms.

2. How firms expect their assessments of Phase I (their response to the question 1 above) to change with the completion of Phase II in 2012.

3. The reasons behind the trend in decreasing share of universities within corporate R&D budget spent on external research contracts: for example, whether the increasing internal R&D capability of firms has reduced—in relative terms—the usefulness of universities for R&D.

4. Some believe that firms sponsor academic research mainly for recruitment and corporate image purposes, and therefore not much can be expected from academic research with corporate sponsorships. Has there been an improvement in this perception when comparing before-and-after Phase I?

5. How firms expect their assessments of (4) to change with the completion of Phase II in 2012.

6. The criteria for selecting research groups to be provided with matching funds and the expectation regarding research outcomes.

7. Evaluation of research outcomes of the projects provided with corporate matching funds from the firm's point of view.

8. The expected benefits of Phase II from the firms' point of view.

9. The "right" way of setting the objectives and the basic course for Phase II.

10. Suggestions for BK21 outcome evaluation methods in the future.

11. Whether job applicants with BK 21 experience are favored for hiring.

Selection Criteria for Applied Science Research Groups: Phase II

Areas	Weighting Scheme	Indicators
Education (25%)	Curriculum (5%)	Excellence of curriculum contents and plan
	Employment of graduates (8%)	Percentage of graduates hired, excellence of employment support plan and goals
	Publications and presentations by graduate students (7%)	Number of papers per student published in SCIE journals and other journals registered at KRF in past three years, number of presentations per students in past three years, excellence of plans to support these activities
	Globalization of graduate education (5%)	Share of lectures in English only, percentage of foreign faculty, percentage of foreign students
R&D (25%)	Government-funded R&D (10%)	Per-faculty R&D funding sponsored by the government in past three years, excellence of plan to link BK21 fund and other government programs
	Faculty research performance (15%)	Per-faculty SCI papers published in past three years and their impact factors (ISI, 2004), plans for per-faculty paper publications and impact factors, per faculty patents in past three years and future plan for them
Link to Industry (25%)	Industry R&D projects (15%)	Per-faculty funding and projects from industry in past three years and future plan, excellence of linkage between the industry projects and research and education in the department

Areas	Weighting Scheme	Indicators
	Technology transfer (5%)	Per-faculty technology transfer cases in past three years, commercialization performance and future plan for it
	Exchanges with Industry (2%)	Exchanges of human resource and materials with industry in past three years and future plan for them
	Supporting systems and plan for university-industry collaboration (3%)	Specialized staff for university-industry collaboration and plan for hiring them, support systems for patenting and other activities to commercialize research results
University Reform and Specialization (25%)	Investment in human resources (3%)	Ratio of faculty to graduate students, ratio of faculty to undergraduate students, plan for improving student-faculty ratio
	Investment in physical infrastructure (4%)	Ratio of matching funds from the university's own investment to the BK21 funding, plan for managing the matching fund
	Specialization to become a research university (5%)	Ratio of full-time professors, institutional reorganization at university level, ratios of graduate students to undergraduates
	Institutional reforms to be a research university (3%)	Centralized system of research fund management, performance-based faculty evaluation system, plans for improving these systems
	Research Group: Goals and visions (3%)	Emphasis on human resource production and excellence of the goal
	Research Group: Structure (3%)	Linkage between the research group and the department, influence of the research group leader on the department's decisionmaking, institutional reorganization at department level
	Research Group: Competition (3%)	Plans to promote competition among faculty members in the department. Plans to promote competition among graduate students in the department
	Research Group: Evaluation Plan (2%)	Plan for self-evaluations and evaluations by outsiders

SOURCE: MoE (2006a), pp.140–141.

Table with Lagged Outcomes

Table D.1
Testing for Common Trends in Pre-BK21 Phase II Data:
1990–2005 (winners vs. losers vs. nonapplicants)

	Science & Technology Publications (1)	Log of S&T Publications (2)
Pre–BK21		
Winner × year 1991	6.87*	0.19
	(3.06)	(0.21)
Loser × year 1991	−4.34*	−0.25
	(2.18)	(0.26)
Winner × year 1992	9.55**	0.28
	(3.29)	(0.21)
Loser × year 1992	−0.82	0.00
	(2.64)	(0.29)
Winner × year 1993	16.17**	0.16
	(5.81)	(0.28)
Loser × year 1993	−1.96	−0.24
	(3.42)	(0.30)
Winner × year 1994	14.75**	0.01
	(5.39)	(0.27)
Loser × year 1994	5.34	0.16
	(3.50)	(0.31)
Winner × year 1995	29.66**	−0.09
	(8.79)	(0.28)
Loser × year 1995	14.08*	0.16
	(6.18)	(0.32)
Winner × year 1996	36.67**	0.07
	(10.28)	(0.28)
Loser × year 1996	14.82*	0.20
	(6.87)	(0.31)

Table D.1—continued

	Science & Technology Publications (1)	Log of S&T Publications (2)
Winner × year 1997	51.96** (13.53)	0.08 (0.28)
Loser × year 1997	25.97** (9.27)	0.32 (0.32)
Winner × year 1998	55.77** (15.83)	−0.03 (0.31)
Loser × year 1998	32.18** (10.97)	0.35 (0.35)
BK21 Phase I		
Winner × year 1999	63.38** (18.11)	0.01 (0.31)
Loser × year 1999	35.20** (13.02)	0.36 (0.36)
Winner × year 2000	78.90** (20.33)	0.25 (0.30)
Loser × year 2000	37.14** (12.81)	0.50 (0.35)
Winner × year 2001	96.01** (23.73)	0.27 (0.31)
Loser × year 2001	53.18** (16.24)	0.52 (0.36)
Winner × year 2002	103.21** (26.71)	0.23 (0.31)
Loser × year 2002	61.29** (17.41)	0.67+ (0.36)
Winner × year 2003	114.26** (28.76)	0.14 (0.31)
Loser × year 2003	56.26** (18.97)	0.41 (0.38)
Winner × year 2004	130.18** (33.34)	−0.01 (0.31)
Loser × year 2004	66.39** (21.88)	0.30 (0.38)
Winner × year 2005	158.11** (38.54)	0.22 (0.31)
Loser × year 2005	89.38** (28.13)	0.57 (0.38)
Selected for BK21 Phase I	25.75** (5.38)	1.31** (0.31)
Applied but not selected	14.31* (7.13)	0.61 (0.38)
Observations	2,990	2,504

OLS regressions; standard errors clustered at the research group level. * $p<0.05$; ** $p<0.01$. Standard errors are in parentheses. Also included (but not reported) are a full set of year dummies and a constant term.

Research Data Series

On the following pages, we present, in tabular form, the research data series covering university and academic department activities. See Chapter Six for a full explanation of the database worksheet.

Data Series	Description	Time	Type	Level	Used in Measures	Source	Notes
R-1	Laboratory, special equipment funding, and in-kind support from government entitlement sources, by department	Biennial	R	Department	2.2.1.2		
R-2	Laboratory, special equipment funding, and in-kind support from government competitive sources, by department	Biennial	R	Department	2.2.1.2; 2.2.2.5a; 2.2.2.5b		
R-3	Laboratory, special equipment funding, and in-kind support from university central resources, by department	Biennial	R	Department	2.2.1.2		
R-4	Laboratory, special equipment funding, and in-kind support from private foundation sources, by department	Biennial	R	Department	2.2.1.2; 2.2.2.5a; 2.2.2.5b		
R-5	Laboratory, special equipment funding, and in-kind support from corporate sources, by department	Biennial	R	Department	2.2.1.2; 2.2.2.5a; 2.2.2.5b		
R-6	Laboratory, special equipment funding, and in-kind support from direct earnings from licenses and other intellectual property payments, by department	Biennial	R	Department	2.2.1.2		
R-7	Laboratory, special equipment funding, and in-kind support from government entitlement sources, by department	Biennial	N	Department	2.2.1.2		
R-8	Laboratory, special equipment funding, and in-kind support from government competitive sources, by department	Biennial	N	Department	2.2.1.2; 2.2.2.5a; 2.2.2.5b		
R-9	Laboratory, special equipment funding, and in-kind support from university central resources, by department	Biennial	N	Department	2.2.1.2		
R-10	Laboratory, special equipment funding, and in-kind support from private foundation sources, by department	Biennial	N	Department	2.2.1.2; 2.2.2.5a; 2.2.2.5b		

Data Series	Description	Time	Type	Level	Used in Measures	Source	Notes
R-11	Laboratory, special equipment funding, and in-kind support from corporate sources, by department	Biennial	N	Department	2.2.1.2; 2.2.2.5a; 2.2.2.5b		
R-12	Laboratory, special equipment funding, and in-kind support from direct earnings from licenses and other intellectual property payments, by department	Biennial	N	Department	2.2.1.2		
R-13	Research project funding from government entitlement sources, by department	Biennial	R	Department	2.2.1.4; 2.2.2.1; 2.2.2.3		
R-14	Research project funding from government competitive sources, by department	Biennial	R	Department	2.2.1.4; 2.2.2.5a; 2.2.2.5b; 2.2.2.1; 2.2.2.3		
R-15	Research project funding from university central resources, by department	Biennial	R	Department	2.2.1.4; 2.2.2.1; 2.2.2.3		
R-16	Research project funding from private foundation sources, by department	Biennial	R	Department	2.2.1.4; 2.2.2.5a; 2.2.2.5b; 2.2.2.1; 2.2.2.3		
R-17	Research project funding from corporate sources, by department	Biennial	R	Department	2.2.1.4; 2.2.2.5a; 2.2.2.5b; 2.2.2.1; 2.2.2.3		
R-18	Research project funding from direct earnings from licenses and other intellectual property payments, by department	Biennial	R	Department	2.2.1.4; 2.2.2.1; 2.2.2.3		

Data Series	Description	Time	Type	Level	Used in Measures	Source	Notes
R-19	Research project funding from government entitlement sources, by department	Biennial	N	Department	2.2.1.4; 2.2.2.1; 2.2.2.3		
R-20	Research project funding from government competitive sources, by department	Biennial	N	Department	2.2.1.4; 2.2.2.5a; 2.2.2.5b; 2.2.2.1; 2.2.2.3		
R-21	Research project funding from university central resources, by department	Biennial	N	Department	2.2.1.4; 2.2.2.1; 2.2.2.3		
R-22	Research project funding from private foundation sources, by department	Biennial	N	Department	2.2.1.4; 2.2.2.5a; 2.2.2.5b; 2.2.2.1; 2.2.2.3		
R-23	Research project funding from corporate sources, by department	Biennial	N	Department	2.2.1.4; 2.2.2.5a; 2.2.2.5b; 2.2.2.1; 2.2.2.3		
R-24	Research project funding from direct earnings from licenses and other intellectual property payments, by department	Biennial	N	Department	2.2.1.4; 2.2.2.1; 2.2.2.3		
R-25	Register of funded research projects by principal investigator(s) and co-investigator(s), by department	Annual	R	Department	2.2.2.1; 2.2.2.3		
R-26	Register of funded research projects, by principal investigator(s) and co-investigator(s), by department	Annual	N	Department	2.2.2.1; 2.2.2.3		

Data Series	Description	Time	Type	Level	Used in Measures	Source	Notes
R-27	MS- and PhD-level research workers in Korean government institutions	Annual	—	National	1.2.2.4a; 1.2.2.4b; 1.2.2.1a; 1.2.2.2; 1.2.2.1c		Including government research laboratories, testing facilities, regulatory agencies, nuclear facilities, etc.
R-28	MS- and PhD-level research workers in Korea-based nongovernment organizations	Annual	—	International	1.2.2.4a; 1.2.2.4b; 1.2.2.1a; 1.2.2.2; 1.2.2.1c		Including NGO and international organization research laboratories, testing facilities, monitoring facilities, etc.
R-29	MS- and PhD-level research workers in non-Korean government institutions who hold Korean passports	Annual	—	International	1.2.2.4b		
R-30	MS- and PhD-level research workers in nongovernment and international organizations outside Korea who hold Korean passports	Biennial	—	National	1.2.2.4b		
R-31	Register of published papers, by author and co-author, by department	Annual	R	Department	2.2.2.2a; 2.2.2.2b; 2.2.2.4a; 2.2.2.4b; 2.3.1.1a; 2.3.1.1b; 2.3.1.2a; 2.3.1.2b; 2.3.1.3a; 2.3.1.3b; 1.2.2.1a; 1.2.2.1bi; 1.2.2.1b(ii); 1.2.2.1c; 2.2.3.6	May be derived from data bases associated with ISI	

Data Series	Description	Time	Type	Level	Used in Measures	Source	Notes
R-32	Register of published papers, by author and co-author, by department	Annual	N	Department	2.2.2.2a; 2.2.2.2b; 2.2.2.4a; 2.2.2.4b; 2.3.1.1a; 2.3.1.1b; 2.3.1.2a; 2.3.1.2b; 2.3.1.3a; 2.3.1.3b; 1.2.2.1a; 1.2.2.1b(i); 1.2.2.1b(ii); 1.2.2.1c; 2.2.3.6	May be derived from data bases associated with ISI	
R-33	Register of published papers with non-Korean co-authors	Annual		Department	2.2.2.2a; 2.2.2.2b	May be derived from data bases associated with ISI	
R-34	Register of impact factors for scholarly journals, by journal	Annual		International	2.3.1.1b; 2.3.1.2a; 2.3.1.2b; 1.2.2.1a; 1.2.2.1c; 2.2.2.2b; 2.2.2.4b	May be derived from data bases associated with ISI	
R-35	Register of highly cited papers, by field	Annual		International	2.3.1.3a; 2.3.1.3b; 1.2.2.1b(i); 1.2.2.1b(ii)	May be derived from data bases associated with ISI	
R-36	Survey of (Korean) expert opinion assessing quality of research by academic departments	Biennial		Department	1.2.2.3a; 2.3.1.4a; 2.3.1.5; 1.2.1.1b(ii)	Two survey instruments would be prepared with one circulated to (1) individual Korean researchers working in the appropriate field as well as to leading scientists and researchers with national prestige, and the other to (2) a small sample of non-Korean leading field specialists and others familiar with the Korean academy. The surveys would seek ratings of departments on the	

Data Series	Description	Time	Type	Level	Used in Measures	Source	Notes
							quality of the research staff, contribution to the field, subjective judgment of international standing, preparation of researchers, contributions to national interests and general scientific and technology development in Korea. Individuals may also be asked what they find attractive about departments as a way to gain insight into the strength and nature of signals being developed and perceived
R-37	Survey of (non-Korean) expert opinion assessing quality of research by academic departments	Biennial		Department	1.2.2.3b; 2.3.1.4b; 2.3.1.5; 1.2.1.1b(ii)		
R-38	Interviews with present employers of graduates being tracked in longitudinal survey	Biennial		National	1.3.1.1c; 2.3.1.5; 1.2.1.1b(ii)		
R-39	Delphi-type survey among industry R&D directors	Triennial		Industry sector	3.3.1.6	Delphi surveys are used to canvass subjective opinion and determine consensus beliefs on trends. The Delphi would ask questions about present circumstances and directions of perceived change in areas such as: university-industry linkages; ability of Korea to create new-in-world innovations in various areas; adequacy of training and orientation toward industry needs; differentiation and specialization among academic research departments; legal and institutional barriers to flow of information between industry and university research, etc. The Delphi becomes meaningful when observed over time after several iterations.	

Education Data Series

On the following pages, we present, in tabular form, the data series covering the educational activities of universities and departments. See Chapter Six for a full explanation of the database worksheet.

Data Series	Description	Time	Type	Level	Used in Measures	Source	Notes
E-1	Total graduates from Korean BA, BS or equivalent programs	Annual	—	University	2.1.1.1		
E-2	Graduate students enrolled in Korean departments	Annual	R	Department	1.1.1.1; 2.1.1.1; 2.1.1.2; 2.2.3.1; 2.2.3.5		
E-3	Graduate student applicants to Korean departments	Annual	R	Department	2.2.3.1		
E-4	Graduate students enrolled in Korean departments	Annual	N	Department	1.1.1.1; 2.1.1.1; 2.1.1.2; 2.2.3.1; 2.2.3.5		
E-5	Graduate student applicants to Korean departments	Annual	N	Department	2.2.3.1		
E-6	Graduate students enrolled in foreign departments	Annual	—	University	1.1.1.2; 2.1.1.1; 2.1.1.2	May be available from undergraduate institutions, selective service rolls	Potentially sensitive information may be collected in aggregate from agencies holding raw data
E-7	Graduate students from foreign universities enrolled in Korean departments	Annual	R	Department	{?}		
E-8	Graduate students from foreign universities enrolled in Korean departments	Annual	N	Department	2.3.1.7a; 2.3.1.7b		
E-9	MS- and PhD-level non-faculty researchers in Korean departments	Annual	R	Department	1.1.1.3		Graduates of Korean or foreign universities hired to work as research assistants not enrolled as graduate students
E-10	MS- and PhD-level non-faculty researchers in Korean departments	Annual	N	Department	1.1.1.3		Graduates of Korean or foreign universities hired to work as research assistants not enrolled as graduate students

Data Series	Description	Time	Type	Level	Used in Measures	Source	Notes
E-11	MS- and PhD-level non-faculty researchers in foreign departments	Annual	—	University	1.1.1.4	May be available from undergraduate institutions, selective service rolls	
E-12	New MS- and PhD-level hires in universities, Korea	Annual	R	Department	1.2.1.1a; 1.2.1.1b(i); 1.2.1.3; 2.2.3.3; 1.2.1.1b(ii); 2.2.3.2	May be obtained from university, department and faculty Web pages	(1) from BK21 recipient department to BK21 recipient department; (2) from BK21 recipient department to non-BK21 recipient department; (3) from non-BK21 recipient department to BK21 recipient department; (4) from non-BK21 recipient department to non-BK21 recipient department
E-13	New MS- and PhD-level hires in universities, Korea	Annual	N	Department	1.2.1.1a; 1.2.1.1b(i); 1.2.1.3; 2.2.3.4; 1.2.1.1b(ii); 2.2.3.2	May be obtained from university, department and faculty Web pages	(1) from BK21 recipient department to BK21 recipient department; (2) from BK21 recipient department to non-BK21 recipient department; (3) from non-BK21 recipient department to BK21 recipient department; (4) from non-BK21 recipient department to non-BK21 recipient department
E-14	New MS- and PhD-level hires, other professional	Annual	—	National	1.2.1.3	May be obtained by subtracting (E-5 + I-1+ I-2 + E-8) from E-7, by field, if not available from direct sources	
E-15	New MS- and PhD-level hires in universities, abroad	Annual	—	International	1.2.1.3; 1.2.1.4a; 1.2.1.4b		
E-16	MS- and PhD-level transfer hires between universities, Korea	Annual	R	Department	2.2.3.2; 2.2.3.3; 2.2.3.4	Simple tally can be obtained by observing faculty size by department and subtracting new PhD hires. More detailed information on original and	To the extent possible, gain information on the departments of origin and of destination: (1) from BK21 recipient department to BK21 recipient department; (2) from

Data Series	Description	Time	Type	Level	Used in Measures	Source	Notes
						destination department for faculty transfers may be obtained from university, department and faculty Web pages	BK21 recipient department to non-BK21 recipient department; (3) from non-BK21 recipient department to BK21 recipient department; (4) from non-BK21 recipient department to non-BK21 recipient department
E-17	MS- and PhD-level transfer hires between universities, Korea	Annual	N	Department	2.2.3.2; 2.2.3.3; 2.2.3.4	Simple tally can be obtained by observing faculty size by department and subtracting new PhD hires. More detailed information on original and destination department for faculty transfers may be obtained from university, department and faculty Web pages	To the extent possible, gain information on the departments of origin and of destination: (1) from BK21 recipient department to BK21 recipient department; (2) from BK21 recipient department to non-BK21 recipient department; (3) from non-BK21 recipient department to BK21 recipient department; (4) from non-BK21 recipient department to non-BK21 recipient department
E-18	MS- and PhD-level faculty in universities, Korea	Annual	R	Department	1.2.2.4a; 1.2.2.4b; 1.2.2.1a; 1.2.2.2; 1.2.2.1c; 2.3.1.6	May be obtained from university, department and faculty Web pages	
E-19	MS- and PhD-level faculty in universities, Korea	Annual	N	Department	1.2.2.4a; 1.2.2.4b; 1.2.2.1a; 1.2.2.2; 1.2.2.1c; 2.3.1.6	May be obtained from university, department and faculty Web pages	
E-20	MS- and PhD-level faculty in foreign universities holding Korean passports	Annual	—	National	1.2.2.4b		

Data Series	Description	Time	Type	Level	Used in Measures	Source	Notes
E-21	Total MS and PhD production	Annual	—	Department	1.2.1.3; 3.2.2.12		By field
E-22	THES or ARWU world university rankings	Annual	—	International	1.2.1.1b(i); 1.2.1.4b; 3.2.2.12; 2.3.1.7a; 2.3.1.7b		
E-23	Library funding from government entitlement sources, by university	Biennial	—	University	2.2.1.1		
E-24	Library funding from government competitive sources, by university	Biennial	—	University	2.2.1.1		
E-25	Library funding from university central resources, by university	Biennial	—	University	2.2.1.1		
E-26	Library funding from private foundation sources, by university	Biennial	—	University	2.2.1.1		
E-27	Library funding from corporate sources, by university	Biennial	—	University	2.2.1.1		
E-28	Library funding from direct earnings from licenses and other intellectual property payments, by university	Biennial	—	University	2.2.1.1		
E-29	General facilities funding from government entitlement sources, by university	Biennial	—	University	2.2.1.3		
E-30	General facilities funding from government competitive sources, by university	Biennial	—	University	2.2.1.3		
E-31	General facilities funding from university central resources, by university	Biennial	—	University	2.2.1.3		
E-32	General facilities funding from private foundation sources, by university	Biennial	—	University	2.2.1.3		

Data Series	Description	Time	Type	Level	Used in Measures	Source	Notes
E-33	General facilities funding from corporate sources, by university	Biennial	—	University	2.2.1.3		
E-34	General facilities funding from direct earnings from licenses and other intellectual property payments, by university	Biennial	—	University	2.2.1.3		
E-35	GPS location of Korean university department facilities	One-time	—	Department	3.2.2.3; 3.2.2.4-5; 3.2.2.6-7; 3.2.2.8-9; 3.2.2.11		
E-36	Register of lectures, seminars, performances, extension and special courses, and permanent programs originating from, or in cooperation with the university designed for the benefit of non-university communities	Annual	R	University	3.2.2.10; 3.2.2.11	Register may be derived from university Web sites and calendars, department Web sites and calendars, community Web sites and calendars, and cultural Web sites and calendars	
E-37	Register of lectures, seminars, performances, extension and special courses, and permanent programs originating from, or in cooperation with the university designed for the benefit of non-university communities	Annual	N	University	3.2.2.10; 3.2.2.11	Register may be derived from university Web sites and calendars, department Web sites and calendars, community Web sites and calendars, and cultural Web sites and calendars	
E-38	Longitudinal survey of Korean holders of advanced degrees	Biennial	—	National	1.3.1.1b	Survey would track the professional life course of individual PhD (or PhD and Masters) recipients. Details on the equivalent U.S. longitudinal survey may be found at: http://www.nsf.gov/statistics/srvydoctoratework/	

Data Series	Description	Time	Type	Level	Used in Measures	Source	Notes
E-39	Interviews with present employers of graduates being tracked in longitudinal survey	Biennial	—	National	1.3.1.1c; 2.3.1.5; 1.2.1.1b(ii)		
E-40	External review of PhD dissertations	4-year rotation through departments	R	Department	2.3.1.5; 1.2.1.1b(ii)	External reviewers would be engaged to provide assessment of the quality of selected PhD dissertations.	This is the most direct indicator of quality and change in quality for a graduate education program. Due to the nature of graduate level studies, it is not practical to apply a common test instrument to PhD graduates in the manner now beginning to be pursued in the undergraduate setting.
E-41	External review of PhD dissertations	4-year rotation through departments	R	Department	2.3.1.5; 1.2.1.1b(ii)	External reviewers would be engaged to provide assessment of the quality of selected PhD dissertations.	This is the most direct indicator of quality and change in quality for a graduate education program. Due to the nature of graduate level studies, it is not practical to apply a common test instrument to PhD graduates in the manner now beginning to be pursued in the undergraduate setting.

Industry Data Series

On the following pages, we present, in tabular form, the data series covering innovation and R&D within industries as well as industry structure and interactions with academic researchers. See Chapter Six for a full explanation of the database worksheet.

Data Series	Description	Time	Type	Level	Used in Measures	Source	Notes
I-1	New MS- and PhD-level hires in industry, Korea	Annual	—	Industry sector	1.2.1.2; 1.2.1.3		
I-2	New MS- and PhD-level hires in industry, abroad	Annual	—	International	1.2.1.3; 1.2.1.5		
I-3	Formal cooperative contracts between faculty, departments and industrial firms	Annual	R	Department	3.1.1.1; 3.2.2.1; 3.2.1.3a; 3.2.1.3b; 3.2.2.3; 3.2.2.4-5; 3.2.2.6-7; 3.2.2.8-9; 3.2.1.6		
I-4	Formal cooperative contracts between faculty, departments and industrial firms	Annual	N	Department	3.1.1.1; 3.2.2.1; 3.2.1.3a; 3.2.1.3b; 3.2.2.3; 3.2.2.4-5; 3.2.2.6-7; 3.2.2.8-9; 3.2.1.6		
I-5	Value of formal cooperative contracts between faculty, departments and industrial firms	Annual	R	Department	3.1.1.2; 3.2.2.2; 3.2.2.4-5; 3.2.2.6-7; 3.2.2.8-9; 3.2.1.6		
I-6	Value of formal cooperative contracts between faculty, departments and industrial firms	Annual	N	Department	3.1.1.2; 3.2.2.2; 3.2.2.4-5; 3.2.2.6-7; 3.2.2.8-9; 3.2.1.6		

Data Series	Description	Time	Type	Level	Used in Measures	Source	Notes
I-7	Number of technological product/process innovations introduced during year	Annual	—	Industry sector	3.3.1.3; 3.2.1.3a	These data would need to be obtained from other agencies of the Korean government who routinely make this assessment	Technology product and product innovation as defined in the Oslo Manual (OECD)
I-8	Value of technological product/process innovations introduced during year	Annual	—	Industry sector	3.3.1.4; 3.3.1.5; 3.2.1.3b	These data would need to be obtained from other agencies of the Korean government who routinely make this assessment	Technology product and product innovation as defined in the Oslo Manual (OECD)
I-9	U.S., EU, and Japan patents granted to Korean firms	Annual	—	Industry sector	3.3.1.1		
I-10	Patents granted to Korean firms	Annual	—	Industry sector	3.3.1.2		
I-11	Total output from industrial sectors	Annual	—	Industry sector	3.3.1.5		
I-12	MS- and PhD-level research workers in Korean industry	Annual	—	National	1.2.2.4a; 1.2.2.4b; 1.2.2.1a; 1.2.2.2; 1.2.2.1c		
I-13	MS- and PhD-level research workers in foreign industry holding Korean passports	Annual	—	International	1.2.2.4b		
I-14	U.S., EU, and Japan patents granted to Korean university researchers, by investigator, by department	Annual	N	Department	3.2.1.1a; 3.2.1.1b		

Data Series	Description	Time	Type	Level	Used in Measures	Source	Notes
I-15	Patents granted to Korean university researchers, by investigator, by department	Annual	N	Department	3.2.1.1a; 3.2.1.1b		
I-16	U.S., EU, and Japan patents granted to Korean university researchers, by investigator, by department	Annual	R	Department	3.2.1.1a; 3.2.1.1b		
I-17	Patents granted to Korean university researchers, by investigator, by department	Annual	R	Department	3.2.1.1a; 3.2.1.1b		
I-18	GPS location of Korean industrial facilities	One-time	—	Firm			
I-19	Value (KRW) of license fees and other intellectual property payments, by department	Annual	R	Department	3.2.1.2		
I-20	Value (KRW) of license fees and other intellectual property payments, by department	Annual	N	Department	3.2.1.2		
I-21	Firm size, industrial sector	One-time with biennial check	—	Firm; industry sector	3.2.1.6		Obtainable from existing business directories
I-22	Register of nonfinancial contacts with business and industry including sabbatical exchanges, guest lecture exchanges, internship exchanges, seminars on specific industry-department collaborations	Annual	R	Department	3.2.1.5		Register may be derived from university Web sites and calendars, department Web sites and calendars, firm Web sites and calendars, and business and industrial association Web sites and calendars
I-23	Register of nonfinancial contacts with business and industry including: sabbatical exchanges, guest lecture exchanges, internship exchanges, seminars on specific industry-department collaborations	Annual	N	Department	3.2.1.5		Register may be derived from university Web sites and calendars, department Web sites and calendars, firm Web sites and calendars, and business and industrial association Web sites and calendars

Data Series	Description	Time	Type	Level	Used in Measures	Source and Notes
I-24	Survey of industry expert opinion assessing quality of preparation, training and research input by academic departments among top 20 Korean universities	Biennial	—	National	1.3.1.1a; 2.3.1.5; 1.2.1.1b(ii)	Survey instrument would be prepared and circulated to research and technology directors of Korean firms in all sectors. The surveys would seek ratings of departments on the quality of the research staff, contribution to the field, subjective judgment of contribution to Korean industry, preparation of researchers, and contributions to national interests and general scientific and technology development in Korea. Individuals may also be asked what they find attractive about departments and relative strengths among departments as a way to gain insight into the strength and nature of signals being developed and perceived.
I-25	Interviews with present employers of graduates being tracked in longitudinal survey	Biennial	—	National	1.3.1.1c; 2.3.1.5; 1.2.1.1b(ii)	

General Data Series

On the following page, we present, in tabular form, the general data series, including data on the Korean economy, geographical information, and other information necessary for some candidate measures. See Chapter Six for a full explanation of the database worksheet.

Data Series	Description	Time	Type	Level	Used in Measures	Source	Notes
G-1	Labor productivity in Korea	Annual	—	National	3.3.2.1		
G-2	Industrial output, by sector	Annual	—	Industry sector	3.2.1.4		
G-3	GPS location of Korean communities	One-time	—	National			

Bibliography

Accelerating Innovation Foundation Conference presentations, Washington, D.C.: The National Academies, October 2005. As of December 12, 2007: http://www.innovationconf.org/2005/presentations.asp

Angrist, Joshua D., and Alan B. Krueger, "Empirical Strategies in Labor Economics," chapter 23 in O. Ashenfelter and D. Card, eds., *The Handbook of Labor Economics*, Vol. III, Elsevier-North Holland, 1999.

ARWU—*See* Institute of Higher Education, Shanghai Jiao Tong University.

Bloom, Howard, James Kemple, Beth Gamse, and Robin Jacob, "Using Regression Discontinuity Analysis to Measure the Impacts of Reading First," conference paper from American Educational Research Association, 2005. As of February 12, 2007: http://www.columbia.edu/cu/ssw/faculty/famdem/bloomdoc.pdf

Brewer, Dominic J., Susan M. Gates, and Charles A. Goldman, *In Pursuit of Prestige: Strategy and Competition in U.S. Higher Education*, New Brunswick, N.J.: Transaction Press, 2002.

Carnegie Foundation for the Advancement of Teaching, *2005 Carnegie Classifications, Basic Classification Tables*, 2007a. As of June 24, 2007: http://www.carnegiefoundation.org/classifications/index.asp?key=805

————, *2005 Carnegie Classifications, Basic Classification Technical Details*, 2007b. As of June 24, 2007: http://www.carnegiefoundation.org/classifications/index.asp?key=798

Chang, Hong-Keun, and Jae-Sik Chun, *Investigating Career Paths of Graduate Students Supported by the BK21 Program*, Korea Research Institute for Vocational Education and Training (KRIVET), 2005.

Chang, Soo-Young, "Strengthening University Research Capabilities," Conference for OECD Review on Higher Education Issues in Korea, Korea Education Development Institute, RM-2005-8, 2005.

David, Paul A., Bronwyn H. Hall, and Andrew A. Toole, "Is Public R&D a Complement or Substitute for Private R&D? A Review of the Econometric Evidence," *Research Policy,* Vol. 29, 2000, pp. 497–529.

Goldman, Charles, and William F. Massy, *The PhD Factory: Training and Employment of Science and Engineering Doctorates in the United States,* Bolton, Mass.: Anker Publishing Company, Inc., 2001.

Goldman, Charles A., Traci Williams, David Adamson, and Kathy Rosenblatt, *Paying for University Research Facilities and Administration,* Santa Monica, Calif.: RAND Corporation, MR-1135-1-OSTP, 2000. As of July 13, 2007: http://www.rand.org/pubs/monograph_reports/MR1135-1/

Green, D., "Analysis of panel data," mimeo, Yale University Political Science department, 2005. As of March 27, 2007: http://research.yale.edu/vote/pl504/Lecture on panel data 2005.doc

Guarino, Cassandra, Greg Ridgeway, Marc Chun, and Richard Buddin, "Latent Variable Analysis: A New Approach to University Ranking," *Higher Education in Europe,* Vol. 30, No. 2, July 2005, pp. 147–165.

Heckman, James J., "The Common Structure of Statistical Models of Truncation, Sample Selection, and Limited Dependent Variables and a Simple Estimator for Such Models," *The Annals of Economics and Social Measurement,* Vol. 5, 1976, pp. 475–492.

Herald Economic Daily, July 19th, 2007.

Institute of Higher Education, Shanghai Jiao Tong University, *Academic Ranking of World Universities–2006.* As of January 5, 2008: http://ed.sjtu.edu.cn/rank/2006/ranking2006.htm

International Monetary Fund, *World Economic Outlook (from EconStats),* 2007. As of June 24, 2007: http://www.econstats.com/weo/V015.htm

ISI Web of Knowledge [v.3.0]. As of July 9, 2007: http://portal.isiknowledge.com/

Johnston, Jack, and John DiNardo, *Econometric Methods,* 4th ed., New York: McGraw-Hill, 1997.

Kaplan, Robert S., and David P. Norton, "The Balanced Scorecard: Measures That Drive Performance," *Harvard Business Review,* January–February 1992, pp. 71–80.

———, *Balanced Scorecard: Translating Strategy into Action,* Cambridge, Mass.: Harvard Business School Press, 1996.

Kennedy, Peter, *A Guide to Econometrics,* 5th ed., Cambridge,Mass.: MIT Press, 2003.

Kim, Bok-Ki, et al., *Policy Study for Phase II BK21 Program Development,* Korea Research Foundation, 2005.

Kim, Byung-Joo, et al., *Study on BK21 Program Performance Evaluation,* Korea Research Foundation, March 2005.

Korea Institute of Science and Technology Evaluation and Planning (KISTEP), *Report on Phase I BK21 Program Performance Analysis,* 2007.

Korea Ministry of Commerce, Industry, and Energy (MOCIE), "Technology Transfer Rate of Public Research Institutes Are Increasing," press release, June 8, 2006.

Korea Ministry of Education and Human Resource Development (MoE), *Synthesis of the Phase I BK21 Program Evaluations,* October 2005a.

————, *Brain Korea 21,* 2005b (English Brochure on the BK21 Program)

————, *Plan for the Phase II BK21 Program,* January 2006a.

————, "Announcement of Final Winners of Phase II BK21 Funding," press release, April 24, 2006b.

————, *Year 2006 Basic Managerial Plan for Phase II BK21 Program,* September 2006c.

————, "Findings of Survey on University Research Expenses in 2005," press release, November 27, 2006d.

KISTEP—*See* Korea Institute of Science and Technology Evaluation and Planning.

Korea Ministry of Science and Technology (MOST) and Korea Institute of S&T Evaluation and Planning (KISTEP), *Report on the Survey of Research and Development in Science and Technology,* 2005.

Korea Research Foundation (KRF), *Phase I BK21 White Paper,* 2007.

KRF—*See* Korea Research Foundation.

Lee, Gui-Ro, et al., Phase I BK21 *Program Achievements Analyzed by International and Domestic Experts,* Policy Research Project 2005-26, Ministry of Education and Human Resource Development, 2005.

Lee, Yong-Joon, Sun-Joo Lee, and He-Young Kim, "Assessment of the Brain Korea 21 Program and Policy Implications," Korean National Assembly Budget Office, *Program & Policy Evaluation Brief,* No. 5, 2005.

MOCIE—*See* Korea Ministry of Commerce, Industry, and Energy.

MoE—*See* Korea Ministry of Education and Human Resource Development.

Moon, M., and K-S. Kim, "A Case of Korean Higher Education Reform: The Brain Korea 21 Project," *Asia Pacific Education Review,* Vol. 2, No. 2, 2001, pp. 96–105.

MOST—*See* Korea Ministry of Science and Technology.

National Science Foundation, "Survey of Doctorate Recipients," 2006. As of June 28, 2007:
http://www.nsf.gov/statistics/srvydoctoratework/

————, *webCASPAR Data System,* 2007. As of June 24, 2007:
http://webcaspar.nsf.gov/

Oh, Se-jung, Yong-hak Kim, et al., *Evaluating the BK21 Phase I and Planning the Phase II,* Korea Research Foundation, March 2005.

Organisation for Economic Co-operation and Development (OECD) and Eurostat, *Oslo Manual: Guidelines for Collecting and Interpreting Innovation Data,* 3rd edition, Paris: OECD Publishing, 2005.

Patton, Michael Quinn, *Qualitative Evaluation Methods,* Beverly Hills and London: Sage Publications, 1980.

Ruegg, Rosalie, and Irwin Feller, *A Toolkit for Evaluating Public R&D Investment: Models, Methods, and Findings from ATP's First Decade,* National Institute of Standards and Technology, NIST GCR03-857, July 2003.

Schrader, Richard M., "The Growth and Pitfalls in Federal Support of Higher Education, *The Journal of Higher Education,* Vol. 40, No. 9, December 1969, pp. 704–716.

THES—*See Times Higher Education Supplement.*

The Times Higher Education Supplement. As of January 4, 2008:
http://www.thes.co.uk/

United Nations, Statistics Division, *International Standard Industrial Classification of all Economic Activities,* ISIC Rev 3.1, 2007. As of December 12, 2007:
http://unstats.un.org/unsd/cr/family2.asp?Cl=17

U.S. Census Bureau, International Data Base, 2006. As of July 13, 2007:
http://www.census.gov/ipc/www/idbnew.html

Wooldridge, Jeffrey M., *Econometric Analysis of Cross Section and Panel Data,* Cambridge, Mass.: MIT Press, 2002.